DONALD McKAY'S

FAMILY

DONALD McKAY'S

FAMILY

The story of Donald McKay,

famed clipper ship builder,

His brothers and sisters

and

his children.

PAUL HAMILTON

Including Genealogies McKay, Boole, Litchfield & McPherson

Copyright © 2010 by Paul Hamilton

Printed in the United States of America

By: createspace.com

To share information, or to contact the author, write to:

Paul Hamilton

ph7538@yahoo.com

ISBN: 1449513611

EAN-13: 978-1449513610

TABLE OF CONTENTS

INTRODUCTION

There have been many books written over the years that tell the story of Donald McKay and his illustrious clipper ships. Most of these books stress the ships and the ship's accomplishments and then talk about the genius that created them. This book will take a slightly different tact and tell about the genius and his family who happened to be in the business of building ships. Instead of the ships, it was the people and their accomplishments that I found the most interesting.

It is said that behind every great man stands a surprised wife. I am not sure that this applies to Donald McKay however. I tend to believe that his personality exuded greatness. Even to this day he is known, honored and revered, over 130 years after he died. He was famous in his own time not only in his own country, but also in England and throughout Europe. His youngest brother, Nathaniel, describes him as being 6' 4" tall, which must have made him a very imposing figure for his time. He was known for his entertaining and his affiliation with some of the most important people of his time. The famous poet, Henry Wadsworth Longfellow was a frequent visitor to both Donald's shipyard and his home. In fact, Donald's shipyard was the inspiration for Longfellow's poem "The building of the ship". When the McKay shipyard launched the Great Republic, which was the largest all wooden sailing ship ever built, many businesses closed, they closed the schools, and one newspaper estimated that 50,000 people went to witness its launch. He really knew how to throw a party.

Besides his fame, however, Donald was a family man and a loving husband and father. If the letter to his brother, which is included in Chapter 3, is any indication, he had quite a sense of humor. In spite of the fact that he must have worked long hours six days a week, I have the feeling that he got very deeply involved with all of his children. He experienced times of great sorrow and also great happiness. He was very involved with his family, not only his wife and children, but also his parents, brothers and sisters. After he established his business in East Boston, his family joined him in his good fortune. This is the Donald McKay, and his family, that I wanted to write about.

My reason for writing this book is not because I am a writer. It is because half of my family history is associated with the McKay family and I have found that side of the family so interesting that I just had to learn more about them and share that information with others. My mother, Grace (McKay) Hamilton, was the daughter of Richard Cornelius McKay, who wrote a couple of books and several articles about Donald McKay and the days of the clipper ships. Richard was the son of Cornelius Whitworth McKay, who happened to be Donald McKay's oldest son. For those of you who are doing the math, this makes Donald McKay my great great grandfather.

I learned so much about this wonderful family that I never knew before, that it was a pleasure doing the research. I hope that you enjoy reading the stories about these wonderful people as much as I did writing about them.

DONALD McKAY at age 54

CHAPTER 1
DONALD McKAY'S
ROOTS

Donald McKay was probably the most famous clipper ship builder in the world. He built all styles of ships. He built schooners, barques, packets, steam ships. He even built a Civil War monitor, but his fame was with his clipper ships. He did not invent the clipper ship and he was not the only clipper builder, but the clippers that he did build were some of the best. They were beautiful, innovative, and very fast. Several of his ships broke speed records at a time when speed was so important to both passengers and merchants alike. His clipper, the Great Republic, was the largest all wooden sailing ship ever built. Even today, more than 130 years after his death, his name is still recognized and revered. That is truly a sign of a great man.

In order to really understand Donald McKay, it helps to understand his life and his family. Besides his fame with ships, Donald was a family man who came from a very large and interesting family. Donald's father was Hugh McKay, and Hugh's father was Sergeant Donald McKay who fought in the Revolutionary War, unfortunately on the other side. To begin the story, it probably makes sense to start with Donald's grandfather, Sergeant Donald McKay, and work forward from there.

Sergeant Donald McKay came over to this country in August of 1779 with the Scottish Highlander's 76th Regiment, a green military outfit that the King put together to send over to America to put down this bunch of revolutionaries. The Regiment landed in New York and remained there for a little over a year, training and guarding New York and Staten Island. Then the light infantry of the 76th Regiment was sent down south to Virginia to support Lord Cornwallis, but the grenadiers stayed in New York. Donald McKay, now a sergeant, was part of the grenadiers who had stayed to defend the British stronghold in New York. Lord Cornwallis would later be defeated at Yorktown, Virginia and his troops, including the 76th Regiment, would be taken prisoners. Although it is widely debated, some say that as the British troops marched out of their garrison to lay down their arms and to surrender to General Washington they played one of the popular songs of the day:

<u>"The World Turned Upside Down"</u>.
"If buttercups buzz'd after the bee,
if boats were on land, churches on sea,
if ponies rode men and if grass ate the cows,
and cats should be chased into holes by the mouse,
if summer were spring and the other way around,
then all the world would be upside down."

The battle of Yorktown was the turning point of the war and it was only a matter of time before the rebel Americans would take over. When the revolutionary war was over, there was a lot of animosity against the Loyalists who had supported the King, and this was pay back time. The British sympathizers (the Tories) were being run out of town, or tarred and feathered, or even killed. They were forced to leave everything that they had and flee to either England, or some other British land. Those in the south fled to Bermuda, and those in the north, who did not want to go back to England, fled to Canada. The British troops, whose enlistment was up, were discharged and given the choice of returning to England or moving to Canada. Sgt. Donald McKay, now 32 years old, and after spending 5 years in the King's service, decided to sail to Nova Scotia, Canada. Because he held the rank of Sergeant, the King allotted him 200 acres of virgin land and a year's worth of supplies as a reward for settling in Canada. Donald got passage on one of the last ships to leave New York for Nova Scotia in October of 1783.

The ship, with 383 passengers aboard, headed for Shelburne (then known as Port Roseway). Shelburne was considered an ideal site because of its deep water harbor, but it was rugged virgin land. There had only been a very small settlement there until the mass exodus at the end of the war. When the ship arrived, the settlement was not prepared for them. The people who had arrived many months previous were still clearing their own land and building their own houses. There was no place to put these new arrivals, especially just before winter, so the new folks stayed aboard the ship while the surveyors marked out new plots of land.

Sgt. Donald McKay was not one to stand around and do nothing, so he went ashore and helped the surveyors. It was not until November 22 that the solders and civilians would draw for their small Town lots of land. Donald happened to draw a piece of land that was mostly swamp and wetlands that was not fit for even a temporary shelter. Some passengers doubted that they could build a shelter fast enough to survive the winter cold that had already started, so they decided to stay aboard the ship and sail to England. Donald then was able to buy a small level lot in the North Division of Shelburne from William Randall for £3 on which he built a makeshift hut to survive the winter.

After surviving the Nova Scotia winter, in the spring of 1784, Donald again joined the surveyors in marking out lots east of

Shelburne by the Jordan River, 50 acres for privates, 100 acres for corporals, and 200 acres for non-commissioned officers. After the Jordan River lots were surveyed, the 76th Regiment gathered by the falls of the river to draw their lots. This time Donald won a better 200 acre lot of land on the east bank of the Jordan river about a mile north of the falls on the Lake John Road, which at this time was just a rough path which ran north and south from the Falls to Lake John. The lots were laid out so that everyone would have river front property on the west side of the road for their house, so that it was convenient to draw water, and a larger section on the east side of the road for their farm. Donald cleared the forest land, built a house, and started a farm.

Three years later, in 1787, Sergeant Donald McKay married Margaret (maiden name is unknown) and they had three children. Hugh McKay was born in 1788, and the twins Simon McKay and Margaret McKay were born in 1790. Donald's wife, Margaret, died shortly after the twins were born, and Donald was left to work the farm and raise his children by himself. On April 21, 1793 he married Sarah Ketland and they would have two more children, Robert George Gordon McKay and Elizabeth McKay.

Sgt. Donald McKay's farm was mostly sandy soil with patches of good brown earth. Here he had to cut the trees, pull the stumps, and haul the rocks with the most rudimentary tools in order to grow corn, peas, potatoes, wheat, barley, and, of course, hay for his cattle and sheep. But Donald was not just a farmer. He was also a surveyor and was involved in the government of this area that was now his new home.

In 1797 Donald served on the petit jury, and in 1801 and 1802 he was a member of the General Quarter Sessions for the Township of Shelburne.

In 1819, at 68 years old, he was asked, by the Surveyor General of the Province, to inspect all of the land along the Jordan River, Roseway River, and Clyde River in order to report any land that was not being used. This land could then be taken back and regranted to the poor Welch and other immigrants who were arriving in the area. While he was doing this, he was also asked to survey lots on Long Island in the Roseway River. In 1820, he was appointed Deputy Surveyor.

Marion Robertson, in her book "The Family of Donald McKay - The McKays and McPhersons", writes: *"A few years later Donald McKay was called upon to use the information which he gathered in his journeys through the wilderness in an investigation into the illegal voting in the election of 1826 when Nathaniel Whitworth White obtained votes from persons whom Donald McKay knew lived elsewhere than on their grants and that they had not cultivated nor improved their land and were not entitled to vote. As a result of the investigation Nathaniel White lost his seat in the House and John Alexander Barry was declared the legal member for Shelburne Township."* Ironically, five years later, Donald's son Hugh would name his youngest son, Nathaniel Whitworth McKay.

Sergeant Donald McKay died sometime between December 7, 1826, when his Will was signed, and March 5, 1827, when the Will was probated. The inventory of his estate was valued by John Boole and James Cox to be £259 (about £18,900, or $37,800, in 2009 money).

Back in 1787, the same year that Donald married Margaret, a ship from Scotland heading for Pictou, Nova Scotia was caught in a bad storm and sought refuge in East Jordan harbor. Two passengers on that ship, Lauchlan and Elizabeth McPherson, decided that they liked the place that the storm had forced on them, and they decided to stay. They cleared some land and tried to farm it but found that the land was not suited for farming. They then bought 200 acres by the Jordan river where they built a house and carved their farm from the wilderness. They grew grains and vegetables and raised cattle. Lauchlan also became a fisherman and dried his codfish in his fields. They had 12 children, their first born being Ann McPherson, who was born November 4, 1789. There is a more detailed look at the McPherson family genealogy in *Appendix 5.*

The McPherson and McKay children grew up in close proximity with one another, and the two families were good friends. All of the children worked on the farm. The boys also fished, cut logs, milled lumber and, since they lived by the river, they built boats.

Hugh McKay, Donald's first born, and Ann McPherson were married on October 15, 1808 at St. John's Kirk, Shelburne, by the Reverend Matthew Dripps. They acquired a house on the east bank of the Jordan river overlooking the falls. In 1815, Hugh bought a sawmill from his neighbor Francis Boole for £60 (about £3700, or $7407, in 2009 money) that stood across the river on the west bank. There he built his boats and larger vessels. When the local supply of timber became scarce, he petitioned the Honorable Michael Wallace for a grant to use some woodlands further north. He then was granted 300 acres of good timberland six to ten miles north of the falls. During the winter of 1824, Hugh built a new sawmill to replace the one that he had bought from Francis Boole. This sawmill was located on land that today contains a memorial to Donald McKay's clipper ships *(page 54)*.

Although he was a farmer, ran a sawmill, and built boats, my grandfather, Richard C McKay, wrote that Hugh *"would rather build boats than hoe potatoes"*. Hugh, like his father, also served on the Court of Sessions for the district of Jordan in 1823 and 1824.

Hugh and Ann would have 18 children, all born within a span of 22 years. Two of their children died before they were even given names, and the remaining 16 consisted of seven sons and nine daughters.

These were very hard times for both Hugh and Ann. They were raising 16 children and Hugh was working several jobs just to make ends meet. They were forced to mortgage their house and land and the mill several times, and it was not until 1842 that they got some relief when Hugh sold a third of his sawmill to Ebenezer Martin for £100 (£7,686 or $13,082 in 2009).

There was a period of time when the Shelburne area was declining. Many of the early settlers found that farming on this land was very hard. There were no roads to the outside world, and there were not any navigable rivers, and so the people started moving out. Those who did not return to England or go to India, sailed to Lunenburg, Halifax, Cape Breton, Prince Edward Island, or New Brunswick. Speculators and idle opportunists, trying to take advantage of the King's bounty of provisions and free land, started moving in. Crime was on the rise and Shelburne was turning into the "wild west". By 1791 two-thirds of the town was uninhabited. Merchants were buying their ships from England rather than building them from the abundant local natural resources. The close-knit communities of East Jordan and Jordan Falls would survive and, after roads were built, Shelburne would also survive. But for those who had loftier ambitions, they had to seek their fortunes elsewhere.

CHAPTER 2
DONALD McKAY

Hugh's son Donald had his father's love for ship building. Donald not only worked in his father's shipyard, he also worked with his uncles, John and Lauchlan McPherson, who also were ship builders. Later his uncles would move their families down to East Boston and continue building ships. Donald and his brother Lauchlan built themselves a sail boat which they both enjoyed sailing around the bay.

However, Donald needed more education if he was to become a master ship builder. In 1826, at the age of 16, Donald sailed to Halifax and booked passage on a lumber schooner to New York City. He was headed for the East River shipyards in New York to learn the trade and then he planned to return home to build ships.

Donald headed to the shipyard of Isaac Webb, one of the most eminent shipbuilders of his time. He signed on as a day laborer at the Webb & Allen Shipyard and worked there for almost a year before he spoke to Isaac Webb about his ambition to become a shipwright. On March 24, 1827 Isaac Webb drew up a contract, signed by Isaac, Donald and Donald's father, Hugh, making him an indentured apprentice. He would work there six days a week from sunrise to sunset, about 70 hours a week for $1.25 per day. In the summer they began at 4:30 in the morning and worked until 7:30 in the evening. At 8:00 a.m. They were allowed an hour for breakfast. At 12:00 noon they had two hours for dinner, which had to last them until they had supper after work.

He was later joined at the shipyard by his younger brother Lauchlan. Donald and Lauchlan learned every aspect of the ship carpenter's trade. Just a few months shy of the expiration of his four and a half year contract, Donald approached Isaac Webb and asked to be released from his apprenticeship. His contract expired on October 5th, but if he hoped to build any ships back home in Shelburne before the Canadian winter, he needed to start well before October. He had proven his abilities, and had taken on greater duties and far more important work than the rest of the apprentices, and he felt that he was ready to be a free lance shipwright. Isaac was well aware of Donald's abilities and released him from his contract.

Donald McKay, now almost 21 years old, left the Webb & Allen shipyard and booked passage back to Nova Scotia. After arriving home in 1831, Donald, along with his uncle Robert McKay, began to build a barkentine ship on the Jordan river below the falls. In Marion Robertson's book on the McKays, she states that the Honorable David McPherson and his brother Ebenezer had two different accounts as to what happened to that ship. One of them claimed that they ran out of money and did not complete the ship, leaving it on the stocks for their creditors. The other one claimed that they sailed the ship to Halifax and were cheated out of the money by the ones who bought the ship. Robert had mortgaged his home, which he had inherited from his father, in order to pay for the building of the ship and there was no easy way for him to recoup that money. Robert's ship-building days were over. He would later lose title to his house in a sheriff sale and ended up moving his family to Port Joli where his wife's family gave them some land to farm. Whatever dreams Donald had about a shipbuilding career in Nova Scotia ended with this financial disaster, and he returned to New York City.

Now a freelance shipwright in 1832, Donald had no trouble landing a job with Jacob Bell of the Brown & Bell shipyard, next door to the Webb & Allen shipyard, on the East

River in New York. At this same time, the Boole family, one of Donald's neighbors from Nova Scotia, was also in New York and Donald was starting to date their 17 year old daughter, Albenia Martha Boole. Albenia had been born in Jordan Falls, September 8, 1815, and had lived across the river from Donald's childhood home. She was five years younger than Donald but they had known each other growing up. Albenia's father, John, had sold his home in Jordan Falls and moved his family to New York on October 21, 1831 on the schooner *George Henry*, so that he could take up shipbuilding in the famous New York shipyards. Since Donald had returned home after his apprenticeship in early summer of that same year, and he certainly must have discussed the shipbuilding in New York City, I wonder how influential he was in John's decision to move his family to New York. John Boole became a master shipbuilder and remained in that profession most of his life until the New York ship building started to decline. He remained in New York, except for a brief stint in the late 1840's when he tried his luck in the East Boston shipyards, possibly in Donald's yard. In the Brooklyn, NY city directory for 1870, when John is 77 years old, he is listed as a City Sealer.

Albenia was well educated and excelled in mathematics and, since her father was a shipbuilder, she had a thorough knowledge of the shipbuilding trade. She was a perfect match for Donald, and they were married sometime in 1833. They bought a house on the fashionable East Broadway in New York City where they would start their family. On February 1, 1834 their first son was born. They named him Cornelius Whitworth McKay. Cornelius was followed by his sister Frances Jean, who was born on April 3, 1836, and the following year by his sister Anne Jane, who was born on November 12, 1837.

During all of this time, Donald is still working at the Brown & Bell shipyard and, I am sure, coming home to his wife Albenia and discussing the ships that he is building. The New York shipbuilding scene was a very social one. Donald had many friends in New York. They were not only the men that he had served his apprenticeship with, but also some of the great designers and builders of this era. Even though they competed with each other for business, they had so much in common with each other that they were very active socially. One of these friends was John Willis Griffiths who revolutionized the shipbuilding trade by introducing the first clipper ship model. Many of the ship designers would not agree with his theory that in order to get speed from a ship one had to redesign the stern (back) of the ship as well as the bow (front). John would finally prove his theory when he built the very fast ship *Rainbow* in 1845.

In 1840, Jacob Bell, of Brown & Bell, recommended Donald for a foreman job at the Brooklyn Navy Yard, on the opposite side of the East River. The job was a good one except that the men who worked for Donald did not want to take orders from a "blue-nosed" Canadian. There were so many new immigrants in New York at this time, the population in New York City had almost doubled in just the past five years, that they felt that foreigners were taking over too many jobs there, and the men wanted to work for an American. The pressure on Donald was too much and his friend, Jacob Bell, sent him to Wiscasset, Maine to draft and superintend the building of some ships for New York shipping houses.

Maine had many shipyards. Bath Maine, on the Kennebec river had several yards and is still known for its shipbuilding today. A little further northeast from there is Wiscasset on the Sheepscot river. Because of the natural wilderness and its abundance of trees, Wiscasset was the main lumber port for the state at that time. With lumber readily available, there were several shipyards there. However, these yards were still building relatively small craft, with few of them being more than 150 ton. Also, their shipbuilding methods were pretty primitive compared to the methods in New York, and 1840 was not a good year for Wiscasset shipyards. In spite of the fact that there were at least three shipyards, there was only one ship launched in 1840. That ship was the 130 ton *Crusoe* built by John Clark. It appears that the shipbuilding business in Wiscasset was having a bad year, so Donald did not stay too long. On his way back to New York, he checked out some of the many shipyards along the way, especially in Newburyport, Massachusetts. At least this is what most of the history books claim. I have some doubts. Because of the distance between Brooklyn, New York and Wiscasset, Maine, the fact that they were traveling by horse or stage coach, and coupled with all that Donald was doing in 1840, he could not have spent very much time there. I tend to think that there is the outside possibility that Donald never got as far north as Wiscasset Maine, and only got as far north as Newburyport Massachusetts in his quest for a new job. Whichever the case may be, Wiscasset did not play a large part in Donald's life and his family did not move up from New York until he was established in Newburyport.

Newburyport, on the Merrimac river, had been in the boat making business since the early 1600's because the river was the easiest form of transportation back then. In 1840, when Donald was visiting the town, there were seven shipyards side by side on the Merrimac river near the center of town. Many of them had been in operation since the mid 1700's. Donald was traveling with James Townsend, a friend of his during their apprenticeship at Webb &

Allen in New York. Donald landed a job with John Currier, Jr., but James did not. James then continued on his journey and returned to New York, although he would return to Newburyport in a few years.

Donald became a foreman for John Currier, Jr. and would finish the construction on the 427 ton ship *Delia Walker*. The owner of the ship, Dennis Condry, visited the shipyard often to check the progress on his ship. He was very impressed with the 29 year old foreman, for his mechanical abilities as well as how much work he was able to get out of his men. John Currier, Jr. was just as impressed and, after the *Delia Walker* was launched, he offered Donald a binding five year contract to be the foreman of the shipyard. Donald refused the offer because he wanted to be a partner and help design the ships. He had much higher ambitions and was not content to be just a foreman for the next five years.

John Currier, Jr. was a very well renowned shipbuilder in Newburyport, having built 98 ships during his long career. He pioneered the use of subcontractors who would build parts of the ship and then the parts would be assembled and fitted in place at the shipyard. Therefore it was advantageous to use the same ship plans for as many ships as possible. After Donald left, John continued to make ships for the next 43 years until he closed his yard on April 9, 1883, three years after Donald had died. John Currier, Jr. died in September of 1887.

On October 29, 1840, Donald and Albenia's fourth child, and second son, Dennis Condry McKay, was born in Newburyport. He was named after the owner of the *Delia Walker*.

In 1841, Donald struck up a friendship with William Currier, apparently no relation to John Currier Jr. Both of them decided to form a partnership and setup shop three shipyards west of John's and the Currier & McKay shipyard was born. They built the 322 ton bark *Mary Broughton*, followed by the 449 ton ship *Ashburton* in 1842. Donald then designed and built the 380 ton ship *Courier*. Although the *Courier* would prove to be a very fast ship, which even impressed some of the New York shippers, William Currier and Donald had a huge disagreement that ended with them dissolving the partnership. They divided up everything between them. They even cut the models and moulds in half. Donald then formed a new partnership with William Pickett which became the McKay & Pickett Shipyard.

With Donald gone, William Currier convinced James Townsend to return from New York and they changed the name of the yard from Currier & McKay to Currier & Townsend. This yard would launch 52 ships before they went bankrupt. James Townsend then opened his own shipyard at the site of what was, by then, the old McKay & Picket shipyard, but the financing in Newburyport was becoming very difficult because of the Civil War. In 1864, James closed his yard and bought the Osgood & Pratt shipyard in East Boston, Massachusetts, where he stayed until 1881. Some say that James L. Townsend was one of the great naval architects of his time.

The year 1842 was also an important year in the life of the McKay family. Donald's family was living in the neighboring Town of Newbury where, on May 3, 1842, Donald McKay Jr. was born. They moved back to Newburyport sometime during that same year where their three year old daughter, Anne Jane, died of scarlet fever on October 11, 1842. With the death of his daughter, Donald purchased the McKay Family plot in the Oak Hill Cemetery in Newburyport, Massachusetts for $34.50. Although this looks like an unbelievably small sum of money, it probably amounted to two or three weeks wages for the average worker at that time. $34.50 is equivalent to $940 in 2009 dollars.

Shortly after the McKay and Picket partnership was founded, Albenia gave birth, on August 23, 1843, to another son who, unfortunately, did not live very long. Because there was no death recorded and because they named him Cornelius, even though their first son, Cornelius Whitworth, was still alive, it is assumed that he was either still born or only lived for an extremely short time.

The McKay & Pickett yard was in the old Moggridge yard, which was originally built in October 1744 by Aaron Merrill and named for his wife, Betty Moggridge. This was just west of the John Currier, Jr. yard. In 1843, McKay & Pickett built the 845 ton ship *St. George* and the 930 ton ship *John R. Skiddy*, which were much bigger than most ships then being built in Newburyport at that time. In 1844, Enoch Train, a Boston merchant, was planning a line of packets to sail between Boston and Liverpool. On his trip to Liverpool, to setup the business there, he happened to meet Dennis Condry on board the ship and they discussed ships and shipping on their long voyage. In one of their conversations, Enoch remarked that he could not find a suitable shipbuilder in Boston to build his packets and did not want to have them built in New York. Dennis mentioned his impression of the young foreman who had built his *Delia Walker* and suggested that Enoch lookup this Donald McKay in Newburyport. On his return to the states, Enoch went to Newburyport and gave McKay & Pickett a contract to build the *Joshua Bates*, the first ship of Train's famous White Diamond Line. Enoch train was a constant visitor to the yard as his ship was being built and he was indeed impressed with Donald McKay's abilities. After the ship was launched, Enoch had a long discussion with Donald and promised to back him financially if he would come to Boston. Donald had a good relationship with William Pickett, but this was too great an offer to pass up. With Enoch's help, he bought some land for his shipyard in East Boston, rented a house for the family and moved down to East Boston.

William Pickett, along with his son, continued building in Newburyport for the next five years until 1849 when they auctioned off all of the equipment in his shipyard. William then moved up to Cape Elizabeth in Casco Bay, Maine and continued to build ships for many years. He probably worked at his brother Benjamin's shipyard which was the old Turner and Cahoon Yard. Benjamin had bought the yard from James Cahoon after George Turner died.

Many of Donald's brothers decided to joined him at the Boston yard, and some would even start shipyards of their own. Donald's brothers John, David and Nathaniel joined him at the McKay yard. Even Donald's father, Hugh, joined him. According to the Boston city directory, Donald's brother Simon ran a grocery store near Donald's shipyard. Later he worked for Donald and then he would open his own shipyard in Amesbury, Massachusetts. After he closed that yard he would open one in Charlestown, across the river from East Boston. Lauchlan, who had worked at Brown & Bell, in New York for many years, was not only a shipwright but also would become a ship's captain. He also opened a shipyard in East Boston with his younger brother Hugh Robert which mainly repaired ships, but Hugh also designed and built a few ships.

Donald's shipyard was located in East Boston on Border Street between Eutaw Street and White Street. This whole section of East Boston was mostly dedicated to the shipbuilding industry.

Sail makers, outfitters, wood carvers, iron workers, as well as other shipyards abounded along the wharfs of East Boston. He also bought some property on top of a hill, which overlooked Boston Harbor, where he would build his home with the help of some of his ship carpenters. As the neighborhood grew, and more houses were built on White Street, Donald's view of Boston Harbor slowly disappeared. The house was only about a quarter of a mile from his shipyard, which made it easy to walk to work. The problem with living on a big hill came when it was time to walk home from work and it was all uphill.

Donald's family was not the only Canadian family to move down to Boston. Donald had grown up in Jordan Falls, Nova Scotia with the McPherson and Boole families and all of them had made boats there. Donald's father had married Ann McPherson, and Donald had married Albenia Boole. Albenia's father, John Boole, moved from New York to East Boston around 1846 and lived on Marion Street, near his daughter, and presumably worked in Donald's shipyard. The Boston city directories list him until 1849, when he moved back to New York. All three families saw the opportunities that America had to offer, and many realized the advantages of the Boston area.

The Boston city directories of the mid 1800's show that there were many Booles in East Boston. John, George, Leonard, Francis, Thomas, and William Boole were all shipwrights and were all in the East Boston waterfront area. George and Thomas Boole had the G & T Boole Shipyard at Jeffries Point in East Boston, close to where Logan Airport is today. There they launched the *Weymouth* of 1370 ton in 1854. They launched the 1079 ton *Emerald* in 1855. In 1856 they launched the *Endymion* and the *Plutarch*, both over 1300 ton. They also launched the *Pomona*, 1181 ton and the *Calliope*, 280 ton. George and

Thomas were Albenia's cousins, sons of John Boole's brother George.

The McPhersons were also in the same area. David, Ewell, James, John, John Jr., and Lauchlan McPherson were also all shipwrights. Donald had worked with many of them when he was a teenager in Jordan Falls.

In the McKay family, Cornelius Whitworth, David, Donald, Hugh, Hugh Robert, Lauchlan, and Nathaniel were all connected to ship building in East Boston. Simon was a shipwright in Amesbury, Massachusetts.

On December 11, 1844, Albenia and Donald announced the birth of their son John Boole McKay, named after Albenia's father. Almost two years later on September 20, 1846 their daughter Albenia McKay was born.

Donald's first son, Cornelius Whitworth McKay, spent a lot of time at Donald's shipyard in Boston and was well known to all of the workers. My grandfather, Richard C. McKay, tells the story how 12 year old Cornelius and his father took the ferry from East Boston to Boston in order to go sledding down the snowy hills of Boston Common. Walking the streets on the way to the Common, they came across two men looking in the window of a shoe store and counting their money. They were both looking at work boots but obviously did not have enough money. Donald immediately recognized them as workers in his shipyard, and he also realized that he had reduced their hours to part time because he was not working on any ships at the present time. He walked over to them, shook their hands, and brought them into the store. After talking to the proprietor, the two men walked out of the store, each carrying a package with their new boots. Donald then took Cornelius to the Common for his sledding, and then afterwards they walked over to Enoch Train's house on Mt. Vernon Street. Enoch Train was the wealthy merchant and ship owner who initially helped finance Donald's shipyard. After an *"earnest discussion"*, Donald left the house with a contract to build the largest vessel ever built up to that time. This would become the 1301 ton *Ocean Monarch*. After the *Ocean Monarch* was launched in 1847, there were four more ships launched from Donald's yard by the end of 1848.

In 1848, the business was going very well. Donald and Albenia were looking forward to the birth of another baby, their ninth, when all of a sudden Donald's world fell apart. Albenia and the baby died during childbirth on December 10, 1848. Albenia Martha (Boole) McKay was only 33 years old. Donald was left with six children to take care of, the youngest being only two years old. Albenia and the baby were buried in the Oak Hill cemetery in Newburyport, Massachusetts in the same plot as her four year old daughter Anne Jane and her infant son Cornelius who had both died before her.

Nichols Litchfield was a carpenter in Donald's shipyard. He and his wife Anna, along with their children lived one block south of the McKays on Eutaw Street near Brooks Street. Their daughter, Mary Cressy Litchfield, also worked at the shipyard as Donald's secretary. On October 17th of the following year, 1849, Donald and Mary were married. Mary, now 18 years old, had to take care of the six children, ranging in age from 15 year old Cornelius Whitworth, to three year old Albenia. She also had to care for Donald's 13 year old daughter, Frances Jean, who was suffering from tuberculosis.

In the next three and a half years, from the time that Donald married Mary until the spring of 1853, Donald built 17 ships which included the famed *Flying Cloud* and the *Sovereign of the Seas*. Business was good and Donald's shipyard was busy. On October 31, 1850, Mary gave birth to her first child who she named Lauchlan, after Donald's brother. Exactly one year later, on Lauchlan's first birthday, Donald's 15 year old daughter, Frances Jean, died from her tuberculosis. Only one and a half years later, on April 10, 1853, Donald and Mary's only child, two and a half years old Lauchlan, died of "congestion on the brain", which was a general medical term for brain maladies but it probably referred to meningitis. Can you imagine any 21 year old having to deal with all of this?

The 2421 ton *Sovereign of the Seas*, launched in 1852, was the largest ship ever built in East Boston up until that time. After the *Flying Cloud* had set such speed records the prior year, Enoch Train had asked Donald to build a larger ship. When the *Sovereign* was on the stocks Enoch almost bought it, however for some reason he started to have second thoughts about its size. Donald was so convinced that he could combine both size and speed, that he continued to build it with his own money, and it proved to be his personally most profitable ship that he ever built. The *Sovereign* sailed from New York to San Francisco, under the command of Donald's brother Lauchlan, with almost 3000 tons of cargo. In spite of getting dismasted in a storm, she made the run in 103 days. She set the record of averaging 394 ¾ statute miles in 24 hours. In the nine months that it took for the round trip, the *Sovereign* earned $135,000 (almost $3.9 million in 2009 dollars).

On June 18, 1853, Lauchlan McKay, still in command of the *Sovereign*, left New York for Liverpool with his brother-in-law, Henry Warner, as his first mate. Donald and his wife Mary also accompanied them on this voyage so that Donald could see first hand how she handled so that he could apply this information to his next ship. Of course, this was also a nice way to have a second honeymoon. The Cunard steamship *Canada* left Boston for Liverpool on the same day as the *Sovereign* left New York and it turned into a race. The *Sovereign* made a record passage and when the *Canada* entered Liverpool harbor, the *Sovereign* was already there and flying a large canvas sign which made it quite clear who won. It read:

> **Sovereign of the Seas**
> **Fastest ship in the world**
> **Sailed New York to Liverpool**
> **Record Time - 18 days - 22 hours**

In 11 months, the *Sovereign* had earned almost $200,000 (over $5.7 million in 2009 dollars).

James Baines & Co. then chartered the *Sovereign of the Seas* for their Black Ball Line to make a run to Melbourne, Australia. Donald and Lauchlan had to return to Boston to finish working on Donald's latest creation, the *Great Republic*. They returned on the ship *America* and Henry Warner took over command of the *Sovereign* when he was only in his 30's. Capt. Warner sailed from Liverpool on Sep 7, 1853 with a mixed cargo and made the trip in 77 days, beating the steamer *Great Britain* which had left Liverpool the same day. Since Australia was having their own gold rush at this time, Capt. Warner lost most of his crew to the gold fields. When he tried to hire on a new crew, he pretty much had to take whomever he could find. On the return trip, the *Sovereign* carried over four tons of gold, valued at over a million dollars, with a crew who probably did not have any luck finding their own gold. Being so close to so much gold must have been quite a temptation. While on the high sea some of the crew decided to take over the ship and rushed to seize Captain Warner and his officers. Single handedly, Captain Warner grabbed a cutlass and opened a path right through the center of them while his three mates armed themselves. The four officers quickly put down the mutiny and had the ring leaders in irons. They then continued their journey to Liverpool with almost half of the crew in irons. Upon reaching Liverpool, Capt. Warner was highly praised by the underwriters for saving the gold cargo.

With all of the good publicity, and after earning a small fortune on the *Sovereign of the Seas*, Donald finally sold her to J.C. Godeffroy of Hamburg, Germany for $150,000 ($4.3 million in 2009 dollars). Capt. Muller then took command of the *Sovereign* and Capt. Warner returned to Boston to take command of Donald's new ship, the *Commodore Perry*.

Cornelius started hanging around his father's shipyard from a very early age, and was becoming quite knowledgeable about ship design and ship building. On October 4, 1853, when Cornelius was 19 years old, the McKay shipyard launched the *Great Republic*, the largest all wooden sail ship ever built. The newspaper claims that fifty thousand people turned out for the grand event. The East Boston band played "Hail Columbia" and a canon boomed as Captain Alden Gifford christened the ship with a bottle of Cochituate Water instead of the traditional bottle of champagne. The reason was given that this was done to humor the numerous Boston ladies that were advocating temperance. The superintendent of the shipyard, Mr. E. L. Hersey, would later admit that 19 year old Cornelius and some of his friends had gotten together in the mould loft the night before, and drank all of the champagne.

After the christening, the ship was brought over to the dock to be outfitted with rigging, sail, and all of the amenities that were necessary to make her the finest ship of her time. She sailed from

Boston to New York City and was docked at a pier on the East River at the foot of Dover Street to be loaded with cargo destined for Liverpool, England. She was almost ready to sail when, on December 26th, some buildings on Front street, one block away from the dock, caught fire. Some embers from the fire landed in the ship's rigging and set fire to the sails. Because the ships masts were so high, the firemen could not play water on the fire so Captain Lauchlan McKay and Captain Ellis, representing the underwriters, decided to cut the masts before the whole ship was destroyed. One mast fell on the dock, the main mast and the mizzenmast crushed boats, deckhouses, rails and disabled the steam-engine that was the first ever used on a ship to raise and lower sail. The fore-topmast broke when it was cut and it crashed through three decks and set the deck ablaze. The firemen worked through the night and put the fire out on the deck. After the firemen left, someone noticed smoke coming from the hold. The topmast had set the cargo on fire and had gained such headway that it was completely out of control. Captain McKay scuttled the ship in an effort to save as much as possible. The fire burned for two days until it reached the water's edge. The ships *Joseph Walker* and the *White Squall* were also destroyed in this fire. When they re-floated the *Great Republic*, they discovered that some of the cargo of grain had expanded so much that it buckled the knees and beams of the lower hold and the ship was considered a total loss. This was when Donald decided to take the insurance money of $235,000, even though he had spent nearly $300,000 of his own money on it, and not try to salvage her. She was towed to Sneeden & Whitlock at Greenpoint on Long Island and was rebuilt as a slightly altered ship.

The next year, 1854, was the busiest year for Donald. In this year, he built, or launched, eight ships, which included the clipper ships *Lightning, Champion of the Seas*, and *Santa Claus*.

There were also six other shipbuilders in East Boston who were also building clipper ships. They were: his brother Hugh Robert McKay, Robert Jackson, Samuel Hall, Paul Curtis, Jackson & Ewell, and A & G. T. Sampson.

Also in 1854, just a year after Mary's son Lauchlan died, Mary gave birth to her daughter Frances McKay on April 12, 1854. Almost two years later she gave birth to her second daughter, Mary Cressy McKay, on January 4, 1856.

The year 1857 was the first year, in his 17 year career, that Donald did not build any ships. The Crimean War had just ended in 1856 and England and France were no longer at war with Russia. This meant that Europe could once again buy grain and other commodities from Russia instead of the United States. This had a devastating effect on the US grain prices creating economic misery in our rural areas. Then in August of 1857, the Ohio Life Insurance & Trust Company failed because of widespread embezzlement in the company's New York branch. This created panic on the New York Stock Exchange and sent the country reeling into a recession. British investors were pulling money out of the US Banks and many banks were failing. Companies were going out of business and thousands of people were losing their jobs. This economic disaster, which was worse in the north than in the south, would last for several years. Some believe that this was one of the underlying causes for the Civil War.

In 1858, Donald started to build the 1097 ton medium clipper *Alhambra* for William Thwing & Company of Boston, and launched it in 1859. Although he would help his son Cornelius build four fishing schooners in his shipyard, the *Alhambra* was the only ship that Donald would build until 1861. All of the northern shipbuilders were having the same problem. Ship owners were trying to get by with their present ships and were not adding to their fleets. It must have been very difficult for him to see his shipyard idle for so long a period of time and to see his skilled workers leave for other jobs. He had experienced hard times before, but nothing like this.

When the English and French started building iron and iron-clad steam ships Donald went over to Europe to see how they were building them. On his return to America, he wrote several articles for the "Boston Commercial Bulletin" newspaper under a column called "Marine Affaires". In the November 17, 1860 issue, he states that the design of fighting ships has changed over the past 20 years and that America has to keep up. The sailing ship and the armed paddle-wheel steamers were made obsolete when the French developed the screw line-of-battle ship, the *Napoleon* of 90 guns, in 1850. Now the French have developed the iron-clad frigate *La Gloire* which shows that no world power should be without a number of these frigates for their defenses. Sailing ships can never out maneuver a steamship in battle. When one compares the American Navy with the Navies of the rest of the world, we fall short of even a third rate power. England has 638 steamships totaling 10,920 guns. France has 280 steamships totaling 5678 guns. Russia has 233 steamers of 3200 guns. Even Holland, Italy and Spain have more steamships and firepower than us. America has 38 steamships totaling 458 guns, and of those 38, only 16 can be called ships of war, to protect more than 10,000 miles of coastline. *"If we were ever attacked by either England or France, we would have to surrender."* Abraham Lincoln's new administration needs to create a powerful steam navy fit for a nation of 30 million people.

In the March 16, 1861 issue of "Boston Commercial Bulletin", under the column "Marine Affairs", Donald wrote a follow-up article pointing out the volatile situation in the world at that time. A major war in Europe was almost imminent as well as the volatile situation in this country (several states had already seceded from the Union and this was one month before the start of the Civil War). He recommended that the Navy build heavy screw steam frigates and sloops-of-war capable of at least 12 knots and capable of carrying at least eight days of coal, steaming at full speed. The frigates should be of the Merrimac and Franklin class armed with 40 or 50 Dahlgren breech loading guns of the heaviest caliper. The sloops-of-war should be of the Hartford class with 12 to 18 guns of heavy caliper with a draught of only 8 to 16 feet so that they can go up any of our rivers. The French have tested iron plates on ships and have found that four and a half inch iron plates have proven impenetrable to present French and English guns. France has ordered ten such iron-clad frigates be built immediately with 20 more planned for the future. The English have ordered four iron-clad frigates with ten more to follow. Austria and Russia have also started to build iron-clads and it is imperative that Congress order the construction of such ships for us. Donald recommended starting with six iron-clad frigates of 36 guns and capable of 12 knots to cruise the coast to check all attempts to blockade our ports. He also suggested six to ten light draught iron-clad corvettes with 10 to 14 guns with a speed of at least ten knots to protect our southern seaports.

On March 21, 1861, Donald sent a letter to President Abraham Lincoln's Secretary of the Navy, Gideon Welles, recommending that the Navy build iron-clad frigates and sloops-of-war. He also included copies of his articles from the Boston Commercial Bulletin.

On April 17, 1861, Donald sent another letter to the Secretary of the Navy stating that he had a ship on the stocks being built with the best New Hampshire white oak and that he was willing to change it over to a sloop-of-war. He then listed all of the specifications for it. It would have a screw drive powered by a 250 horse power steam engine capable of ten knots armed with ten 9" Dahlgren guns. It's draught, fully loaded, would not exceed 12 feet, and he could launch the ship in two months with it ready for sea in three and a half months from the time of the order. The cost would be $350,000. The Navy looked at the plans and turned down the offer because it was too expensive. As the Civil War progressed, they would later regret this decision.

Even before Donald had sent these letters, he had already set aside almost a third of his shipyard for the production of iron. This iron business was established as McKay and Aldus, referring to his brother Nathaniel McKay and George Aldus. Nathaniel was the principal partner and George ran the plant. They not only built marine engines and ships of iron, but they also had a plant at the other end of Border street that made boilers and train locomotives. Although steel was invented in 1856, it was not in general use until the 1870's and not used for building ships until after 1880. It was not until 1883 that President Chester Arthur authorized the Navy to build their first steel warships.

At the height of the Civil War, on June 17, 1864, Mary gave birth to her twins Anna Cushing McKay, named after her mother, and Lawrence Litchfield McKay, named after Mary's older brother, who became a Brigadier General in the Civil War.

Also in 1864, the United States Government commissioned the McKay shipyard to build four ships for use in the Civil War. The *U.S.S. Trefoil*, a wooden gunboat with steam propellers, the *U.S.S. Yucca*, also a wooden gunboat with steam propellers, the *U.S.S. Nausett*, an iron clad monitor, and the *U.S.S. Ashuelot*, an iron side wheel steamer. The United States Navy had given Donald, and some other shipbuilders, preliminary plans for them to bid on the contracts. The final plans were supposed to follow, but they were never finalized. It took over a year to build these ships because the government kept changing the designs and delaying their construction while they thought of new changes. When the first monitor was launched, of the same class as the *U.S.S. Nausett*, it rode only three inches out of the water, even without its turrets, guns and all of the other weight that she needed to carry. The Navy then ordered that the deck of all monitors be raised 22 inches. During these delays the prices of iron and other materials was skyrocketing because of shortages caused by the Civil War. The costs of coal and iron went up some 300 percent. Although the government paid for the ships at the price that was originally bid on, they would not pay for the added material caused by their constant redesign, nor would they pay for the higher cost of materials that was caused by all of the delays. This meant that the McKay shipyard lost a considerable amount of money on each of the four ships. The loss was estimated to total more than $300,000 (over $4.2 million in 2009 dollars).

Donald and several other shipbuilders, who had built ships for the Civil War, would petition the government for payment. They even filed law suits against the government. Donald's youngest brother, Nathaniel, would spend many years walking the halls of Congress lobbying to get the bills paid. Finally, in 1888, twenty three years after the ships were turned over to the government and eight years after Donald McKay had died, Congress approved the payment for the added material, but not the appreciation of the material costs caused by the delays. In spite of the fact that the Secretary of the Navy Whitney had earnestly requested him to sign the bill, President Cleveland vetoed it, claiming that it was a raid on the treasury and would offend the loyal south. It would not be until March 10, 1895, 15 years after Donald had died, that the United States Court of Claims would adjudicate that the bills be paid. The government finally paid Nathaniel $101,529.73 (a little over $2.6 million in 2009 dollars) to settle the litigation. It took over 30 years to get the matter finally settled.

In the years after the Civil War, Donald and Mary would have two more children. Nichols Litchfield McKay, named after Mary's father, was born on October 4, 1866. Their last child, Wallace McKay, was born two years later on October 6, 1868.

The financial disaster connected with the ships built for the Civil War put Donald in debt, but it was not going to slow down his creativity. In the next years, from 1866 to 1868, he would build 5 more ships: 2 steamships, 1 brig, and 2 clippers. The two clippers were the *Helen Morris* and the second, and smaller version, *Sovereign of the Seas*. The buyers of these ships wanted them to be able to carry more cargo, so Donald built them wider. Unfortunately, this made them slower. Although these ships allowed him to payoff some of the debt that he had accumulated, because the government was not paying him what they owed, he still owed a considerable amount to some of his lenders and suppliers. To help him solve this problem, he laid out plans for a new, bigger, grander clipper which he would call *Glory of the Seas*. He could have designed a steamship instead of a sail ship, but there was greater profit in a really impressive medium clipper. This ship had the added cargo space that the merchants wanted but would still have the speed. Because the demand for ships had slowed down after the Civil War and the economy was not yet out of the post-war slump, Donald was finding it difficult to find a company willing to put up the financing for such an expensive ship which might end up being as slow as the prior two clipper ships. Since Donald could not find a company to finance the building of the *Glory*, and could not afford to wait for the economy to turn around, he decided to finance the building of it himself. He was confident that a buyer could be found after they saw the ship, and he would be able to satisfy his creditors.

The McKay & Aldus company had gone bankrupt in December of 1868 because they had over extended credit to their customers, so Donald put up its machinery as collateral on a loan to lay the keel of the *Glory of the Seas*. He mortgaged his shipyard to complete the ship. When his creditors started to clamor for payment and no buyer was in sight who was willing to pay the $190,000 ($2.9 million in 2009 dollars) that he was asking, Donald mortgaged the *Glory* on November 25, 1869 to Daniel Sortwell, a prominent Cambridge distiller, for $100,000. Donald accompanied the ship down to New York to find a buyer. Even though he found buyers, he could not find anyone who was willing to pay more than it cost him to build it. Donald then decided that he would accompany the ship to San Francisco, confident that he could get his price once they saw how fast she really was. However, some of his suppliers in Boston were not willing to wait the four or five months, for the ship to reach San Francisco, before they got paid. Donald then borrowed another $70,000 from Daniel Sortwell with the understanding that Daniel would get whatever profit the ship made when the goods were sold in San Francisco. Donald also gave Daniel his power of attorney to take care of any emergency while Donald was away.

When Donald arrived in San Francisco on June 13, 1870, he found out that less than four weeks earlier, on May 18, 1870, Daniel Sortwell had conveyed the *Glory of the Seas* over to Charles E. Brigham, of Gay, Manson and Co., an iron and steel firm in Boston that had supplied most of the iron work for the *Glory*, as trustees of Donald McKay's assets on behalf of his creditors. Donald could not sell the ship because he no long owned it. He was out of business.

When Donald returned to Boston in August of 1870, he tried to get the ship back, but to no avail. Donald was sure that Daniel Sortwell had exceeded his power of attorney and had no right to foreclose, but when the lawyers got finished wrangling, there was little else to do than to quitclaim the *Glory of the Seas* and give up any interest in his shipyard on Border Street in East Boston. All of his debts were considered paid. Although Donald and Mary were left with their house on Eagle Hill, his shipyard was dismantled following the bankruptcy. A shipyard in Maine got his prized steam bevel saw which he had designed himself.

The *Glory of the Seas* had sailed from San Francisco to Liverpool with a load of grain and then returned to New York in ballast. She then remained idle at the dock in New York for three months while all of the legal wrangling was going on in Boston. Charles Brigham was getting tired of paying her expenses and decided to sell her. Twelve of Donald's creditors, plus three other interested parties, decided that they would buy her. They would not only recoup their loses but, because the **Glory** proved to be such a fast ship, they could also reap her profits. As was customary at that time, there were 64 shares made available. Isaac Pratt, the president of Atlantic National Bank, and a friend of Donald's, bought 24/64 of the *Glory*. J Baker and Company, chandlers who supplied ships with groceries and other provisions, bought 16/64. They also owned shares in about 90 other ships because supplying provisions to your own ships was good business. The remaining 24 shares were spread among the other members of the syndicate. The syndicate voted to make J. Henry Sears Company, a Boston shipping merchant, manager of the *Glory of the Seas* and to look after the syndicate's interests.

Donald still had friends in high places. In May of 1873, Donald bid on a contract to build a steam sloop of war for the Navy. When the nine bids were opened, Donald's bid of $168,000 was the second lowest. The lowest bid was from Thomas Stack for $148,500. A dozen of Donald's influential friends wrote letters to George Robeson, the Secretary of the Navy, trying to persuade him to give the contract to McKay rather than Stack because McKay could build a better ship. They also pointed out that Stack had very little experience building ships and McKay was the most famous ship builder of his time. Finally, on September 28, 1873 Isaiah Hanscom, the Chief of the Bureau of Construction and Repair, offered to award the contract to Donald if he would lower his bid to $148,500. Donald reluctantly agreed. Donald received the contract in November of 1873, but there were wording changes that needed to be made in the contract and logistics for using the Boston Navy Yard and some of their materials, so that the work on the ship was not started until January of 1874. The contract and all of the correspondence referred to the ship as the *U.S.S. Guilding,* but it was renamed the *U.S.S. Adams* sometime before it was launched. This was the second Navy ship named after former President John Adams.

All of the history books claim that Donald built two sloops of war at the same time, the *U.S.S. Adams* and the *U.S.S. Essex*. I always wondered how he could have built the *Adams* in the Boston Navy Yard in Massachusetts at the same time as the *Essex* was built in the Kittery Navy Yard, 56 miles away in Maine. This trip between Boston and Kittery would have been almost a full day's ride by horse and carriage. Donald was a 'hands on' sort of person who managed every phase of a project. He often built multiple ships at the same time, but he built them side by side in his shipyard. Why would he build two ships 56 miles apart when he could have built both of them in Boston? In April of 1876, the

Honorable J. H. Burleigh started leaking innuendos to the press that Donald McKay had overcharged the government $22,000 in the building of the *Essex*. Donald's response, as reported in the April 3, 1876 issue of the Boston Daily Globe, was that he did NOT build the *Essex*. This sent me to the National Archives, on my next trip to Washington, to get an answer to this dilemma. I found that the newspaper report was correct. He only had the contract to build the *Adams.* The Navy built the *Essex* in the Navy Shipyard in Kittery Maine. After the *Essex* was launched, the ship was towed down to Boston to be finished and for the engine to be installed. The Atlantic Works, who had taken over the McKay and Aldus company, made and installed the engines in both the *Adams* and the *Essex*. Donald was given a contract for $57,000 to finish the *Essex* at the Boston Navy Yard and make it ready for sea. He was also given a contract for $35,000 to finish the *Adams*. This is probably the reason for the $22,000 question. Isaiah Hanscom, the Navy's person in charge of all ship building and repairs, had commissioned two of his men, Easby and Fernald, to come up with the cost to finish both of these ships. They were the ones who came up with the figures and Donald probably had little say in the matter. The *Essex* obviously needed more work. I suspect that the $22,000 may have had to do with adding iron plate onto the *Essex*. On December 16, 1874, Donald had sent Isaiah Hanscom an itemized list of material and labor supplied by the Boston Navy Yard to iron clad the *Adams*. It totaled $21,985.09. This is why I suspect that the *Essex* did not yet have the iron plate on the sides of the ship.

Most people think that when a ship is launched it has been completed and is ready to set sail, but this is not true. After the launching there is still a considerable amount of work that still remains to be done. This extra work is what they referred to as

"Finishing" the ship. If you look at the picture of the **Great Republic** being launched (page 57), you will notice that there are no sails nor rigging showing on the ship. If you could look inside of the ship you would also notice that the cabins and amenities inside of the ship have not been built yet.

If you think of how a ship was built at that time, it makes a lot of sense not to finish a ship before it is launched. A ship was made on top of the ground, starting with the bottom of the ship which was raised slightly off of the ground on its slipways. Then they slowly built up the supports and then the sides and the deck. They also had to build scaffolding along the side of the ship so that the men could climb up to work on the sides and the top. Originally, the men had to manually carry all of the heavy timber up the scaffolding to reach the top. Now consider that the deck of the ship rose from 30 to 50 feet off of the ground. This is comparable to a four to six story building with the entrance on the roof and no elevator. Apprentices hefted these heavy timbers on their shoulders and carried them up the scaffolding. Donald McKay was the first shipbuilder to solve this problem and to use a steam derrick to lift the heavy timbers. He also used horses, mules, and oxen, instead of men, to drag the heavy materials across the yard over to the derrick. Although this certainly made life easier on all of the workers, it still did not alter the fact that they had to climb up and down the scaffolding perhaps 20 to 30 times per day. This is why they built the ship, caulked it and sealed it to make it water tight; made sure that the ship would float and that the rudder worked. Then the ship was launched. It was then towed over to a dock so that you only needed a gang plank to get on board. You only had to walk up four to eight feet instead of 50 feet. With easy access to the deck, the ship was then finished. Rigging was attached, along with sails, and the 100 miles of rope. The cabins were finished and all necessary equipment installed.

If there were steam engines to be loaded, this was the time that they were loaded. Only after all of this finish work was completed was the ship ready to set sail.

Donald's friend, General Butler, who was instrumental in getting some of the Navy contracts for Donald, had bought the yacht *America* from the government. General Butler was interested in racing the yacht and knew that it needed some modernization to make it successful, so he asked Donald to do it. Although Donald's shipyard was pretty much stripped, he got permission to use part of it. He was able to gather some of his old workers and, over the spring of 1875 he started work on the *America*. He changed her masts, replaced the tiller with a wheel, and rebuilt the cabins in the grand manner that reflected the tastes of her owner. This was the last work that he did in his shipyard.

In his long career, Donald had built 64 ships, finished 2, and helped Cornelius build 4, for a total of 73. There were 3 ships, 2 trading ships, 16 packet ships, 3 barques, 2 clipper barques, 4 clippers, 13 medium clippers, 13 extreme clippers, 2 schooners, 1 brig, 4 steam screw propeller ships, I iron clad monitor, 1 steam side wheeler, 1 steam sloop of war and finished another, and 1 full model ship.

In 1877, Donald sold his house on Eagle Hill in East Boston and moved up to a farm at 1031 Main St. in Hamilton, Massachusetts. This was down the street from his shipyard foreman, Mr. Winslow, who lived at 1079 Main Street. Donald was suffering from consumption and he decided to retire to a nice quiet place. Farming was not his favorite pastime, but he made the most of it.

Donald had been known for his entertaining, both in Boston and in Hamilton. He played the violin and was known as a very gracious host. The famous poet, Henry Wadsworth Longfellow, visited his Boston home on several occasions. After the launching of each of his ships, it was common for dignitaries and friends to gather at Donald's house to celebrate. In a history of the Town of Hamilton, Austin Brown writes that there was a big party at Donald's farm in 1878 where he invited the whole town.

In the Hamilton, Massachusetts Census of 1880, Donald was 69 and living with his wife Mary C. (49); his son Lawrence (20) working as a farm hand; the twins Anna and Nichols (15) in school; his son Guy Allen (13) in school; his youngest son Wallace (11) in school; Ellen (35) and Mary McCarthy (50) both servants; and Mike (58) and Jack Scanlon (25) both farm hands. On July 17th of that same year Donald was struck down with a paralytic stroke. After suffering from consumption for many years, he died in Hamilton at 2 PM on September 20, 1880. He is buried in the family plot at Oak Hill Cemetery in Newburyport, Massachusetts. At the time of his death, there were four of Albenia's children and seven of Mary Cressy's children still living.

Donald had made out his Will on June 19, 1880, less than one month before he had his stroke, and it contained some interesting things. He specified that the house in Hamilton be sold upon his death, and distributed as follows:

- His wife, Mary Cressy (Litchfield) McKay, received 1/4 of the real estate sale, 1/8 of any government settlement of the claims owed on the Civil War ships, and everything else not mentioned in the Will.
- Donald McKay, Jr. and John Boole McKay were not to receive anything from the estate because *"They have already received as much of my property as is just"*.
- Albenia (McKay) Bodemer only receives a silver water urn.

- Cornelius Whitworth McKay, received all of Donald's ship items: library, draughts, models, plus 1/24th of any money received from any government settlement.
- Frances (McKay) Clavel received a silver teapot and bowl, 1/17 of the real estate sale, and 1/24 of any government settlement.
- Mary Cressy (McKay) Bliss received a silver coffeepot, 1/17 of the real estate sale, and 1/24 of any government settlement. Her husband was executor of the Will.
- Anna Cushing (McKay) Burton received a silver sugar bowl and creamer, 3/17 of the real estate sale, and 1/8 of any government settlement. However, she died in January 1885 before the house was sold and before the government settled the claim.
- Lawrence Litchfield McKay received a gold watch and diamond pin, 3/17 of the real estate sale, and 1/4 of any government settlement, 1/4 of the farm tools and livestock, and $500 (about $10,863 in 2009 dollars).
- Nichols Litchfield McKay received a gold watch chain, a silver server, 3/17 of the real estate sale, 1/8 of any government settlement, and 1/4 of the farm tools and livestock.
- Guy Allen McKay received 1/2 dozen small silver forks, 3/17 of the real estate sale, 1/8 of any government settlement, and 1/4 of the farm tools and livestock.
- Wallace McKay received 1/2 dozen small silver forks, 3/17 of the real estate sale, 1/8 of any government settlement, and 1/4 of the farm tools and livestock.

Mary Cressy (Litchfield) McKay continued to live in Hamilton for five more years, until 1885, when she moved to Arlington, Massachusetts. In the 1900 and 1910 censuses she is living with her son Nichols and his family at 73 Jason Street. in Arlington. In the 1920 census, she is 89 and living with her widowed daughter Mary Cressy Bliss at 19 Oakland St. in Lexington, Massachusetts, along with four servants. There was a cook, a maid, a chauffeur, and a nurse attendant. Mary would live to the ripe old age of 91. She died in Lexington on Feb 6,1923 after suffering for several years with arteriosclerosis. She also is buried in the family plot in Newburyport, Massachusetts.

Mary was the type of person who stood up for what she believed in. There was a story in an old Hamilton newspaper that said that one of the McKay neighbors wanted to turn his home into an inn and pub. Mary attended all of the Town's meetings concerning the Inn and pleaded with the Town not to allow alcohol to be served there because it was a residential area with many children living in the area.

It is also interesting to note that Donald's last clipper ship, the *Glory of the Seas*, was scrapped for her metal at Brace Point in Seattle, Washington on May 13th, 1923, three months after Mary's death, and after 53 years of honorable service. The last remaining ship still afloat that Donald McKay was connected with, the Navy's *U.S.S. Essex,* was scrapped Oct 14, 1931 in Duluth, Minnesota. The *U.S.S. Adams* had been scrapped ten years prior.

CONCLUSION

In the course of doing my research on Donald McKay, I read several books that had erroneous information about Donald, or simply drew the wrong conclusions about him, and I think that it is important to correct these errors. I read such things as: Donald was a poor businessman, he was still building wooden sailing ships while others were building iron steamships, he went out of business because he did not keep up with the times. I firmly believe that none of these conclusions are correct.

One of the remarks about Donald's poor business sense was that he paid his workers wages when the economy was down and there was no work for them to do at the shipyard. In today's market that simply is not done. Employer/employee loyalty no longer exists today in "good business practice" but that is a shame because I think it should. He had workers with very specialized skills that he needed to keep for when the business picked up again. He could not afford to lose them. It was in Donald's best interest, as well as the employee's interest, to pay them at least partial wages during such down times.

I believe that Donald proved himself a very good businessman. He made the fastest and most famous ships, sold them to the most illustrious merchants, paid all of his bills, paid his workers excellent wages, and made himself an excellent living while doing all of this. He kept the business going in bad times as well as good. He was not afraid to take occasional calculated risks, as all good businessman have to do from time to time.

Although most ships were built to order, he built a few ships with his own money on speculation hoping that he could find a buyer, and in most cases that paid off very well for him. After the Civil War ended in 1865, the government still owed Donald more than a quarter of a million dollars for ships built for the Navy (more than $4 million in 2009 dollars) which the government was refusing to pay. Donald was not the only shipbuilder with this problem. Many shipbuilders, who had built ships for the Civil War, were not paid in full, and went bankrupt because of it. Although several writers consider that the building of the *Glory of the Seas* as a clipper ship rather than a steamship was Donald's undoing. I do not think that it would have made any difference. A steamship would not have given Donald enough profit to satisfy his creditors. The *Glory of the Seas* indeed proved to be a very fast ship after her sail to San Francisco and Donald could very well have gotten top dollar for it, but the mortgage holder got greedy and foreclosed one month before she reached port. He would not wait one more month to find out how fast it was. If the mortgage holder had waited until the payment was due, or at least the patience to wait a couple more months, this would never have happened and they would have been paid back in full, and Donald would still have his shipyard. The *Glory of the Seas* was a great ship that would earn her owners a great deal of money throughout the years. I believe that if the government had paid their debt, and had paid for the multiple changes that they had made to their specifications, Donald would not have been in debt and would not have had to mortgage the *Glory of the Seas.* He would have stayed in business and have made a handsome profit. If Donald had not been in debt because of the government, it is also possible that he may never have built the *Glory of the Seas* and would have built steamships instead.

England started experimenting with iron ships as early as 1798, but the first iron ship to cross the Atlantic was the S S Great Britain in 1845, many years before the United States started to build them. England had large supplies of iron and coal but a short supply of wood. They had to import most of the wood for their ships. The United States had an abundant supply of wood, which was cheaper and actually built a better ship. Wooden ships were coppered below the water line because copper was poisonous to marine life and kept off the barnacles that would slow down the ship. They also required periodic overhauls in dry-dock about every two years. Iron ships could not be coppered because the copper would eat away the iron. This meant that they had to be dry-docked every 6 months to scrape the barnacles, remove the rust and repaint the bottoms. Although the United States was building fresh water boats and ships out of iron, most builders were still building their salt water, ocean going, steamships out of wood. The steel ship would not be built until well into the 1880's, long after Donald had died.

As far as the statements that Donald went out of business because he did not keep up with the times and was still building clipper ships when the rest of the world was going with steamships is not true. In 1855, Donald joined with George Upton, Enoch Train, Andrew Hall, and James Beebe to incorporate the Boston and European Steamship Company. The plan was to build "*a splendid line of Atlantic steamers rivaling in every respect the Collins Line of New York*". Donald showed them his design for the pioneer steamer of the proposed line, which was to be called *Cradle of Liberty*, and was to cross the Atlantic in six days. Unfortunately, the Collins Line went bankrupt the following year and the partners got cold feet and dissolved the corporation.

Donald had setup his youngest brother, Nathaniel, to run the McKay and Aldus Iron Works for the express purpose of building steam engines and steamships. Besides the steamships that Nathaniel built, Donald built the *Trefoil, Yucca, Nausett, Ashuelot, Geo B Upton, Adams*, and the *Theodore D Wagner*, all steamships. When it started looking like the Civil War was imminent in 1861, Donald wrote several letters to the Secretary of the Navy encouraging him to start building iron, or iron clad, steam driven screw propeller war ships. He pointed out that the sail ships and the side wheeled steamers were obsolete for use in battle because they were not maneuverable enough, and that the new French designed screw propeller iron clad war ships were far superior. And yet, the government continued to build side wheeled steamers and monitors during the Civil War, which were clearly the wrong ships.

One has to remember that the steamships of Donald's time were all fired by coal, and there was also a tendency of the boilers blowing up if they built up too much pressure. Donald's sister-in-law, Eunice C. Boole, was scalded to death, in September of 1878, when the steamship *Adelphi's* boiler exploded off of Gregory Point in Long Island Sound.

In order for a ship to get from point A to point B, they had to carry enough coal to get them there and then they had to reload enough coal to get them back home. There was a limited amount of coal that could be carried on any ship that was also carrying cargo in order for the ship to make any money. Therefore many of the ocean going steamships had masts, and carried sail if the wind was favorable, in order to conserve on the coal. Most steamships were not particularly fast and, if the wind was right, a good clipper was much faster. There were also many parts of the world that did not have a coal supply and therefore steamships could not travel there unless they had some sort of refueling station along the way. The coal fired steamship was inefficient and much more costly to run than a sailing ship. Passengers also complained about the vibrations and noise caused by the engines. In the 1860's, when the ocean going steamships really started coming into prominence, and into the 1870's there was still a reasonably good market for sailing ships as long as they were fast. It was not until 1887, seventeen years after Donald was forced to close the shipyard and seven years after Donald had died, that the steamship tonnage finally surpassed that of the sailing ship. The *Glory of the Seas*, built in 1869, would sail for 50 more years before it was turned into a fish canning plant, and it was almost four more years before it was finally scrapped in 1923 despite a public outcry to save the famous ship.

48

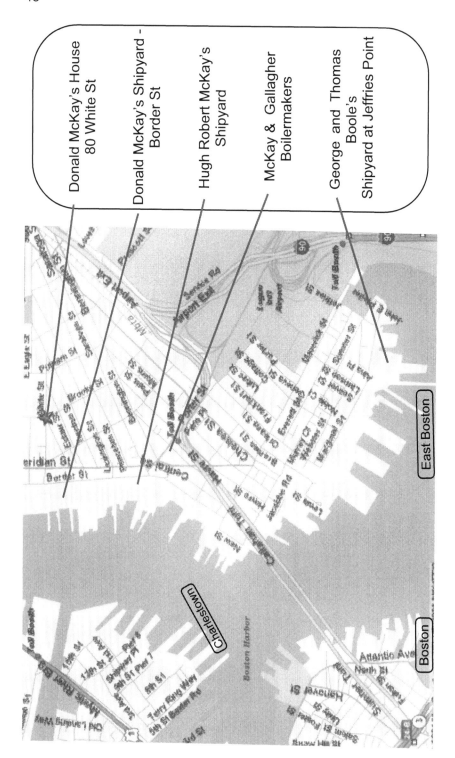

Donald McKay's House
80 White St

Donald McKay's Shipyard -
Border St

Hugh Robert McKay's
Shipyard

McKay & Gallagher
Boilermakers

George and Thomas
Boole's
Shipyard at Jeffries Point

Charlestown

East Boston

Boston

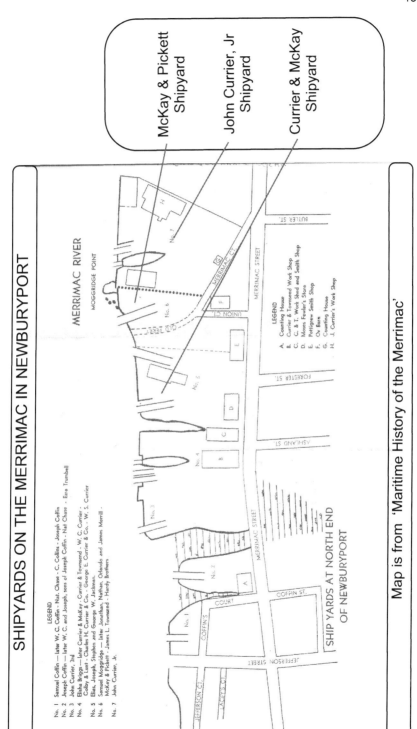

SHIPYARDS ON THE MERRIMAC IN NEWBURYPORT

McKay & Pickett Shipyard

John Currier, Jr Shipyard

Currier & McKay Shipyard

MERRIMAC RIVER

MOGGRIDGE POINT

LEGEND

No. 1 Samuel Coffin — later W. C. Coffin - Nat. Chase - C. Collins - Joseph Coffin
No. 2 Joseph Coffin — later W. C. and Joseph, sons of Joseph Coffin - Nat Chase - Ezra Trumbell
No. 3 John Currier, 2nd
No. 4 Elisha Briggs — later Currier & McKay - Currier & Townsend - W. C. Currier - Colby & Lunt - Charles H. Currier & Co. - George E. Currier & Co. - W. S. Currier
No. 5 Elias, Joseph, Stephen and George W. Jackman.
No. 6 Samuel Moggridge — later Jonathan, Nathan, Orlando and James Merrill - McKay & Pickett - James L. Townsend - Hardy Brothers
No. 7 John Currier, Jr.

LEGEND

A. Counting House
B. Currier & Townsend Work Shop
C. C. & T. Work Shed and Smith Shop
D. Moses Fowler's Store
E. Pettigrew Smith Shop
F. Ox Barn
G. Counting House
H. J. Currier's Work Shop

SHIP YARDS AT NORTH END OF NEWBURYPORT

Map is from 'Maritime History of the Merrimac'

McKay's home at 80 White Street (Eagle Hill),
East Boston - 1850's

McKay's house in 2006
as a 3 family house.

The side parlor in the McKay house
at 80 White Street in 2006

The dining room in the McKay house
note the rounded walls

52

Donald McKay's house in Hamilton, MA
1031 Main St. (Rt 1a)
1992 and 2007

ANNA LITCHFIELD   NICHOLS LITCHFIELD
Picture courtesy of Kate Silvernale

MARY CRESSY LITCHFIELD McKAY
Pictures courtesy of Kate Silvernale

Donald McKay Memorial
Castle Island in Boston Harbor

Donald McKay Memorial
In Jordan River, Nova Scotia
near the site of his father's sawmill

Picture is from the Nova Scotia Electric Scrapbook on the ns1763.ca web site.

The Donald McKay bust
in Bremen Park - East Boston, MA

Donald McKay stained glass window
in the chapel of Tabor Academy

Diorama of the McKay Shipyard of East Boston
in the Boston Museum of Science

John Brooks took over part of the McKay Shipyard after Donald closed
the yard in 1870. The McKay yard was to the right of the picture. Note the curb-
cut, which is still there today, that acts as a reference point to the McKay Yard.
John was Donald's foreman for 6 years.

Launching of the Great Republic
McKay Shipyard, East Boston on October 4, 1853
Picture is from the Richard C. McKay collection

U.S.S. Adams at anchor about 1880 - same design
as the U.S.S. Essex

58

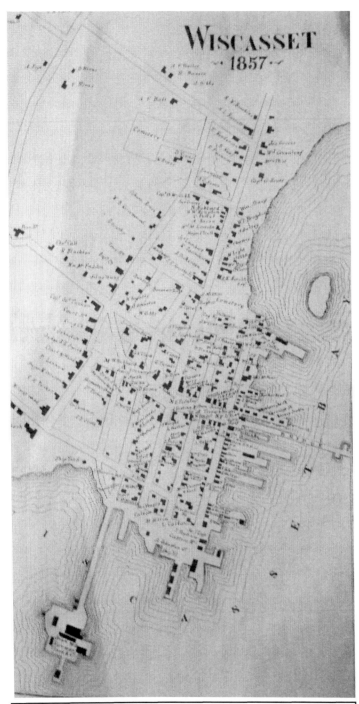

1857 Map of Wiscasset, Maine on the Sheepscot River

CHAPTER 3

A LETTER THAT DONALD McKAY WROTE TO HIS BROTHER LAUCHLAN

Growing up with 15 brothers and sisters, there are bound to be times when some personalities might clash. In 1856, Lauchlan was suing Donald, and Donald was counter-suing Lauchlan over thousands of dollars and all sorts of properties in East Boston and Roxbury. I read Donald's lawyer's notes several times, at the Peabody Museum's Phillips Library, and I still could not understand what was really going on, other than the fact that Lauchlan's case against Donald was vacated (thrown out).

The following is a copy of a letter that Donald wrote to Lauchlan at the time that all of this was going on. The letter was printed in 1856 by William P. McCue for Donald. After Mr. McCue's death in 1893, his son submitted this material to the historical archives in Boston.

"To: Lauchlan McKay   * The Great Business Man *

Sir:

You have frequently, during the past two months, stated that I am insane; and, I am sorry to say, a review of my conduct towards you for many years, proves your statement correct. As a boy, I knew you to be mean and selfish; but, as a man, I forgot those early traits of character, and loved you affectionately as a brother. Had I been sane, I would have bestowed my affection upon you with prudent caution, and have only believed your statements after I had proved them true.

You doubtless remember the INSANE credence I gave to your tale of destitution, when I resided in Newburyport. You were then, you stated, sick and penniless. I INSANELY believed you, and though very poor at the time myself, living from hand to mouth, surrendered to you and your wife the best room in my house, and shared with you my scanty fare. My wife too, washed for you and your wife , for the latter was too much of a lady to moisten her hands in a washtub. I subsequently learned you had ample means to support yourself during the months you resided with me, but being a SANE man you preferred to sponge your poor INSANE brother and thus husband your resources until your health was restored. You believed I was a fool, that I would never make any charge for the expense you caused me, and the sequel proved you were correct. But had I been a SANE man, like yourself, I would have made strict inquiries about your circumstances, have drawn up a bill of costs, and have refused to give up your clothing and other effects until I had been paid, or had received ample SECURITY. This would have been, agreeable to your views, "In strict accordance with sound business principles, for the protection of property and character".

Permit me to call your attention to another act of INSANITY; you had no visible means of support when I used my influence to procure you the command of the ship Jenny Lind, although I had reason to believe that you were as ignorant of seamanship as I knew you to be of shipbuilding. But I hoped by procuring a sailor for your mate, you might manage to pass muster. In this I was mistaken. My INSANE affection for you blinded my understanding to the fact that you were as presumptuous and self-willed as you were ignorant and incompetent, and the result was, that you had to throw overboard part of the ship's deck-load of cotton, through stupidity in loading her; and on the next passage, from the same cause, had to put back and discharge. This was the only ship I ever built that had to make a port in distress through the ignorance of her commander. But I had charity. I knew you were green, and made all the excuses for you that my INSANE affection could suggest.

Again INSANE; contrary to the advice of my best friends, I placed you in command of the "Sovereign of the Seas" with a picked crew of a hundred men, but you could not carry her to her destination without disaster. It is an old saying that "He who knows nothing, fears nothing", and so it was with you. I need not remind you of the lubberly way you carried sail, which brought the ship's topmasts on deck, not the biting remarks made by your officers about your stupidity. I closed my ears to them and INSANELY went to work to prove that you were a great man! God forgive me for my wicked partiality towards you! Not satisfied with having you praised throughout the length and breadth of the land during your absence, I had your praise revived and reechoed when you returned. And all this for what? Because you had ignorantly dismantled my ship and with a crew of a hundred men, had barely managed to refit her again. But this is not all; when I sold the ship I took care that you should be amply rewarded for your services. Previous to your departure I agreed to give you the wages out of the port, about $250 a month, but I threw this agreement away, and stipulated that you should receive $6,000 for this voyage. You received it, and with it a service of plate for 9 month's work. I was overjoyed at your success, for I was INSANE and went along blundering as before. I placed you in command of the "Great Republic" and foolishly gave you the superintendence of her outfits. The extravagance of the expenses you lavished on her, the stupid increase of her spars, and the fact that you were continually at war with the mechanics, failed to shake my attachment to you. I sustained you everything, and although I saw with regret, when too late, that the ship could not even carry her top-gallant masts aloft when laden, I did not complain. You were still my affectionate brother, and after the ship was burned, and you again out of employment, I did not desert you. INSANE to the last I employed you as my agent at a salary of $10,000 per annum, exclusive of traveling expenses. When I took you up you were so poor that you could not pay your expenses, at least you told Mr Ayres so; yet in thirteen months I paid for services $18,480, and as already stated, have given you from that time until within a few weeks $10,000 per annum and traveling expenses.

Now mark the result of my INSANE liberality, when you were in Liverpool I partly revealed to you the state of my affairs, and furnished you with ample means to raise money to enable me to meet my liabilities; but you disregarded my positive instructions and wrote me insolent letters. You promised to send me $220,000 but only sent me $180,000, nor have you to this day explained the causes why you could not perform what you had promised, when I respectfully requested you to explain you answered to the following effect: "You are surrounded by a parcel of dxxxxd thieves, and those nearest you are the biggest thieves, there is Pratt, Osgood, Porter - all dxxxxd thieves and they fail you yet. I have told you this again and again. I say discharge every one of them". Your whole conduct towards me was entirely changed. Repeated personal insolence was substituted for brotherly affection, and has been continued to this day.

When you returned from Liverpool I respectfully, even kindly, asked you to render an account of your business and was answered as follows: "I'll see you dxxxxd first. God dxxxxn you, I'm prepared for you; pay me $25,000 or I'll ruin you." A stranger would hardly credit that at the time you made this demand you were $7,000 in my debt, and also held in addition, my drafts for $25,000; yet such was the fact, and you knew it. But you also knew that I was INSANE and believed that I must fail, therefore you determined to kick up a row with me in order to cover up the manner in which you had mismanaged my business in Liverpool. Who ever heard of an agent who demanded his pay before he rendered an account of his doings? Yet you did this, and because I demanded your accounts, you went whining to your friends and represented that I had refused to pay you. A more infamous falsehood was never uttered. I objected to your making a grab of $57,000, and for this you denounced me as insane. But at the same time, to your pious friends you pretended to be deeply penetrated with "Great pain and sorrow" and said all you wanted was security - you did not wish to embarrass me; and to show further how good you had been, you circulated a sworn statement that you had never spoken a word against me or my ships in Liverpool. You perjured loafer! Both Captains Gardner and Beauchamp, as well as the others, heard you frequently in Liverpool, denounce the best ships I ever built as unseaworthy. This was done, no doubt, to make people believe that you were the great man of the establishment, and that I was only your ignorant wood-chopper, a kind of servant that required to be strictly watched. I was a cheat too, for you disputed the bills I sent you to collect, and made a long statement that I had overcharged for my work; and since your return you have boasted that you cut $9,000 off my bills. What a generous brother!

You expected that I would fail, and like the unjust steward, went to work to make friends of my debtors. Of course they thought you very conscientious and a person wholly worthy of their confidence. This is apparent by their refusing to answer my letters until they first hear from you. Satisfied within your own mind that I must fail and thus afford you an opportunity to make a grand grab out of my ruins, you not only turned against me yourself, but labored to turn everyone else against me at the same time. You made long homilies about what you were pleased to term my extravagant mode of living, wrote letters to show that you, like a kind brother, had warned me of the result, but that I was deaf to your remonstrances. But your cunningly devised scheme miscarried, I have not failed, nor will I fail, even should you succeed in cheating me of every cent within your control. You want security to the last cent. I must yield to your insolent demand or you will "ruin" me. You will expose my mode of shipbuilding. Pray where did you acquire a knowledge of shipbuilding? The only thing of your production I ever saw was the bark "Odd Fellow" and she was the laughingstock for the mechanics while she remained in East Boston.

You lazy ignorant loafer! I say ships are my monuments and they float triumphantly on every sea. Two of them, the "Flying Fish" and "Santa Claus" are now in port, and I challenge you to produce their superiors. But you want security, though you owe me over $7,000, or you will run them and me down. To strangers, during the past year, I have been indebted over a million, yet not one of them asked me for security. It was reserved for you, my affectionate brother, to be the first to question my honesty, the first to misrepresent my workmanship. Nay more, a few days since you hawked a note of mine about the street before it was due, offering it for sale, for the benevolent purpose of impairing my credit. You have left no stone unturned to crush me. But I paid your note as I have all my other notes, when it comes to maturity. Can you say as much, you cheat, and speak the truth? But you are the "Great Businessman" according to your estimate of yourself and your conduct towards me, in your view, has been in accordance with "Strict Business Principles". Your maxim is that "Business knows neither relations nor friends, it is purely selfish". This maxim has been your cardinal point through life. Before I took you up and gave you wealth and position, there were many strange stories in circulation about you. Stories which, if I had not been INSANE, I ought to have investigated before I trusted you. But I was too busy, and moreover, had little desire to overhaul the weaknesses of a favorite brother, so I took you to my heart and gave you my entire confidence! How well you have repaid it!

Your first prominent business transaction was with Mr. Ayres in Lowell. When he was embarrassed you came into possession of his property without consideration, and when he requested you to restore it you declined, and even threatened him if he dared to insist upon restitution. You hold his property, valued at $10,000, to this day, or I ought rather to say Capt. Warner holds it for you.

The next great business you were engaged in was raising funds to build the bark "Odd Fellow". The simpleton who furnished you with the means failed, but you, like a 'wise business man' held on to the bark, sailed her and sold her, but never gave the man who furnished the funds a cent.

Your great business talent was again displayed when you were in company with your Uncle in New York. You received $9,000 for an insurance job, but only accounted for $6,000 on the books. Did you pocket the balance $3,000, and then quarrel with your partner in order to hide the fraud you had perpetrated? It is a patent part of your policy to cheat, and then kick up a row. But this is not all; you schemed to sponge your partner out of a year's board for yourself and family; but in this you made a slight mistake. For once you were compelled to pay a just debt, your partner, in the matter of board, made you honest by law. Still you triumphed for he allowed you to cheat him out of $3,000, rather than take the trouble to make you disgorge. The remembrance of this triumph has no doubt had a powerful influence in deciding your conduct towards me.

It is hardly worth while to allude to the knavish way you ran away from your creditors in Virginia, how you treated your brother Simon in getting him to father your debts, for these are mere trifles; nor will I inquire into the cause of your imprisonment in Lowell, nor why you committed perjury in New York, because you escaped justice by the exercise of your "great business talents"; but I must not forget to call your attention to the funds collected from visitors to the Great Republic. These funds, designed for charitable purposes, were carried to your house every night and counted, yet when the ship was destroyed, with (great business talent) you made the press of New York believe that the money was destroyed in her. The sum was about $4,000, which you put 'business like' in your own pocket. This you deny, and will probably swear to before some Justice of the Peace "with great pain and sorrow".

But you are a great business man for though worth over $100,000, a very large part of which is in real estate, yet it is all covered so that your creditors can not compel you to be honest. Your business talents consist of cheating your creditors. Why have you deeded part of your property to me, without my knowledge? And why does Capt.

Warner hold your estates in Lowell and Roxbury? Because you are deeply in debt and because you are determined not to be honest and pay what you owe. Why do you not pay the note of $4,800 which you owe Mr. Ayres, and which Mr. Hicock has now in court against you? Because by the exercise of your "business talent" you hope to cheat him. And you will do it too. You have been kindly pleased to represent me to strangers as entirely ignorant of business and that I have been indebted to your GREAT TALENTS for whatever success I have achieved; in other words you have been my thinking machine and balance wheel. So far is this from truth that everything I have left to your superintendence has been done wrong. The sparring of the Great Republic was a masterpiece of stupidity. You also sparred the Comm. Perry and when she arrived in Liverpool, you wrote that her spars were all wrong, and spent much money in having them altered; but when you returned to Boston, and faced the mechanics who made the spars by our direction, you swore they were all right and that I lied if I said anything to the contrary; but you took care not to state the reason of the alteration you said something about her going a southern voyage; but is it customary to lay out money in altering ship's spars every time they change their trade? An increase in the size of her light sails would have been all that was necessary.

If you have been so successful in thinking for me, how is it that you failed in every honest enterprise you have undertaken yourself? You built the steamer Independence, and estimated she would cost $45,000 yet she cost over $70,000; a small schooner too, the result of your thinking, cost $3,000 over your estimates. You also planned a line of packets between this port and Liverpool, and where is it? You have been successful only in cheating; and so well are you convinced of this, that you have reduced it to a system. You are pious to the pious, profane to the worldly, all things to all men whenever you can have a chance to make a grab. After you have cleaned me out, if I permit you, some other insane victim will be selected for the exercise of your great business talents.

You propose going to the Crimea to join a partner there; and if you do not cheat him, it will be because he will not give you the opportunity. But you are a religious man, you fear God and have a conscience; only, my dear brother, you are a little given to sins of the flesh. Can you tell the reason why Mr. Simpson turned a certain lady out of his house? Was it because you were found in rather delicate contact with her? I suppose you have forgotten all about the time, your own Mother and Sister found you in sweet communion with a young woman, when you and she were pretending to watch with a dying man in the next room. But you cannot have forgotten the night when I took you out of a girl's bedroom, though your own wife slept in the next apartment.

In continuation, permit me to revive your memory about the time you were in Liverpool. On account of "pressing business" you could not accompany your wife in a proposed trip to Paris, so she proceeded as far as London without you, but there changed her mind and returned unexpectedly to Liverpool where, of course, you were deeply immersed in business. Nothing of the kind Dear Brother; you were on a cruise elsewhere, which lasted several days; no doubt exercising your great "Business Talent". At least your wife said so, and dressed you down in decent style. But you were penitent, so meek and so self-abashed that she forgave you, and you promised not to sin again. Why is it, Brother, that you always seem to shun your wife? Why do you not take her with you in your travels? You have no children, and I think economy, not to speak of love, ought to keep you together. Everyone to whom she is known can bear testimony to her affectionate devotion toward you. Why then, seem to shun her? Because, you lecherous scamp, you are void of manly principle. Your proper place is among the Turks or Mormons.

In your estimation however, these derelictions from duty are only small love affairs, and amount to nothing in the eyes of business men. Besides, if occasion required it, you could easily obtain sworn certificates that these frail sisters seduced you, that they took advantage of your fine, pious conscientious feelings to overcome you! You are so good, so sane, so honest, so conscientious, and have withal, such brotherly love and meekness of expression, that nobody but an INSANE person would believe anything against you. How can you do wrong?

Brother, forgive this long epistle, written "in great pain and sorrow", and which would never have seen the light had you not set me the example by circulating perjured affidavits to prove me a liar! Still I ought to feel that I am very INSANE, a mere "WOODCHOPPER", void of all "BUSINESS TALENT". Proof of this can be found in the facts that, though I have done over five millions worth of business, since I have been in East Boston, yet I have cheated no one, and though I own about $400,000 in real estate, yet not a dollar of it is covered to shield it from attachment, should my creditors seek security. This is not the way you do business, consequently I am wrong. Having such a conscientious brother, am I not INSANE to call in question his conduct towards me? Ought I not rather, in deep humility to surrender all I possess to him? He knows so much more than I do, has such an affectionate heart for the sisters, that, with my means at his disposal, he might found a harem or some other female institution upon "great business principles".

Brother, forgive my hardness of heart and waywardness of disposition, and believe me, were it not that I still desire to guard your poor soul against taking another step towards perdition, you might grab and run with all I own in the world, and I would not even turn upon my heel to cry "Stop Thief".

PS When you again find a fool, who will give you $18,480, exclusively of what you can steal and sponge for less than thirteen months' services, or even $10,000 a year (with traveling expenses), please send me his address that I may pay my respects to him, and present him with my "Cap and Bells".

D. McKay "

CHAPTER 4
DONALD McKAY TIMELINE

Sep 4,	1810	**Donald McKay** is born in Shelburne, Nova Scotia to Hugh and Ann (McPherson) McKay
May 20	1817	**Jennett McKay** (Donald's sister) dies at 2 yr in Shelburne, NS
Feb 10	1824	**Ann McKay** (Donald's sister) dies at 7 yr in Shelburne, NS
	1826	Left Shelburne - took boat to Halifax - from Halifax to New York City
Mar 14,	1827	Signs 4 ½ year contract with the Webb & Allen Shipyard in NY to become indentured apprentice
Spring	1831	Returns to Shelburne and builds a barkentine with his Uncle Robert
	1832	Returns to New York to work for the Brown & Bell shipyard
	1833	**Donald** marries **Albenia Boole** in Manhattan NY
Feb 1,	1834	**Cornelius Whitworth McKay** is born in Manhattan, NY
Apr 3,	1836	**Frances Jean McKay** is born in Manhattan, NY
Nov 12,	1838	**Anne Jane McKay** is born in Manhattan, NY
	1840	Becomes foreman at the Brooklyn Navy Yard
	1840	Goes job hunting in Wiscasset, Maine
	1840	Becomes foreman at John Currier, Jr. shipyard in Newburyport, MA and supervises the building of the *Delia Walker*
Oct 29,	1840	**Dennis Condry McKay** is born in Newburyport, MA
	1841	Donald McKay and William Currier become partners in shipyard In Newburyport, MA - builds *Mary Broughton* 322 ton
	1842	Currier and McKay build the *Ashburton* 449 ton, and *Courier* 380 ton
May 3,	1842	**Donald McKay, Jr** is born in Newbury, MA
Oct 11,	1842	**Anne Jane McKay** dies at 3 yr 11 mo. In Newburyport, MA of scarlet fever
	1843	Donald McKay and William Picket become partners in shipyard In Newburyport, MA - builds *St. George* packet 845 ton
Aug 23,	1843	**Cornelius McKay** is born in Newburyport, MA and died same day
	1844	McKay & Picket build 2 packet ships *John R Skiddy and Joshua Bates*
	1845	Donald McKay moves the family to East Boston
Sep 15,	1845	*Launches Washington Irving* - packet ship 751 tons
Sep 5,	1846	*Launches Anglo Saxon* - packet ship 894 tons
Sep 9,	1846	*Launches New World* - packet ship 1404 tons
Sep 20,	1846	**Albenia McKay** is born in East Boston, MA
Jul	1847	*Launches Ocean Monarch* - packet ship 1301 tons

Oct	1847	Launches *A.Z.* - *packet ship 700 tons*
Feb	1848	Launches *Anglo American* - *packet ship 704 tons*
May	1848	Launches *Jenny Lind* - *packet ship 533 tons*
Dec	1848	Launches *L.Z.* - *packet ship 897 tons*
Dec 10,	1848	**Donald's wife Albenia (Boole) McKay** dies in childbirth at 33 in Boston. She is buried in Newburyport, Mass. The child also died and is buried with his mother.
Feb 13,	1849	Launches *Plymouth Rock* - *packet ship 960 tons*
May	1849	Launches *Helicon* - *barque 400 tons*
Jun	1849	Launches *Reindeer* - *ship 800 tons*
Oct 17,	1849	**Donald McKay** marries **Mary Cressy Litchfield** in East Boston
Dec	1849	Launches *Parliament* - *packet ship 998 tons*
Mar	1850	Launches *Moses Wheeler* - *trading ship 900 tons*
Jun	1850	Launches *Sultana* - *barque 400 tons*
Jun	1850	Launches *Cornelius Grinell* - *packet ship 1118 tons*
Sep	1850	Launches *Antarctic* - *packet ship 1116 tons*
Oct	1850	Launches *Daniel Webster* - *packet ship 1187 tons*
Oct 31,	1850	**Lauchlan McKay** is born in East Boston, MA
Dec 7,	1850	Launches *Stag Hound* - *extreme clipper 1534 tons*
Apr 15,	1851	Launches *Flying Cloud* - *extreme clipper 1782 tons*
Jun 17,	1851	Launches *Staffordshire* - *extreme clipper 1817 tons*
Sep	1851	Launches *North America* - *extreme clipper 1464 ton*
Sep	1851	Launches *Flying Fish* - *extreme clipper 1505 tons*
Oct 31,	1851	**Frances Jean McKay** dies at 14 in East Boston, MA
Jul	1852	Launches *Sovereign of the Seas* - *extreme clipper 2421 tons*
Sep 14,	1852	Launches *Westward Ho!* - *extreme clipper 1650 tons*
Nov 25,	1852	Launches *Bald Eagle* - *extreme clipper 1704 tons*
Jan 14,	1853	Launches *Empress of the Seas* - *extreme clipper 2200 tons*
Apr	1853	Launches *Star of Empire* - *extreme clipper 2050 ton*
Apr 10,	1853	**Lauchlan McKay** (Donald's son) dies at 2 yr in East Boston, MA
May	1853	Launches *Chariot of Fame* - *extreme clipper 2050 tons*
Sep 4,	1853	Launches *Great Republic* - *4 masted clipper barque 4555 tons. When the ship was rebuilt, after the fire, it was only 3357 tons*
Nov 15,	1853	Launches *Romance of the Sea* - *extreme clipper 1782 tons*
Jan 3,	1854	Launches *Lightning* - *clipper 2083 tons*
Apr 12,	1854	**Frances McKay** is born in East Boston, MA
Apr 19,	1854	Launches *Champion of the Seas* - *clipper 2447 tons*
Jul 25,	1854	Launches *James Baines* - *clipper 1787 tons*
Sep 5,	1854	Launches *Santa Clause* - *medium clipper 1256 tons*
	1854	Builds *Blanche Moore* - *extreme clipper 1787 tons*
	1854	Builds *Benin* - *schooner 692 tons*

	1854	Builds *Commodore Perry* - medium clipper 1964 tons
	1854	Builds *Japan* - medium clipper 1964 tons
Jan	1855	Launches *Donald McKay* - clipper 2594 tons
	1855	Builds *Zephyr* - medium clipper 1184 tons
Jul 28,	1855	Launches *Defender* - medium clipper 1413 tons
Jan 4,	1856	**Mary Cressy McKay** is born in East Boston, MA
	1856	Builds *Henry Hill* - clipper barque 568 tons
Feb	1856	Launches *Mastiff* - medium clipper 1030 tons
Mar 22,	1856	Launches *Minnehaha* - medium clipper 1695 ton
	1856	Builds *Amos Lawrence* - medium clipper 1396 tons
	1856	Builds *Abbott Lawrence* - medium clipper 1497 tons
Oct	1856	Launches *Baltic* - medium clipper 1372 tons
Oct	1856	Launches *Adriatic* - medium clipper 1327 tons
Nov 14,	1856	**Ann (McPherson) McKay**, Donald's mother, dies in Boston,MA
	1858	Cornelius builds *R.R. Higgins* in Donald's shipyard - a schooner
1858 -	1859	Launches *Alhambra* - medium clipper 1097 tons
	1859	Cornelius builds *Benj. S. Wright* in Donald's shipyard - 107 tons
Jan 25,	1860	**Lawrence Litchfield McKay** is born in East Boston, MA
	1860	Cornelius builds *Mary B. Dyer* in Donald's shipyard a schooner
	1860	Cornelius builds *H. & R. Atwood* in Donald's shipyard - a schooner
Feb 02,	1861	**Dennis Condry McKay** dies at 20 in East Boston, MA of convulsions
1861 -	1862	Builds *General Putnam* - ship
	1863	Donald equips his yard to build iron ships, marine engines
Jun 17,	1864	**Anna Cushing McKay** is born in East Boston, MA
Jun 17,	1864	**Nichols Litchfield McKay** is born in East Boston, MA
1864 -	1865	Builds *Trefoil* - wooden screw propeller ship for US Navy
1864 -	1865	Builds *Yucca* - wooden screw propeller ship for US Navy
1864 -	1865	Builds *Nausett* - iron clad monitor for US Navy for $578,100.98
1864 -	1865	Builds *Ashuelot* - iron side-wheel double ended ship 1030 tons for US Navy, cost $297,415.92
Jun 25,	1866	Launches *Geo. B. Upton* - wooden screw propeller ship 604 ton
Jul 4,	1866	Launches *Theodore D. Wagner* - wooden screw propeller ship
Oct 4,	1866	**Guy Allen McKay** is born in East Boston, MA
	1867	Builds *North Star* - brig 410 tons
Aug 29,	1867	**Margaret (McKay) Salisbury** (Donald's sister) dies at age 53
1867 -	1868	Builds *Helen Morris* - medium clipper 1285 tons
	1868	Builds *Sovereign of the seas* - full model ship

		1502 tons
Sep 22,	1868	**Sarah (McKay) Thurston** (Donald's sister) dies at 54
Oct 6,	1868	**Wallace McKay** is born in East Boston, MA
	1869	*Builds* ***Frank Atwood*** *- schooner 107 tons*
Oct	1869	*Launched* ***Glory of the Seas*** *- medium clipper*
		2102 tons
Feb 18,	1869	**Elizabeth Ann (McKay) Major** (Donald's sister) dies At age 60
Jun	1870	Donald is forced into bankruptcy and closes the Boston Shipyard
Dec 30,	1871	**Hugh McKay,** Donald's father, dies at 83 in Roxbury, MA
1874 -	1875	*Builds* ***U.S.S. Adams*** *- sloop of war 615 tons built for the US Navy at the Boston Navy Yard*
1874 -	1875	*Finishes* ***U.S.S. Essex*** *- sloop of war built by the US Navy at the Portsmouth Navy Yard in Kittery, ME and finished by Donald at the Boston Navy Yard*
	1875	*Repair and update* ***America*** *- schooner yacht*
	1877	**Donald McKay** moves his family to 1031 Main St. Hamilton, MA
Sep 30,	1880	**Donald McKay** dies at 70 in Hamilton, Mass., buried in Oak Hill Cemetery Newburyport, Mass.
	1885	**Mary Cressy McKay** sells the house in Hamilton, MA, moves to Arlington, MA. In 1900 she is living with her son Nichols in Arlington
Feb 10,	1888	Congress passes bill to finally pay the McKay Shipyard for 4 ships built for the US Navy in 1864-65 for the Civil War
Apr 4,	1888	President Cleveland vetoes this bill because it would offend the "Loyal South"
Mar 10,	1895	**Nathaniel McKay** is awarded $101,529.73 as settlement for the Civil War ships that he and Donald had built in 1865
Feb 6,	1923	**Mary Cressy (Litchfield) McKay** dies at 91 at her daughter's, Mary Cressy Bliss, house in Lexington, MA
May 13,	1923	The *Glory of the Seas*, the last clipper ship that Donald built is scrapped for her metal at Brace Point In Seattle, Washington
Oct 14,	1931	The *U.S.S. Essex*, the last remaining ship still afloat that Donald had worked on, is scrapped for her metal in Duluth, Minnesota

CHAPTER 5
DONALD McKAY'S
BROTHERS and SISTERS

From all of my reading about the McKay family, I got the impression that after Donald opened his shipyard in East Boston, he brought his family down from Nova Scotia. As I researched this wonderful family a bit closer, I found out that much of the family had moved down to Maine before moving to East Boston. His sisters Elizabeth, Sarah and Margaret all had children who were born in Maine, most of them in Bristol, Maine. Lauchlan married Judith Coombs from Bath, Maine and Nathaniel married Adeline Smith in Kennebec, Maine. Although I have not been able to find out what their attraction was to coastal Maine, nor why they decided to leave Nova Scotia, they all seemed to congregated around the maritime communities. Bristol was known to have a large Scottish community, and perhaps there were relatives there.

Although Donald McKay is probably the most famous of his family, his brothers and sisters were just as interesting. Many of them did some extraordinary things. This is what I have learned about these fascinating people.

ELIZABETH ANN McKAY was one year older than Donald, born October 14, 1809 in Jordan Falls, Shelburne, Nova Scotia. She married John Crocheron on August 23, 1827 in Christ Church, Shelburne. John was the son of Abraham and Penniah (Jones) Crocheron, and they lived on land that formerly belonged to Penniah's grandfather, Abraham Jones, on Jones' Point on McLean Island in the Jordan river. John was a farmer and he and Elizabeth had one son named:

- 1. Thomas Jones Crocheron was born on May 8, 1829.

Thomas married Catherine S. Bowers on New Years Day in 1850 and they would have seven children, one boy and six girls.

Sometime following the death of her husband in a drowning accident in Shelburne harbor, Elizabeth married Robert Major and they would have five children. The first four were born in Nova Scotia, and the last was born in Maine. These are their children:

- 1. Eliza Major was born about 1836.
- 2. John Major was born about 1838.
- 3. William Major was born about 1843.
- 4. Robert Major was born about 1844.
- 5. Mary Major was born in Maine about 1849.

Sometime between 1849, when Mary was born, and the 1860 census, the family moved from Maine to East Boston, MA. In 1860, Robert is working as a ship carpenter along with his 22 year old son, John. Their son William, then 17, is an apprentice to a boiler maker in East Boston, possibly with Elizabeth's brother Nathaniel.

Elizabeth Ann died in East Boston on February 18, 1869 at the age of 60. I have not been able to find Robert or any of their children in any of the US Census after 1869. Perhaps they may have returned to Nova Scotia.

LAUCHLAN McKAY,

named after his grandfather Lauchlan McPherson, was one year younger than Donald, born in Jordan Falls on December 16, 1811. He followed Donald down to New York a year after Donald in 1827, and became an apprentice with Donald in the

shipyard of Isaac Webb and worked at the Webb and Allen Shipyard for a while after his apprenticeship. In June of 1836, he decided to join the infant United States Navy and was a ship carpenter on the sloop of war *Natches* and on the frigate *Constellation* and other ships until he resigned from the Navy in 1840. He had joined the Navy to learn to sail the ships as well as build them. He really wanted to know everything there was to know about ships and learn first hand what ship designs worked and which did not. In 1839, the Navy gave him a leave of absence so that he could write "**The Practical Ship-Builder**", which was the first American treatise on shipbuilding. This was the most influential text on the subject for almost 20 years, until Griffith published his work on Clipper Ships in the 1850's. A copy of Lauchlan's book was selling on the Internet in 2004 for $12,000. Lauchlan and his wife Judith lived with his brother Donald in Newburyport, Massachusetts while he wrote the book, and Donald and Albenia assisted him.

Lauchlan married Judith Coombs. Judith was born in Bath, Maine, the daughter of Nathaniel and Rebecca (Turner) Coombs. Although Lauchlan and Judith did not have any children of their own, they adopted Judith Thurston who was the daughter of Lauchlan's sister, Margaret McKay and her husband Solomon Thurston. Unfortunately, she died at only 12 years old. Later in life, Lauchlan adopted William Lawrence Kean, the son of Lauchlan's sister, Mary Ann McKay, and her second husband John Kean. William Kean was the author of the McKay genealogy, "*Hugh McKay and His Lineal Descendents*", which is part of Appendix 4. William married Eliza Jane Hacker, daughter of Judith Coombs' sister Mary Hacker, in Boston on February 11, 1895.

Upon leaving the Navy, Lauchlan left Newburyport and moved to New York City to work as a master shipwright at the Brown and Bell Shipyard. He later opened his own shipyard in Boston with his younger brother Hugh Robert, where their main business was repairing ships, but they also designed and built a couple of ships. In 1846, he designed and built the barque *Odd Fellow* and also sailed it as master. In 1848, he captained the *Jenny Lind*, which Donald had built, and made such quick trans-Atlantic passages that Donald put him in charge of the *Sovereign of the Seas*.

When Lauchlan captained the *Sovereign of the Seas* on her maiden voyage to San Francisco in 1852 - 1853, he set a record of averaging 394 ¾ statute miles per day over four consecutive days. He also made a most respectable run to San Francisco in 103 days, which set a record for that time of year, even though he lost his masts in a storm off the coast of Valparaiso, Chili. He repaired the masts on the open seas without even stopping in port. He jury rigged one mast so that he could keep going, and had all of the masts fixed within 12 days. Donald would later admonish him for carrying so much sail during a storm.

On Lauchlan's return trip from San Francisco, the *Sovereign* carried as cargo, one grizzly bear, a rainbow bear, a wolf, a coyote, a wildcat and a leopard, all destined for the Crystal Palace in New York. Whereas most Clipper ships on the Pacific run headed to China to pickup tea and other items to bring back to New York, Lauchlan headed to Honolulu to pickup whale oil, which was much in demand. This also created a boon for the whaling industry because the whaling ships no longer had to make the long trip to the Atlantic ports. This nine month round trip earned about $135,000 ($3.8 million in 2009 dollars) for the ship. Also on the return trip from San Francisco, the Sovereign of the Seas only had 34 crew members, out of the original 103 member crew, because most of the sailors jumped ship and headed for the California gold fields. Lauchlan was known as an excellent Captain who got the most from his men without the use of force or abuse which most Clipper Ship captains were known to use. In spite of the small crew, the *Sovereign* made it back to New York in only 82 days.

Then on June 18, 1853, Lauchlan took the *Sovereign of the Seas* on its next voyage from New York to Liverpool in the record time of 13 days 22 hours, which was faster than the steamship *Canada* which left Boston on the same day. Lauchlan's brother-in-law, Henry Warner, was his first mate on this voyage, which also included Donald and Mary McKay. After arriving in Liverpool, Henry Warner took command of the *Sovereign* for a trip down to Melbourne, Australia. Lauchlan, Donald and Mary returned to Boston on the ship *America* so that they could put the information that they had gathered on this trip to good use in their building of the *Great Republic*.

After he sailed the *Great Republic* from Boston to New York in 1853, and after the tragic fire that destroyed it, Lauchlan sailed to Liverpool on Donald's *Lightning* as a companion and advisor to Captain James Nicol Forbes. Later he sailed the British ship *Nagasaki* from Liverpool to Australia. While in Sidney, he proved his advanced knowledge of ship construction by raising a sunken ship in a week which others had failed to raise in a month. On this same voyage, Lauchlan rescued the Captain and crew of a vessel in distress. Upon boarding the ship with his carpenter he discovered that they had bored holes in the hull in order to collect the insurance money. Lauchlan's crew plugged the holes and pumped out the ship, and then Lauchlan placed his mate in command, along with some of his own crew, to sail it to an East Indian port where he received a reward from the underwriters for saving the ship.

In the early 1860's, while the Civil War was raging, the cost of living in the United States was sky rocketing. There were shortages of almost everything and prices had doubled or tripled. Southern privateers were capturing and sinking northern shipping so the prospects for a northern captain sailing a northern ship were not good. Lauchlan and his brother-in-law, Capt. Henry Warner, were no longer sailing. Henry joined into a partnership with Benjamin Palmer and they ran a sail-making loft in East Boston. After a while they ended up making tents for the Union army instead of sails.

Lauchlan and Henry decided that the best course of action for them was to build ships in Canada where the economy was better and far less expensive. Henry went up to Quebec and found a large farm on the St. Charles River in Quebec that would be an ideal location for a shipyard. On October 31, 1863, Henry bought a large farm house for both families on lot 437 on the northeast shore of the St. Charles River, in what is now known as the Limoilou section of Quebec City, for $4,000. This lot contained not only the house (it was more like a stone mansion), but also included a barn, stables, and a coach-house. Since it was located on a good sized piece of land right on the river, it would also be used for their shipyard. The property was put in the name of both Henry's wife Elizabeth and Lauchlan's wife Judith. The Coombs sisters then turned around and leased the property to Lauchlan on a five and a half year lease for $700 per year. Lauchlan made it a point never to put his property in his own name. If someone were to sue him, or McKay and Warner, they would not be able to touch the shipyard, nor his property, because he did not own it. Lauchlan had a reputation of not always paying his bills.

Both families lived in the large stone house and, although neither family had any children of their own, there were often nieces and nephews staying there. In Frederick Wallace's book "*In the Wake of the Wind-ships*", he says that above the fireplace in the drawing-room was a picture of the *Sovereign of the Seas*, painted by a well known artist. There was also a painting of the ship *Donald McKay*. These paintings were then copied by one of Lauchlan's nephews, and reproduced in books about the clipper ships.

During the ten years that they were in Quebec, from 1863 to 1873, they launched 28 ships and boats of various sizes with eighteen of them larger than 500 tons. None of these ships were clippers since they were built for freight and not passengers. One of their more famous ships was the 825 ton *Rock City* which was built in 1868 for Henry Fry of Quebec. Mr Fry owned her for ten years and the ship was still sailing 37 years later, in 1905, under a Russian Flag.

When Henry's wife, Elizabeth, died on September 9, 1871, half of her share of the property went to her husband, and half went to her sisters Judith McKay and Mary Hacker. Henry later bought back the shares from her two sisters.

On December 23, 1873, Henry sold his share of the shipyard, along with his shares in several of the ships that they had built, to Lauchlan for $50,000 ($928,030 in 2009 dollars). He then moved back to East Boston. Lauchlan also left Quebec shortly after, but he moved down to New York City. Quebec historian Eileen Marcil claims that Lauchlan left many of his personal belongings in the house when he left. Whether this was because he left in a hurry, or just did not want to move it to New York, we will probably never know. Some time between December 1873 and October 1874 the shipyard was put back into Henry's name because, on October 31, 1874, Henry sold the Quebec shipyard property to Owen Murphy for $6,000 ($117,012 in 2009 dollars). In 1877, Henry returned to Quebec and built the 381 ton barkentine *Chelmsford*, which he sailed and operated on his own account. He also owned two ships, the *Samuel and Florence Wackrell* and the *Frank Lambirth*, which had been built in Bath, Maine. At some point he ran into financial problems and was forced to sell his business. Henry died in February 1893 at the age of 73 and is buried in the Woodlawn Cemetery in Everett, MA.

Lauchlan entered into a partnership with Captain Charles B. Dix to form the firm of McKay and Dix. This was a general shipping business in New York with interests in the Greenland and Newfoundland trade with the ports of Boston, New York and Philadelphia. Much of their business was the importation of cryolite from Greenland which was used in the manufacture of aluminum. To meet the demands of their growing trade, they built, or had others build, 14 more ships. Of these 14 ships, one was built by Lauchlan in 1877 which he named *Ivigtut* (the name of the port city in Greenland where the cryolite came from), and four ships where built in Parrsboro, Nova Scotia.

In 1900, five years after Lauchlan died, Charles B. Dix opened the McKay and Dix Shipyard on Verona Island, Maine across the narrow channel of the Penobscot river from Bucksport, Maine. The McKay and Dix Company apparently lived on for ten more years after Lauchlan died. Captain Dix built the four masted schooner *Edward T. Stotesbury*, the schooners *Thallium, Geo G. Thomas, James W. Paul Jr.*, and his last ship the bark *Roosevelt* of 650 tons which he launched in March of 1905. This was the first ship ever designed as an icebreaker (they called it an ice cutter). This was the ship that Robert E. Perry used to discover the North Pole, but Captain Dix died shortly after its trial run and never knew how famous his ship would be.

Lauchlan died of cancer on April 3, 1895 at his home at 620 Warren Street in the Roxbury section of Boston. Judith had died from influenza three years before Lauchlan, on January 5, 1892, and is buried in the Mt. Auburn Cemetery in Cambridge, MA with Lauchlan and their 12 year old adopted daughter Judith who had died in 1855. Also buried in that same plot is Judith's sister Elizabeth (Coombs) Warner, William and Eliza (Hacker) Kean and Eliza's sister Judith A. (Hacker) Morrison, and Eliza's parents Capt. William and Mary (Coombs) Hacker.

In Lauchlan's Will, he left everything, totaling close to $250,000 ($6.6 Million in 2009 dollars), to his adopted son William Kean. Lauchlan's youngest brother Nathaniel was so upset that he contested the Will and claimed in court, on December 2, 1896, that his brother, Lauchlan, was 80 years old and mentally incompetent when he formally adopted William. He also claimed that the signature was obtained by fraud and undue influence on the part

Lauchlan McKay

Henry Warner

Cutting ice on the St Charles River in Quebec, Canada
McKay & Warner Shipyard is in the background

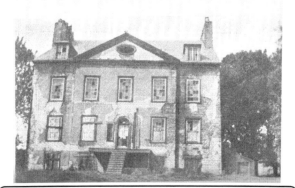

The McKay & Warner house in Quebec
Pictures on this page are from "In the Wake of the Wind-Ships" - 1927

of the Keans. In his own inimitable style, Nathaniel hired the well known George F. Hoar, U.S. Senator from Massachusetts, as counsel to represent him in court against the Keans. Nathaniel withdrew his objection to the Will two years later on April 8, 1897, but the Will was not finally settled in William Kean's favor until July 28, 1914. Several microfilm volumes were missing from the Massachusetts Archives so I could not find out why it took so long to settle. When the Will was finally settled, the estate was worth $111,454.04 (almost $2.5 million in 2009), which was made up of $75,000 from Charles B. Dix, Lauchlan's partner in McKay and Dix; Bank deposits of $19,631; Insurance policies for $7,440; stock shares worth $7,280 (58 shares Quebec Bank and 66 shares Montreal Telegraph); plus $2,103 in miscellaneous income. It is also interesting to note that in the 1900, 1910, and 1920 censuses, William Kean is listed as retired, no occupation, or living on his own income, and in 1900 he was only 46 years old. William and Eliza are also buried at the Mt. Auburn Cemetery, in the same family plot as Lauchlan.

Sarah McKay, one year younger than Lauchlan, born February 26, 1813 in Jordan Falls, married George Washington Thurston, a master mariner from Bristol, Maine. George was the son of William and Nancy (Foster) Thurston. Sarah and George had eight children, all born in Bristol, Maine. They had six daughters and two sons:

- 1. Emma Louisa Thurston was born January 19, 1842. She married John R. Major and they had six children (Elizabeth, Ralph, Sarah,Reginald, Mabel and Donald).
- 2. Susan Alice Thurston was born November 1, 1843. Susan died at the age of 22 on January 15, 1866 of tuberculosis in East Boston and is buried in the East Boston Cemetery.
- 3. Henry William was born October 19, 1846. Henry married Margretta Gilmore and they had five children (Donald, Lottie

Elizabeth, Alice, Ida, Lottie Alice). After Margretta died, Henry married Sarah Dove in 1882 and they had two more Children (Susan and Henry). Henry William died sometime before the 1920 census.

- 4. Donald Thurston was Henry's twin brother, born October 19, 1846. Whereas Henry lived to a ripe old age, Donald died when he was only 15.
- 5. Lucretia McClure Thurston was born March 19, 1848 and died at the age of 20 on April 19, 1869.
- 6. Margaret Thurston was born November 30, 1850. She also died at 20 in 1870.
- 7. Annie Thurston was born August 31, 1852 and died on January 19, 1868 at only 15.
- 8. Harriet Thurston was born on February 25, 1858 and died at the age of 12 on March 13, 1870.

In the 1860 Census, the family was still living in Bristol, Maine, but by 1862 they had moved to East Boston were their son Donald died. In 1866, they were living at 20 Eutaw Street, which was one block away from Donald's house on White Street.

Sarah died on September 22, 1868 at the age of 55 of dysentery. She had suffered from a disease of the spine for 16 years before she died. At the time of her death they were living at 62 Marion Street in East Boston, three blocks away from her brother Donald's house.

Margaret McKay, one year younger than Sarah, was

born May 2, 1814 in Jordan Falls, Nova Scotia. Just as her sister Sarah had moved down to Bristol, Maine, so did Margaret. It was in Bristol where Margaret married Solomon Thurston on January 14, 1833. Solomon was a Sea Captain and the son of William and Nancy (Foster) Thurston. Solomon and Margaret had six children, three boys and three girls, all born in Bristol, Maine. Their children are:

- 1. Ann Elizabeth Thurston was born September 22, 1836 and died May 30, 1896 at the age of 59. She married Montague Burke and they had two sons (Lauchlan and Walter), who both died before they were five years old. After Montague died, she married Joseph F. Taylor and they had three children (Fannie, Frank, Annie).

- 2. Franklin Thurston was born February 14, 1837 and died at age 32. He married Mary Major.

- 3. Eugene Thurston was born January 13, 1841. He married Elnora Roff about 1890 and they had one daughter, Linda Judith.

  In the 1900 census, he was listed as a janitor in Manhattan, NY.

- 4. Judith Thurston was born February 18, 1843 and died at the age of 12 on June 2, 1855. Judith was adopted by Lauchlan and Judith McKay, perhaps because she was sick and needed special attention.

- 5. Albenia Thurston was born November 8, 1844. She married George A. Wadleigh and they had one daughter, Jennie Buxton Wadleigh.

  In 1870, the family was living in Jersey City, NJ and George was working in the County Clerk's Office.

  In 1900, Albenia, a widow, was working as a dressmaker in Weymouth, MA.

- 6. Oscar Thurston was born July 11, 1846 and died at the age of 34 on July 11, 1880. Oscar married Addie White and they had four children (Albenia, Eugene, Ernest and Oscar). They lived in Weymouth, MA where Oscar worked in a boot factory in 1870, and a book store in 1880.

Margaret and Solomon moved to East Boston sometime between 1846, when Oscar was born in Maine, and November 8, 1849 when

Solomon accidentally fell off of the Welles Wharf in East Boston and drowned in Boston harbor.

After Solomon died, Margaret married Ambrose Salisbury. Ambrose was born in Weymouth, MA in October 1808 to Abiah Whitman Salisbury and Patience Pratt. Ambrose and Margaret had two sons:

- 1. Ambrose Salisbury was born April 28, 1854. Ambrose married Estella Meyer and they had one son, Lauchlan McKay Salisbury.
  In 1920, Ambrose was retired at the age of 65 and living with his wife, Estella, in Brooklyn, NY.
- 2. Nathaniel McKay Salisbury was born on December 22, 1855 and died October 22, 1872, at the age of 16, in Weymouth, MA. Since his mother had died in 1867, Nathaniel was living with his half sister, Ann Elizabeth Thurston, at the time of his death.

In 1860, Margaret and Ambrose were running a boarding house in Boston, MA with their two sons, Ambrose 6 and Nathaniel 5, along with Margaret's children, Frank 21, Albenia 16 and Oscar 14, and Ambrose's children Sarah 16 and Ella 13.

Margaret died of cancer, one year before Sarah, in Weymouth, MA on August 29, 1867 at the age of 53.

Jennett McKay, one year younger than Margaret, was born May 4, 1815, and died on May 20, 1817 in Jordan Falls, Shelburne when she was only two years old.

ANN McKay was born one and a half years after Jennett on January 27, 1817 and died on February 10, 1824 in Jordan Falls, Shelburne when she was only seven years old.

Hugh Robert McKay was seven years younger than his

brother Donald and 1 year younger than Ann, born March 21, 1818 in Jordan Falls, Nova Scotia. Hugh Robert married Margaret McKay in Nova Scotia. Margaret was the eldest daughter of Robert and Janet (Murray) McKay. Hugh Robert's grandfather, Sergeant Donald McKay, had a brother named Robert, and several genealogies show that there were other McKay families in the Jordan River section of Nova Scotia who were from Scotland, but I do not know if Margaret was related to him or one of the other McKays.

Hugh Robert and Margaret had eight children. The first five children, one boy and four girls, were born in Nova Scotia. The last three children, two girls and one boy, were born in East Boston, Massachusetts. There are conflicting dates for the birth dates of Gurden and Anna Jane, so I will give you all of the dates and you can pick whichever one you want. The conflicting dates came from William Kean's book "*The Genealogy of Hugh McKay and His Lineal Descendents*" and Marion Robertson's book "The Family of Donald McKay.

- 1. Gurden McKay was born in Jordan Falls on February 22, 1844 according to William Kean, or on February 2, 1842 according to Marion Robertson. Just to make it more confusing, the 1870 and 1880 census both indicate a birth in 1843.

When the Civil War broke out, Gurden enlisted in Company B of the 5th Massachusetts Infantry Regiment on April 16, 1861. On July 31, 1861 he was transferred to Company G of the 22nd Massachusetts Infantry Regiment. In the fall of 1861, he recruited 20 men from the Melrose area to join the Union Army. Because of his keen leadership abilities, Gurden was Commissioned a 2nd Lieutenant on September 4, 1861.

In October of 1861, the 22nd Regiment left Massachusetts and traveled down to Baltimore, Maryland. The train ride from

Boston to New York City, with a few stops along the way, took 18 hours. The train stopped to feed the troops lunch and supper. The train arrived in New York at 10:00 AM in time for a late breakfast. Today's train takes three and a half hours from Boston to New York.

The Regiment then traveled by boat from New York City to South Amboy in New Jersey, on the other side of Staten Island. Two soldiers fell asleep on the boat, fell overboard, and drowned. One of those soldiers was William Noyes, one of the 20 that Gurden had recruited. Lieut. McKay then had to escort William's body back to his family in Massachusetts, and then make arrangement to meet the Regiment in Baltimore, Maryland.

Lieut. McKay rejoined the Regiment in Baltimore, which later moved over to Hall's Hill on the Virginia side of the Potomac River for further training. On March 10, 1862 they marched to Fairfax, Virginia and secured the Town. The Regiment then started their march to Yorktown, Virginia. On April 5, 1862 they met their first engagement and lost three men and 12 were wounded. There was another engagement in Yorktown on May 4, 1862 where Gurden was wounded, and because of his injuries, he was dismissed from service on August 3, 1862.

The 22nd was engaged in almost all of the battles that took place in Virginia and Pennsylvania. Antietam, Fredericksburg, Chancellorsville, Gettysburg, Spotsylvania and Petersburg are just some of the battles. The 22nd lost 59% of its regiment at Gettysburg. Of the 1300 soldiers that left Massachusetts in October 1861, only 124 returned with the regiment at the end of the war.

In the 1870 census, Gurden is a carpenter in Baltimore, Maryland. In 1880, he is a widower and a doctor in Philadelphia, Pennsylvania.

Gurden died in his mid 40's on December 15, 1888, probably in Philadelphia.

- 2. Anna Jane McKay was born in Jordan Falls on March 16, 1846, according to William Kean, or on February 20, 1844, according to Marion Robertson. The 1870 and 1880 census indicates the birth in 1845. The 1900 census shows March 1850.

  Anna married a Methodist minister, Edmund White, and they had three children (Lorenda, Eliza Jane, and Edmund).

  In 1880, they were living in Mahoning, Pennsylvania.

- 3. Margaret Elizabeth McKay was born April 16, 1847 and she died very young. She was three years old in the 1850 census, but had died before the 1860 census.

- 4. Sarah Margaret McKay, Margaret's twin sister, was born April 16, 1847. She married William R. Gwinn and they had six children (William, Margaret, Hugh, Georgia, Sarah, and Charlton). William R. Gwinn was a minister in Baltimore, Maryland in 1880.

- 5. Albenia McKay was born October 10, 1849 in Jordan Falls. She married William E. Davis, an insurance agent, and they had two daughters. One daughter died very young and the other girl, Lorenda, grew up to become a school teacher in Baltimore, Maryland.

- 6. Lorenda McKay was born February 4, 1854 in Massachusetts. In 1880, she was a music teacher in Philadelphia.

  She married Vincent McKim and they had two children (Vincent, and Margaret). Vincent was a physician in Derry, Pennsylvania and he was still practicing medicine in 1930, when he was 73 years old. Lorenda lived to be 80.

- 7. Eliza McKay, Lorenda's twin sister, was born February 4, 1854. In 1880, she was a music teacher in Philadelphia when she was still single. She later married Joseph G. McGill and they had one daughter, Josephine, who was born in Philadelphia, Pennsylvania.

- 8. Robert was born March 17, 1856 in East Boston and died June 5, 1945 at 89 years old.
  Robert married Harriet C. Selsor and they had two children. Their daughter Nellie only lived two months. Their son Robert Barnes became a minister like his father. Robert and Harriet lived in Chester, NJ in 1900 where he was an Episcopal Minister. In 1920, he was still a Minister but they were living in Daytona, Florida.

Hugh Robert and his father Hugh are listed in the East Boston city directory in 1852 and 1853 as shipwrights, either in his own shipyard or working in Donald's Shipyard.

A couple of histories say that Hugh Robert and his brother Lauchlan opened their own shipyard in East Boston in the 1840's where they mainly repaired ships, though they did build a couple. In 1846 they built the *Odd Fellow*. Hugh then returned to the Jordan river and built two more vessels. There are records of his purchases for the ships in Shelburne in 1847. In 1850, he sold his land in Jordan River to Samuel and Robert Harlow and returned to East Boston.

In 1854, Hugh Robert has his own shipyard in "the 4th section near Ocean Highway" in East Boston. Ocean Highway is no longer there. I would assume that it was in the vicinity of Donald's yard because Hugh Robert is still living in the area of Princeton Street. Lauchlan is no longer involved in the shipyard because he is now sailing ships. In 1854, Hugh designed and built *Barreda Brothers* of 770 tons, and *Indiaman* of 1165 tons. In 1855, he built the *Ganges* of 1253 tons and in 1858 he built *Princess* of 1080 tons. The Boston city directory lists Hugh up until 1858, and then he seems to have left Boston. In 1861, when his son Gurden joined the army, the family was living in Melrose, Massachusetts.

In 1864, Hugh Robert and his family are down in Baltimore, Maryland at 309 East Eager Street. In the 1870

Census, Hugh and his oldest son Gurden, 27 years old, are listed as carpenters in Baltimore. The Census also lists the three older girls as being home, and Robert and the twins, Lorenda and Eliza, are still in school. In the 1880 census, the family is in Philadelphia, Pennsylvania and Gurden is 37, a doctor and a widower.

Hugh Robert McKay died on April 23, 1886 at the age of 68, presumably in Philadelphia.

David McKay, born October 14, 1819 in Jordan Falls, Nova

Scotia, was one year younger than Hugh Robert. David married Mary Riley in Gloucester, MA on January 7, 1849 when she was about 19 years old. Mary was born about 1830 in Ireland and she died before the 1900 census. David and Mary had six children, three boys and three girls, all born in East Boston. Their children are:

- 1. Annie McKay was born on August 24 1850. She married John Mulloy and they had five children (Mary, Catherine, John, Frederick, Annie).
- 2. John McKay was born on October 14, 1853 and died at the age of 38 on July 22,1892.
  In 1870, at 17 years old, he was working as a waiter at the Moinken Oyster House in Boston.
- 3. William McKay was born on May 30, 1854 and died 1 month later on June 30, 1854 of convulsions. The family was living on Trenton Street in East Boston at that time.
- 4. Matilda McKay was born in August of 1855 and died at two years old on February 15, 1857 of Scarlet Fever. The death certificate gives the address as Marion St. & Trenton St. Matilda is buried in the East Boston Cemetery.
- 5. Nathaniel Joseph McKay was born on February 14, 1860 and died prior to the 1910 census. Nathaniel married Elizabeth

Mary Shea about 1866, and they did not have any children. In 1900, he was a day laborer in East Boston.

- 6. Mary Elizabeth McKay was born on November 9, 1865. She was married to John Frederick Lang on August 11, 1886 in East Boston by the Rev B.P. McCarthy. John is listed on the marriage license as a salesman. Mary and John had six children (Mary, Annie, Frederick, Francis, Margaret & an unnamed baby).

  In 1910, their daughter Mary was a bookkeeper, daughter Annie worked in an office, son Frederick worked with his father in the grocery store, son Francis was in school, daughter Margaret and an unknown child had both died.

David worked in his brother Donald's shipyard for a time. When Matilda dies in 1857 the family was living on the corner of Marion and Trenton Streets in East Boston. In the census of July 1870 and in the City directories up through 1884, he is listed as a shipwright in East Boston and living on Decatur Street. The next time that I find him is on the 1900 census, at 80 years old, living with his daughter Mary Elizabeth (McKay) Lang and her family at 147 Maverick Street in East Boston, Massachusetts.

David died of "old age" on February 12, 1907 at the age of 87. He is buried in the Woodlawn Cemetery in Everett, Massachusetts.

John McKay, born January 20, 1822 in Jordan Falls, Nova Scotia, was two years younger than David and he too went with his family to East Boston and worked in his brother Donald's shipyard. He married Mary Brothers and they would have eight children, four boys and four girls. Their children are:

- 1. Richard Brothers McKay was born in Boston on November 2, 1845 and died November 23, 1895 when he was 50 years old. Richard married Mary Bill on November 8, 1875 in Shelburne and they had four children (Jesse, Elizabeth, Gordon and John).

In 1881, he was an engineer in Lockport, Shelburne. NS

- 2. Hugh McKay was born on March 8, 1847 in Boston and died 22 years later on October 7, 1869.
- 3. Nathaniel Lang McKay was born on December 13, 1848 in Boston. Nathaniel married Ida Gray in Nova Scotia and they had 4 children (Mary, Nina, Jesse, Annie).
- 4. Mary Ellen McKay was born on June 12, 1852 in Boston. She married Donald McKay and they had three children (Mary, William and Warren).
- 5. John Lauchlan McKay was born on January 30, 1854 in Boston and died prior to the 1920 census.
  John was married to Emily B. Margeson on November 21, 1883 in Boston, MA by the Rev. William W. Colburn.
  In the 1900 and 1910 census, John is a building superintendent, and the family is living at 46 Francis Place in Melrose, Massachusetts. John and Emily had four children (Marion, Ermina, Richard and Marjorie).
- 6. Barbara McKay was born on January 19, 1857 in Jordan River, Nova Scotia.
- 7. Elizabeth Jane McKay was born on September 22, 1858 in Jordan River, Nova Scotia.
- 8. Annie Cornelian McKay was born on April 14, 1860 in Nova Scotia. She married Michael Fitzgerald and they had one son named Austen in 1880.

John was the only one of the McKay brothers to move down to Massachusetts and then return to Nova Scotia to stay. This was sometime before January 19, 1857, when his daughter Barbara was born at Jordan River. He later settled in Summerville, Queens County, Canada, where he remained until he died on May 13, 1897 at the age of 74.

Simon McKay was one year younger than John and 12
years younger than Donald, born February 6, 1823 in Jordan
Falls, Nova Scotia. In 1846, he is listed on the Boston City
Directory as a grocer on Meridian St. in East Boston in the vicinity
of Donald's shipyard. On February 21, 1848, Simon married
Sarah Jane Osgood in Amesbury, Massachusetts. Sarah was the
daughter of Timothy and Eunice (Varnum) Osgood.

There were Osgoods building ships in Amesbury along
the Powwow river since at least 1784 when Oliver Osgood
launched the sloop *Sally*. There was also a Jacob Osgood and
an R. Osgood building ships in the early 1800's. Timothy Osgood,
Sarah Jane's father, and Sarah's two brothers, Edwin and
Samuel, were also shipbuilders. Timothy Osgood was a "head
workman" at Donald's yard from 1845 to 1847. Timothy and
Simon formed the partnership of Osgood & McKay Shipyard on
the Powwow river in Amesbury. The yard was on the north bank
where the Powwow river enters the Merrimac river, just across
the river from Newburyport, Massachusetts. Although the credit
for a couple of the ships goes to Osgood & McKay, most of the
ships are credited to just Simon, so I do not know how active
Timothy was in the business.

On March 5, 1849 Simon launched the 410 ton bark
Homer, which was the largest ship launched in Amesbury in 13
years. On March 8, 1850 Osgood & McKay launched the
Swallow. This launching just happened to be 12 days before
Simon's only son, Roland, was born.

Roland was born March 20, 1850, and I think that Simon's
wife Sarah Jane may have died in childbirth, or very soon
thereafter. I have not been able to locate Sarah's death
certificate, but someone on the Family Search web site has
Sarah's death as April 20, 1850. At any rate, the June 1850
census shows Simon and Roland living with the Osgood family
but Sarah is not there with them.

Simon later married Mary Jane Worthen. Mary Jane was born in Amesbury, Massachusetts about 1833 to Joseph and Dorothy Worthen. In 1860, her father, Joseph, was a ship carpenter, and her two brothers, John and Charles were shoemakers in Amesbury.

On April 9, 1851, Simon launched the *Wildfire* of 380 tons. She was a very fast ship, and in 1853 went from Boston to Gibraltar in only 14 days. The *Wildfire* saw many years of service, but in its last years it's owners used it as an infamous slave ship.

Simon launched many ships on the Powwow River. These are some of them: the bark *Alma* on December 5, 1854, the three masted schooner *Charles Smith* of 400 tons on October 6, 1856, a schooner of 1000 tons on Mar 15, 1859, a schooner of 140 ton Aug 1859. There was a newspaper article on February 24, 1863, during the Civil War, that stated that Simon and Ben Dutton had moved from Amesbury to a shipyard in Charlestown and were finding plenty of work. They had already launched a ship that is believed to have been the *Lady Washington*, a bark of 900 tons, and they had on the stocks a bark of 240 ton.

In 1866, the Boston City Directories show him back in East Boston as a Ship carpenter and living in the vicinity of Donald's yard. However, he continues to be listed as a ship carpenter up until 1881, long after Donald has closed his yard and after Donald had died. In the 1880 Census, Simon and his wife Mary are living at 168 Lexington Street with his sister Matilda and her family.

Simon died of consumption (tuberculosis) in East Boston on November 25, 1882 at the age of 59. At the time of his death he was living with his sister Charlotte at 38 White Street. His wife Mary Jane would die of pneumonia 12 years later on February 9, 1895 in Cambridge, Massachusetts.

Simon's son, Roland, moved down to Philadelphia, Pennsylvania and married Celia C. Smith where they had two children (Clement and Harold). Roland worked for a naval contractor in Philadelphia in 1880. He died on September 28, 1885 at the age of 35.

Mary Ann McKay, born one and a half years after

Simon, on September 11,1824, in Jordan Falls, Nova Scotia. She married Patrick McKenzie of Jordan Bay and they had three children in Shelburne, Nova Scotia. Unfortunately, they all died very young.

- 1. Alexander McKenzie was born in August 1841 and died of measles at eight years old. He is buried in the East Boston Cemetery.
- 2. Hugh McKenzie was born in May 1845 and died of diarrhea on August 2, 1850 at five years old. He also is buried in East Boston.
- 3. Unnamed child was baptized on September 15, 1848 and died shortly after.

As if loosing three children were not enough, her husband, Patrick, also died.

After she moved down to East Boston with the rest of the family, she married John Kean, a ship carpenter in East Boston, and they would have two sons and one daughter:

- 1. William Lawrence Kean was born September 23, 1854. William was the one who wrote the McKay family genealogy which is the basis for much of the McKay Genealogy in Appendix 4.

  In 1880, William was a bookkeeper in a bank in East Boston. By 1900, William is married to Eliza Jane Hacker and is retired at the age of 46, living in the Roxbury section of Boston. He died June 15, 1923 at the age of 68 and is buried with Lauchlan McKay in the Mt. Auburn Cemetery in Cambridge, Massachusetts.
- 2. Matilda Kean was born on August 11, 1856, but she died only five years later on September 10, 1861.

- 3. Alonzo Kean was born September 13, 1859 in East Boston.

  In 1880, at the age of 20, he is working in a grocery store, is not married, and is living at home on Saratoga Street in East Boston.

  In 1900, he is married to Martha Jackson, is an electrician, and has his mother-in-law, Lydia, living with them on Princeton Street in East Boston.

  In 1920, he is divorced and has moved to Los Angeles, California where he is working as an electrician for a railroad. Martha and her mother, age 86, are still living on Princeton Street.

Mary Ann was still living at 114 Saratoga St. in East Boston when she died of apoplexy (stroke) on April 14, 1888 at the age of 63.

Charlotte Sprot McKay, born June 14, 1826 in Jordan

Falls, Nova Scotia, was named for Charlotte Sprot, the wife of the Rev. John Sprot, a Presbyterian Minister who held services in Jordan River. She married James Albert German, of Jordan Bay, sometime before 1846. In 1860, the family is down in East Boston and James is a ship carpenter. In 1880, James is listed as a ship joiner and they are living at 38 White Street, just down the street from where her brother Donald used to live. Charlotte and James had five children, three boys and two girls. They are:

- 1. Walter McKay German was born April 14, 1846 in Nova Scotia. In 1870, at the age of 24, he is living in Cleveland, Ohio and working as a coachman. Eight years later he died at the age of 32 on May 14, 1878.
- 2. John Crocheron German was born September 16, 1848 in Nova Scotia. He married Eliza Golden and they had two daughters (Florence Gertrude and Georgie Evelyn).

  In 1880, John is a machinist in East Boston, living with his wife Eliza and their two daughters in the same house as his parents.

- 3. Mary Annie German was born on September 14, 1852 in Nova Scotia and died at the age of two on Sep 18, 1854.
- 4. Annie McPherson German was born on December 23, 1854 in Massachusetts just three months after her sister, Mary, had died. Annie married William C. Pinney.
  Annie died one month after her brother James, on May 23, 1883 at the age of 28.
- 5. James Albert German, Jr. was born on October 21, 1856 in East Boston. James married Katherine F. Creelman and they would have one daughter, named Annie McPherson German, born Oct 12, 1880. James was a flagstone dealer and they were living at 38 White Street, in the same house as his parents and his brother's family. James died on April 22, 1883 at the age of 26, one month before his sister Annie. James' daughter died three years after her father, on May 8, 1886 at only five years old.

Charlotte died in East Boston on November 19, 1899 at 73.

Anna Lang McKay, born December 11, 1829 in Jordan Falls, Nova Scotia, was named for Anna Lang, the wife of the Rev. Gavin Lang who baptized her. Anna married James D. Alley on July 7, 1853 in East Boston, Massachusetts, but shortly afterwards they moved across the river to Chelsea. James was a painter and they lived at 114 Chestnut Street in Chelsea. Anna and James had one child.

- 1. Alden Alley was born May 9, 1854 in Chelsea, Massachusetts. At about 24 years old, he married Hannie O. Dixie in 1878 and they would have two children, a son named Alden Gifford Alley, and a daughter named Anna Lang Alley.
  In 1900, Alden and his family are living in his mother's old house in Chelsea and he is a salesman.

In 1910, he is a widower, living alone at 31 Crescent Avenue in Chelsea, and is working for a manufacturer.

Anna died at her home in Chelsea of dilation of the heart (enlarged heart) on November 30, 1894 just a few days before her 65th birthday. Six years later, in 1900, at age 69, her husband James was living in a boarding house in Lynn, Massachusetts and was working as a sexton in a church.

Nathaniel McKay

seems to have been the 'character' in the family. He definitely had an entrepreneurial spirit and the uncanny knack for bouncing back after hitting life's little pitfalls. He also had a penchant for getting his name in the newspapers, which is why I have been able to find out so much about him. During his remarkable life, he was a grocer, shipbuilder, boilermaker, made railroad locomotives, a huge market building, built a bridge, was a Boston City Councilman, owned a hotel, was a Washington lobbyist, was a

Nathaniel McKay photo taken in Matthew B. Brady's studio, famed Civil War Photographer

Director of the Washington Savings Bank, owned homes in Brooklyn, Washington DC, and Oklahoma, all at the same time, owned 40 acres on Grand Exuma (One of the Bahama Islands), and traveled all over the world. It seems like he was a "jet setter" before they even invented the airplane.

Nathaniel was Donald's youngest brother, born March 4, 1831, almost 20 years younger than Donald, and only three years older than Donald's oldest son, Cornelius Whitworth McKay. On November 13, 1851, at 20 years old, he married Adeline Smith at the County Hall in Kennebec, Maine. Nathaniel and Adeline had three children:

- 1. Edward Orison McKay, was born June 4, 1853 in East Boston, Massachusetts but tragically died when he was only two years old, on August 2, 1855 of encephalitis.
- 2. Elizabeth Rebecca McKay was born on May 30, 1857 in East Boston. Elizabeth married Theodore Wiedersheim in 1881 and they had three children, one girl and two boys (Katherine, Edwin and William). Theodore was a banker.
- 3. Harriet Augusta McKay was born on March 23, 1859, also in East Boston. Harriet married Charles C. Kneisly and they had two boys, Wallace and Nathaniel McKay Kneisly. In 1880, Charles was a wholesale grocer in Dayton, Ohio.

Sometime between 1860 and 1870, Nathaniel and Adeline divorced. The 1870 census shows Adeline, her two daughters, and Nathaniel's father, Hugh, living together on Princeton Street in East Boston without Nathaniel and shows that Adeline is blind.

In 1852, Nathaniel is listed in the Boston city directory as a grocer with his brother Simon just a couple of blocks away from Donald's shipyard. Nathaniel then worked with Donald in his shipyard from 1853 to 1857. In 1858, he formed a partnership with John Gallagher and they opened the McKay and Gallagher Boilermakers near Central Square in East Boston, making large steam boilers for the many factories around the Boston area.

When, in 1860, Donald set aside a third of his shipyard for the fabrication of iron for ships, marine engines, and locomotives, Nathaniel, then 29 years old, used his expertise to put together the McKay & Aldus Iron Works Company, named after Nathaniel McKay and George Aldus. From the start of McKay and Gallagher to the height of McKay and Aldus, he went from a handful of employees to almost 1000.

McKay & Aldus built many marine engines that powered ships. However, when you check the history, it is the ship builder that gets the credit for the ship, not the firm that made the engine. The one exception that I found was the *Charles Houghton* side wheeler that boasted that it had a McKay & Aldus stroke engine.

McKay & Aldus also built ships. In March of 1864 Nathaniel launched the *Azalea*, a wooden hulled steam driven screw tug that was sold to the Navy and used in the Civil War.

In August 1864, he launched the *F. W. Lincoln,* a wooden side wheeled steamer which was sold to the Navy. Except on the day that the Navy received the ship, they renamed it the *Phlox*.

In December 1864, he launched the steamship *Squando*, also for the Navy, at a cost of $589,535.70, but it never saw action during the Civil War.

In 1865, he launched the *Edward Everett*, a wooden hulled side wheel steamship.

Edward Everett   1865

In 1864, 1865 and 1867, Nathaniel was on the Boston City Council, as well as holding other positions in the Boston City government.

McKay & Aldus, begun in 1860, was probably better known for their locomotives and their attention to detail, especially in the cabs, that gave the locomotives a touch of class that set them apart from other manufacturers. They supplied locomotives to several railroads on the east as well as the west coast. Since the transcontinental railroad was not completed until May 10, 1869, the cars and rails manufactured before that time were all shipped by sail to the west coast, first around Cape Horn, and later to Panama. Locomotives were also shipped the same way except that they

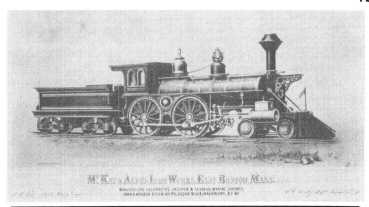

1868 Locomotive - McKay & Aldus Iron Works

were too big to fit through the ship's hatches and too heavy to be lifted by any existing crane on the west coast. Consequently they were shipped in several crates to be assembled when they got there. Sometimes there were several locomotives being shipped at the same time and all of the pieces for any particular locomotive may end up on two different ships, arriving in port at two different times, sometimes months apart. This problem was especially prevalent when they completed the Trans-Panama railroad and parts were shipped to Panama, off loaded onto a train that took them to the Pacific, where they were loaded onto other ships to complete their voyage to Los Angeles or San Francisco.

According to a railroad history by Wendell Huffman that was published in 1999, there were 197 locomotives known to have been imported to the west coast by ship, coming from fourteen different builders. The largest single share of these (forty one) were from McKay and Aldus. Most of these were for the Central Pacific RR. One of the McKay & Aldus locomotives shipped to the Central Pacific was the first to cross over the Rocky mountains. Another one was one of the fastest passenger locomotives that the Central Pacific had and it was used to bring dignitaries from San Francisco to Lang for the laying of the golden spike which connected the tracks from San Francisco to Los Angeles.

The Central Pacific RR purchased 147 of those 197 locomotives that were sent by ship. Because of their volume, they had a tendency to play one manufacturer against the other in order to get the lowest price. They also made it clear that they would favor the ones that would extend them credit and take promissory notes instead of cash. Nathaniel had also purchased new machinery to streamline his manufacturing process. It appears that these purchases coupled with the Central Pacific credits, may have over extended Nathaniel's credit and cut into his cash flow. When he declared bankruptcy in December of 1868, there were still four unfilled orders for locomotives for the Central Pacific. The company was then taken over by the Atlantic Works Company.

After the failure of McKay and Aldus in December of 1868, George Aldus and his son became boilermakers in New London, Connecticut and Nathaniel went to Jersey City, New Jersey and founded the McKay Iron and Locomotive Works. In January of 1869 he rented the building of the former Jersey City Locomotive Works, which had produced more than 100 locomotives before they went out of business the prior year in 1867. From what I could gather, he only made a few locomotives before he too decided to close shop and move on. Whether this was caused by the ever changing technology of this growing industry, the economic slump after the Civil War, or whether it was just the difficulty of the "new kid on the block" competing with the older and larger companies, we probably will never know. We do know, however, that it did not slow him down. Nathaniel had a knack for finding new opportunities. Even while he was still working at McKay and Aldus, three years earlier, he joined with Moor Falls, William Kimberly and James Hunt to incorporate the Cherrystone Steam Navigation Company on February 8, 1866. This company, incorporated in Maryland, ran steamboats along the waters of Chesapeake Bay in Maryland.

On September 12, 1874 the Navy Department held an auction in New Orleans in order to dispose of several ships and monitors that had been used during the Civil War but were no longer needed. Nathaniel attended the auction and bought at least two monitors. He bought the *Umpqua*, a single turret, twin screw monitor which was a Casco class monitor designed to be used in the shallow rivers and inlets of the Confederacy. These ships sacrificed armor plate in order to have a shallow draft. They were also fitted with a ballast compartment that would lower them in the water during a battle and reduce the target they provided for enemy guns.

The *Umpqua* was one of the first light draft monitors, similar to the *USS Nausett* that Donald had built, that had serious errors in the original plans when they calculated its displacement. When they launched the very first monitor of this design, they found that it rode only three inches out of the water, and this was before they mounted the turret, guns and all of the other weight that the ship would carry. As a result, the Navy ordered that the deck be raised 22 inches, on all such monitors, to provide sufficient freeboard.

The second ship that Nathaniel bought was the *USS Winnebago*, which was a twin turret, twin screw monitor that had patrolled the Mississippi river and was

U.S.S. Winnebago

in the battle of Mobile Bay. It also saw action against Ft. Morgan and Ft. Blakely. It also served on the Tombigbee river against Confederate forces in Montgomery and Selma, Alabama. After Nathaniel bought it, some say that he sold it to the Peruvian Navy and the ship was renamed the *Manco Capac*. Nathaniel is also known for buying ships, fixing and refitting them and then leasing them to the Navy for $150 per day.

I have found several references that Nathaniel built ships in Brooklyn, New York, but I can not substantiate it. He certainly is well known by the Brooklyn Eagle newspaper, had a house in Brooklyn, and, of course, he was a shipbuilder, but I have not been able to connect the dots. The newspaper also refers to him as Colonel. He is listed among the members recruited to the "Honorable Artillery Company of Massachusetts" in 1868, but he left Massachusetts in 1869 so I doubt that he made the rank of Colonel. More than likely it is just an honorary title.

The Brooklyn Public Library in New York City was good enough to place copies of the Brooklyn Eagle newspaper, from 1841 to 1902, on their web site. As a person who has himself been misquoted many times in the local newspaper, I can certainly attest to the fact that one can not believe everything that one reads in the paper. The reporters of the 1800's and early 1900's wrote stories from their own perspective and, by and large, did not even pretend to be objective about the news. Keeping these things in mind, a lot of the following information was taken from this newspaper. Although I could have summarized these news accounts, I think it is more interesting reading the actual articles.

May 9, 1873 - Washington, D. C. - *"Edwin C. B. Garcia, consul General to the United States from Uruguay, and whose office is in this city, was arrested this morning by Deputy U. S. Marshal James Turney, in a civilian suit instituted against him by Nathaniel McKay to recover about $12,000 which Garcia is charged with having misappropriated to his own use.*

"... It appears from the papers that some four years since the South American Steamship Company, of Buenos Ayers, purchased from McKay and Aldus, well known ship and locomotive builders of Boston, the steamer Yi for $158,000, leaving a balance due of $11,000 on the payment made.

"An arrangement was made by which the Captain of the steamer was to leave this amount in the hands of Garcia, in trust for McKay and Aldus. The money was so received by Garcia, who failed to make the payment in accordance with the arrangement,... "

Having sent five separate drafts for payment that were dishonored by Garcia, McKay and Aldus assigned the drafts to Nathaniel McKay, who has brought the suit. Since Garcia had sold his seat on the Stock Exchange, and could not be found in his office, it was feared that he might leave the city to prevent arrest. McKay's counsel asked the judge to set bail at $12,000 to cover the $11,000 plus interest.

In **1874,** Nathaniel is back in East Boston, living at 96 Lexington Ave. With his brother Simon. In **1876**, he is listed in the Boston City Directory as a Box maker, living at 42 Decatur Street in East Boston with his brother David. At this same time his former wife, Adeline, is still living at their old house at 73 Lexington Street.

April 17, 1877 - Philadelphia - *"Colonel A. K. McClure, Editor of the Philadelphia Times was attacked by Nathaniel McKay on Chestnut Street, Philadelphia yesterday. McKay tried to horsewhip him on account of a series of articles in the Times charging McKay with fraud in connection with certain Navy contracts. McClure received two or three blows before his assailant was stopped. Both were taken before a magistrate and held on $500 bail. Colonel McClure was not seriously hurt."*

September 5, 1879 - Current Events - *"A Philadelphia gentleman, Mr. Nathaniel McKay, has recently returned from a visit to Demerara, where he made a thorough examination into the alleged adulteration of sugar imported from the island into this country. Mr. McKay was sent there by the Committee of Ways and Means of the House of Representatives. It is understood that the result of his inquiries has demonstrated that there is no* *artificial coloring used in Demerara sugars, and that the discrimination of the Treasury Department against them is arbitrary and unjust."*

1880 - In the 1880 census, Nathaniel is in Philadelphia and listed as a contractor at 312 Stock Exchange Place. He is living with his second wife, Ellen J. Kneisly, his two daughters, Elizabeth (Lizzie) and Harriet (Hattie), and Ellen's son by a prior marriage William (Willie). Sometime in this same time frame he went to Demerara in British Guyana to negotiate a contract to build a railroad in the colony. I have not been able to find any information that he ever was awarded that contract.

1881 - When the government of Guyana wanted to rebuild their town marketplace in Georgetown out of steel, because the two prior wooden markets had burned down, Nathaniel easily won the contract, because he was the only bidder who did not demand full payment up front. The Edgemoor Iron Company of Delaware did the actual fabrication and construction. Nathaniel did the design and was the engineer in charge of building the Stabroek Market in Guyana in 1881. The building is made out of steel beam and all steel fabrication that is still in use today. This market contains 77,000 square feet of selling space inside as well as market areas outside, and is a main tourist attraction in the city. As a testament to how well the building was built, in 2002, 121 years after the market was built, Guyana had two experts from the Smithsonian Institute inspect the clock to see what it would take to fix it. The experts said that

the clock tower and its faces were in fine condition, but that the original huge clock works, that was running the four clocks, would take a lot of work to rebuild because it was so old. They recommended that it be replaced with four electric clock works.

January 11, 1884 - New York - Nathaniel McKay, a broker, who was charged with assault and battery by George T. Stearns at No. 39 Broadway, New York, where both have their offices, was tried today in the Court of Special Sessions.

The complainant repeated his story of the affair and McKay in his defense denied having struck his accuser, maintaining that when the latter accused him of dishonesty in connection with a check, he demanded a retraction of the allegation and merely gave him a shaking up. After consulting his colleagues, Justice Smith announced that the defendant had had considerable provocation for his action and adjudged him not guilty.

April 4, 1888 - Washington, D. C. - *"President Cleveland has sent in a veto of the bill referring the claim of Nathaniel McKay, of Brooklyn, for extras on ships constructed, to the Court of Claims."*

September 20, 1888 - Brooklyn - In a rather long and convoluted story, the Brooklyn Eagle reported that Mr. Nathaniel McKay and R. P. Porter went to England to study the working conditions of the ordinary workers. They reported back that the working conditions were horrible. The laborers were working for $1.00 per day and that they were living in squalor because they could not afford better. The reason for this was that the country had a Free Trade policy. Since President Cleveland was running for reelection on the platform of reducing the trade tariffs in this country, this was in essence Free Trade and would lead to the same sort of working conditions as they had in England. If the workers did not want that to happen they had better vote for

Harrison and Morton, or else they would have to compete with workers from other countries that are paid 75 cents per day and can live on $2.00 per week.

As added information that was not in the newspaper, Nathaniel had booklets and hand bills printed and organized a workforce to make sure that every worker in all of the large cities was given one before the election. Because of this, Nathaniel was credited with President Cleveland's re-election defeat and President Harrison's win in the election.

January 10, 1889 - Brooklyn - *"A very fashionable wedding was quietly and unostentatiously celebrated last evening at 323 McDonough street, the residence of Mr. John Barstowe Pope, the brother of the bride. Mr. Nathaniel McKay, the New York shipbuilder and prominent Republican worker in the late campaign, was married to Miss Jenney Wilson Pope. Daughter of the late Gideon Barstowe Pope, who died about four years ago. The Rev. Dr. J. D. Fulton performed the ceremony ... A reception, largely attended by many of the leading Republicans of this city and New York, followed the marriage and a supper by Maresi concluded the evening's festivities. Mr. and Mrs. McKay departed early for a honeymoon tour, which will include visits to Washington D. C. and points south."* The newspaper then printed a listing of over 100 quests, among whom were Mr. and Mrs. Donald McKay. Since Donald had died in 1880, this must be his son Donald, who would be about 47 years old, and his soon to be second wife Mary .

April 22, 1889 - The United States government opened up 1.92 million acres of the Indian territory of Oklahoma to homesteading on this day. 100,000 men waited on the border for the gun shot that would start the stampede for land. By nightfall, the towns of Guthrie and Oklahoma City were established and every available acre had been claimed. The rules stated that in order to register your claim, the property had to contain a structure no less than 12 by 14. One clown built a doll house on his land because the rules did not specify feet or inches. Since Nathaniel owned property in Guthrie, and had an eye for adventure, I would not be surprised if he was one of the 100,000 that participated in this stampede. Guthrie was the town where Nathaniel owned a building, had residency and filed for divorce from

Guthrie, Oklahoma 5 days later. By the end of the week there were 30 saloons.

his third wife, Jenney Pope, just before he married Mable Geyer.

August 30, 1889 - The Brooklyn Eagle printed a long story about how the politicians have a hard time getting along, and it included this sentence:

"Last night Collector Erhardt, encountering the Hon. Nathaniel McKay in the corridor of a New York hotel, informed that eminent shipbuilder and friend of labor that he amounted to no more than a flyspeck on the wheel of time, or words to that effect."

October 6, 1889 - Brooklyn - *"Mr. Nathaniel McKay, of Brooklyn, the famous shipbuilder, has sent the following letter to the Secretary of the Navy Tracy:"*

The letter simply states that the United States unarmored cruiser *Dolfin* was homeward bound from its trip around the world. Nathaniel requests that a full, exhaustive and critical report of the ship's behavior at sea and its current condition be made public upon its return, because it is important to know for the building of future ships. It seems that the Democrats had said the

the ship was a "crazy quilt", structurally weak, and a Republican sham of no possible benefit to the Navy. It is important to get the facts straight and show that the ship is indeed of great benefit to the Navy.

February 12, 1890 - Washington D. C. - *"Nathaniel McKay, of Brooklyn, took a colored man in to dinner with him at the Riggs House last Monday afternoon and sat at a table with Representative Grimes of Georgia. As soon as Mr. Grimes noticed the complexion of Mr. McKay's guest he rose from his unfinished meal, walked to the office, paid his bill and had his effects moved over to Vice President Morton's hotel. Other Southern people who are guests at the hotel, which is patronized largely by Southern people, have given the proprietors notice that they will leave if such an occurrence is repeated. Mr. McKay says his guest was H. C. C. Ashwood, ex-minister to San Domingo, and he invited him to dine, as he would have invited the President of the United States under the circumstances. He claims that though Ashwood's skin is dark, his heart is as big and true as that of Grimes or any other man. Mr. McKay regrets nothing and declares he will not hesitate to repeat his action at any time."*

February 19, 1890 - Washington D. C. - *"Nathaniel McKay, of Brooklyn, who is quite as well known in the corridors of the Capital as he is at home, is just now in what may be called, for want of a better term, a state of mind. Two years ago yesterday the Democratic House of Representatives passed the bill for his relief that had been before Congress for about twenty years. There were subsequent events which caused Mr. McKay, who was posing as a Democrat, to make a complete somersault and come out flat footed as a Republican. Almost everyone is familiar with the gymnastics of Mr. McKay in the last Presidential election, when he was getting even with President Cleveland for vetoing his bill.*

"... The bill is before the present Congress and Mr. McKay has had every reason to believe that now, when the Republicans had full control of all legislation, that they would lose no time in paying the great debt of gratitude they owe him for the election of Benjamin Harrison. Mr. McKay had a right, or at least thought he had, to expect the Republicans in Congress to act as speedily as its predecessors. But at this late date his bill has not even progressed beyond the committee stage. The Democratic committee had reported it early in January; the Republicans have not been half as prompt. . . . Mr. McKay. . . is constantly on hand and working for a report, which he hopes will be made in a week or two."

February 26, 1890 - Washington D. C. - *"The Committee on War Claims has ordered a favorable report on the bill for the relief of Nathaniel McKay for balances due on the construction of the vessels **Ashuelot, Squando** and **Nauset.** This is the bill which Cleveland vetoed. It will probably become a law at this session, allowing the claimants to prove their case in the Court of Claims. McKay will get $500,000 very soon after Harrison signs the bill."*

April 6, 1890 - Washington D. C. - *"Nat McKay, who is scarcely better known in Brooklyn than his celebrated claim is all over the country, is not having nearly so much success with his measure before the present Republican Congress as he had two years ago, when the Democrats had the upper hand..."*

The newspaper then printed portions of Nathaniel's logbook, that he had kept in 1888, when he was trying to see President Cleveland to get his bill passed. This is a synopsis of it:

March 20, 1888 - Cleveland's private secretary told a senator in confidence that his bill would be vetoed.

April 3, 1888 - Mr. Whitney tells him that there is trouble about the bill. He goes to the White House at 1 o'clock, sends in his card, waits an hour and is told to go.

April 4, 1888 - Goes to White House with his lawyers, sent in their cards stating their business, wait three and a half hours and are told to go away. At 2:30 the veto of the bill comes in.

May 24, 1888 - Sent letter to White House stating the facts and thinking that after he read the letter he would see the injustice. The President never replied.

June 5, 1888 - Called at the White House, sent in his card, waited an hour and the President refused to see him.

June 6, 1888 - Called at the White House, sent in his card, waited an hour, and the President refused to see him.

"So my only alternative was to aid in removing him from the White House after he had treated me in this manner. I took the steamer to Europe and obtained all the photographs of the poor working women and men there, with the small pittance they received per day, and presented them to the National Republican Committee free of charge. They printed millions of them and I distributed them in every place where man and woman worked."

May 4, 1890 - Washington D. C. - *"The Senate bill for the relief of Nathaniel McKay and of the executors of Donald McKay ... was taken up and discussed. The bill was explained and advocated by Mr. Higgins and was opposed by Mr. McPherson, who intimated that favor was shown to Nathaniel McKay because of his service to the Republican party in the last presidential election. ... The bill was passed. Yeas, 38; nays, 10 (all Democrats)."*

May 11, 1890 - Brooklyn - *"The bill for the relief of Nathaniel McKay passed the Senate on Saturday last and is now before the House, where it will no doubt have a favorable consideration. ... it looks now as if McKay will get his money from the Government; others have been paid large sums of money on the same kind of vessels. The bill gives McKay the right to proceed in the Court of Claims to prove his case. The bill is well guarded so as to protect the*

Government and give McKay all the rights he requires. The claim amounts to between $400,000 and $500,000."

July 13, 1890 - Washington D. C. - *"The Eagles' Washington bureau has received the following type written memorandum from an anonymous, but readily traceable source:*

"Nathaniel McKay, of Brooklyn, N. Y. has had a very sever attack of inflammatory rheumatism for the last week and he is completely helpless. He consented to go to the hospital and remained there for two days. They gave him a room 8x10, with a window about 2x5. The temperature in this room ranged, night and day, from 82 to 86. He states that he could look over the footboard of his bed and see the bolts of fire shoot from the sky for two nights. There was no air in the room whatever, as the window was tightly screened and kept out what little air there might have been. So McKay informed the doctor that he must be removed from the hospital at once, and they sent for the ambulance and took him back to his quarters on New York Avenue, where he now is and seems to be improving. As soon as he is able to walk he will make for Brooklyn.

"This hospital was a homeopathic one, where everything was done up in very small shape. When McKay got there they gave him a cord with a little knob to it (an electric bell) to ring for an attendant, and one could ring for four or five hours before anyone would come during the night. The watchman, who took care of the fires, cut the grass, milked the cows (if they had any), was the male nurse; all the patients in the house were under his charge, and Mr. McKay states that had he not left as soon as he did he believed he would have died, and he soon came away in an ambulance."

July 20, 1890 - Brooklyn - *"Mr. Nathaniel McKay, whose lamentable prostration with inflammatory rheumatism was the subject of a communication in last Sunday's Eagle, is now* convalescing, as evidenced by the following note, which is published to afford some pleasure to his numerous friends: **Washington, D. C., July 17.**

"Mr. Nathaniel McKay, of Brooklyn, NY, is up today with his clothes on for the first time in four weeks; this has been four weeks of life spent in a fiery furnace. The only way he could survive was to get a colored woman to fan him for $100 per day. His rheumatism is now better and he will strike for McDonough street Saturday if he can walk to the carriage. Never in his life has he suffered so much as in this last four weeks. He will come back next week to look after his claim before congress, which Cleveland vetoed."

April 22, 1893 - Washington D. C. - "Nathaniel McKay, the ex-shipbuilder of Brooklyn, is in a state of mind over the removal of his nephew, Cornelius W. McKay, as inspector of steamboats at New York. McKay is very angry, but just why he should be is somewhat surprising, after the very active part that he took against Mr. Cleveland during the last election. Cornelius McKay's papers show that he was recommended for the post of inspector by Nat McKay, Thomas C. Platt and Frank Hitchcock. He has the uncertain satisfaction of having been the first man bounced at the New York custom house since the new deal began."

July 30, 1893 - Washington D. C. - "Mr. Nathaniel McKay of Brooklyn is out gunning after a young colored office seeker named H. C. C. Astwood, who is a candidate for the consulship of San Domingo. McKay says: "Astwood is as smart as a steel trap and is the cleverest colored man I ever met. He is also a great talker and can make a man believe most anything if he has a chance to argue with him;" but McKay does not have much faith in his Democracy. "Astwood," he says, "was always a Republican and was appointed by Arthur from New Orleans. In 1889, Secretary Bayard dismissed him from the consular service on account of his effort to obtain the *bones of Christopher Columbus at San Domingo and have them exhibited in the United States. When dismissed he refused to surrender the office and a cable was sent ordering his successor to take forcible possession. Astwood was John Wanamaker's agent in San Domingo for some time and through him Wanamaker furnished war material for the revolutionists; he was also secretary of a lottery company there. After his dismissal by the state department he published, and placed on sale all over the West Indies, his biography."*

January 13, 1895 - Brooklyn - When private shipbuilders were trying to convince the House Committee on Appropriations that the government was wasting money trying to build ships themselves, and that private shipbuilders could build them much cheaper, this article appeared in the newspaper.

"Mr. Nathaniel McKay of Brooklyn, one of the oldest living ship builders, and who has had an experience of forty-five years in the construction of ships, in speaking to the Eagle correspondent tonight as to the cost of building ships at the Navy Yard, said: "The government should keep the Navy Yards in working shape, for if we have a war and have no tools in our navy yard or plant to build a ship we would be in very bad shape. Every other nation knows our strength just as well as we do. They know every tool that we have in the shops and the government should keep those tools continuously at work. It matters not if the item of cost is 10, 20, 40 or 50 percent higher than the contracting shipbuilder can do the work. This money is paid to the various local mechanics, and it goes into our local industries. We should appropriate as much money for the navy yard, and even more, than for the outside builders. I never believed in closing any of the Eastern yards. They afford work for thousands who are worthy and hardworking citizens, and in these days, when there is a great agitation as to the expediency of the government

Nathaniel McKay
Picture is from an 1895
Brooklyn Eagle newspaper

appropriating money for the building of roads and canals and in other ways finding employment for idle labor, it does seem to me folly, almost criminal folly, to talk about shutting up the navy yards."

March 10, 1895 - Washington, D. C. - *"The judgment in the claim of the late Donald McKay for $101,529.73 has been settled, and all the litigation in the famous case is ended. After thirty-two years of constant work at the national capital, Nathaniel McKay of Brooklyn has thus succeeded in securing his late brother's rights, and the success of his efforts are owing entirely to his untiring will and energy, backed up with his Scotch pluck and persistency. He has walked the marble halls of congress for thirty-two long and weary years, for his claim would pass one branch or the other and then drop through. Then he would be obliged to commence all over with a new congress and explain the claim to new members. His bill was vetoed twice, once by General Grant and once by President Cleveland. It took fourteen congresses to pass it and nearly all the members and senators who rallied to his support when his bill first came up have passed out of public life. Nearly a third of a century has been used up by McKay in getting justice from the government; and there is no man living today who has had such an experience in legislative work. McKay received his money from the treasury department today and carried it to the bank in a small hand satchel.*

"Speaking of his legislative experience he said to the correspondent of the Eagle tonight: "Every time I received a rebuff it always made me more zealous. There are hundreds of demagogues in congress who think that if a man has a claim

against the government he wants to loot the treasury for his own benefit. ..."

"Mr. McKay is now engaged in writing a book giving his thirty-two years experience of how to pass a bill through congress."

April 4, 1895 - Brooklyn - *"Mr. Nathaniel McKay of Brooklyn left for Boston today to attend the funeral of his brother Lauchlan, who died yesterday. Captain McKay was born December 16, 1811, at Shelburne, Nova Scotia. He was one of a family of eighteen children and was a man of considerable note and achievement in ship building."*

April 26, 1895 - Brooklyn - This was a story about collectors and antiques, and mentions that Mrs. Nathaniel McKay is quite a collector. It then goes on to mention many of her items, such as a china closet, tea set from 1830, old pewter plates, old silverware, mahogany tables, and two chairs with claw feet over 200 years old.

July 17, 1895 - Washington, D. C. - *"Nathaniel McKay of Brooklyn arrived here today from Boston, where he has been engaged in contesting the will of his late brother, Captain Lauchlan McKay."*

October 6, 1895 - Washington, D. C. -
"The American Tariff league will shortly publish and distribute a document, the contents of which were compiled by Nathaniel McKay of Brooklyn, while on a recent trip through Europe. Mr. McKay did not go, as has been claimed by some, as the representative of Mark Hanna, and his trip had no connection whatever with the Republican Party or its managers. In speaking to the Eagle correspondent today about his European visit Mr. McKay said:

"I went abroad for the purpose of personally studying the condition of the laboring man in Europe as compared with that of the laborers in this country. I also wanted to find out what difference was occasioned in the big manufacturing cities of England by the change from the McKinley to the Wilson tariff. I made personal investigations into the condition of the laboring people in the big cities of England and took a number of photographs in the various sections of the country. I find that no actual comparison can be drawn between the American laboring man and the working people of England. ... Low tariffs in this country do not effect the condition of the working people abroad... I found the most interesting condition arising from the recent changes in the American tariff rates. They exported from Bradford to the United States during the last nine months of the existence of the McKinley bill $4,478,000 worth of goods. This was from January 1, 1894, to September 30, 1894. During the corresponding eight months of 1895 they exported under the Wilson bill, $21,171,000 worth of their product. Their exports to the United States were five times greater under the Wilson law than under the McKinley tariff. ... The sentiment among the business men of England is decidedly opposed to Bryan and the the principles which he advocates. They are in hopes that he will be defeated, for they know McKinley to be a straightforward business man, and although the latter is in favor of a high protective tariff, the Britons would prefer to see him elected than Bryan."

December 2, 1896 - Boston, Mass. - Senator George F. Hoar, as counsel for the appellant in the pending contests between Nathaniel McKay of Brooklyn, NY, and Mr. And Mrs. William L. Kean over the property left by the late Captain Lauchlan McKay of East Boston, appeared in the supreme court yesterday to defend the right of his client to a jury trial upon the questions which he raises in respect to the adoption of Mr. and Mrs. Kean by his late brother, Captain McKay. Mr. McKay claims that when the decree of adoption, which was made on January 18, 1892, his brother being more than 80 years of age, and the Keans of mature age was signed, his brother was mentally incapable and also that the signature was obtained by fraud and undue influence on the part of the Keans.

"The amount of the property left by Captain McKay is about $250,000." Decision on the pending issue was reserved.

June 20, 1897 - Washington, D. C. - *"Nathaniel McKay of Brooklyn today sent the following open letter to Senator Jacob H. Gallinger of New Hampshire:*

"I see that Senator Pritchard, chairman of the committee on civil service, has made a report from that committee ... That no laborers of any class, employed by the government, shall be included in the classified executive service. ... I am surprised that the committee on civil service should strike first at the laboring man, who is the poorest paid all over the world. ... The poor laboring man who watches the treasury and does your bidding as your poor messenger and gets but $660 to $700 a year is the first to be attacked by the civil service committee, while the clerk who has been fortunate enough to be educated and the statesman who receives his yearly salary of from $3,000 to $5,000 remains untouched. ... We can not afford to pass any such bill as this and discriminate against the laboring man."

March 24, 1898 - Washington, D. C. - *"Nathaniel McKay, the well known Grand Army man, was seen today in reference to his advertisement in last night's Eagle. In this Mr. McKay notified the public that he refused to be responsible for any debts incurred by his wife, Mrs. Jennie Pope McKay, of 323 McDonough street, Brooklyn. Mr. McKay lives at 1003 Thirteenth street, this city, with his children by a former marriage."* He then goes on to say that he has given her large sums of money amounting to about

$23,000. He had refused to live with her and had told her to stay away from him, but that she had continually come to his home, sometimes in disguises, and had taken things from it. He had given most of his things to his children and she had taken their things too. He tried to have her arrested, but the police would not because she was his wife."

The last paragraph reads: *"I married her in 1889," said Mr McKay. "The marriage has been a very unfortunate one, as we have not had one happy day since we were married."*

March 27, 1898 - Washington, D. C. - *"Nathaniel McKay of Brooklyn today applied for a decree of absolute divorce from his wife Jenny Pope McKay. The papers were issued and were served on Mrs. McKay at the Shoreham Hotel, Washington, where she is staying."*

June 25, 1898 - Washington, D. C. - *"Nathaniel McKay of Brooklyn, who, it is said, received a commission of one-third of the famous Roach claim of $350,000, recently allowed by Congress, has just come in for another stroke of good luck.*

"The Solicitor of the state Department announced this morning that the arbitration in the claim of Nat McKay against the San Domingo government for damages resulting in the building of a bridge for the Brooklynite at San Domingo City, has made an award in favor of McKay for something like $85,000.

"About ten years ago McKay secured a concession from the government of San Domingo to build and operate a toll bridge at San Domingo City. As the structure was about completed a revolution occurred in the island, during which the bridge was seized. It has been in the hands of the San Dominican government since, and McKay lost all the money he put into the enterprise, as well as all tolls collected from it. This occurred in September, 1895 ... Nat McKay is well known in Brooklyn as a member of the firm of ship builders who for years have had a yard in that city. For some

time past he has resided in this city. Somewhat of a sensation was caused a few weeks ago by McKay filing a bill for divorce from his wife, who lives in Brooklyn."

NOTE: After Nathaniel's death in 1902, Henry William Thurston, the son of Nathaniel's sister Sarah, filed claim against the estate claiming that he was the owner of the bridge and Nathaniel had owed him half of the $91,000 that he was paid for the bridge, and that Nathaniel had only paid him $4,500. His claim was for $45,711.69, which included interest, less the $4,500. As a negotiated settlement of this claim, in the Washington Post story of March 31, 1905, the lawyers agreed to $12,000 as a full settlement. The story did not elaborate Henry's roll in the bridge.

July 18, 1898 - Washington, D. C. - *"There was an exciting scene in the lobby of the Navy Department this morning between Nathaniel McKay of Brooklyn and George E. Ducker, also of Brooklyn, and the representative of the General Construction Company of New York. It seems that Ducker and a man named Thomas Dirvan had a contract for furnishing hospital tents for the Bureau of Medicine and Surgery of the Navy Department. McKay supplied the money for carrying out the contract and was to receive one-third of the profits. He was given an order on Ducker and Dirvan on the department for payment on the contract. Ducker and Dirvan, however, retained certain papers and when McKay met them at the department today, he claimed that they were not treating him properly.*

"When the men came together in the corridor there was a lively scene. Ducker defended himself vigorously. McKay finally called on Secretary Long and explained his part in the transactions and persuaded the secretary to stop the payments until the tangle was straightened out."

September 9, 1899 - Washington, D. C. - *"Nathaniel McKay of Brooklyn, the famous old ship builder, who has been residing in Washington for a number of years, and whose dinners and entertainments have become famous the world over, is dangerously ill at his residence in this city. Mr. McKay left Washington for Europe early in July. About a month ago he was stricken with a complication of diseases in Paris and on the advice of his physician as soon as he was able to travel he returned to this country. He reached Washington about a week ago and yesterday was reported to be at the point of death. Today he is a little better, but little hope is entertained for his recovery. He has Bright's disease (acute kidney disease) and heart trouble. Mr. McKay is one of the picturesque characters of the Capital. He has had claims before Congress for the past twenty years and has been extraordinarily successful in winning his cases. It is believed that he has been paid nearly half a million dollars by the government since he came here. He owns considerable property in Brooklyn, is the owner and proprietor of the Dewey Hotel in this city and has invested a great deal of money in Oklahoma and other Western parts. A few months ago he began divorce proceedings against his wife and the case was to have been brought to trial this fall. Mr. McKay's Washington home is filled with rare and beautiful things, collected from all parts of the world. Every other week during the session of Congress he has been in the habit of entertaining at dinner prominent senators and members of Congress. These dinners have become famous. Among his particular friends are numbered senator Burrows of Michigan, Thurston of Nebraska, Hoar of Massachusetts, Warren of Wyoming. ... His time and his money have been ever ready to advance the interests of the American merchant marine."*

1900 - The 1900 census for Washington lists Nathaniel living at 1008 Thirteenth street, around the corner from the Dewey Hotel, which is on L Street. He is 69 and owns his house without a mortgage. He is living with Leila Blanchard, 36, white, his housekeeper; Julia Daily, 20, white, his maid; William Mitchell, 50, black, his coachman; and James S. Mumy, 22, black, his valet.

April 16, 1901 - Brooklyn - *"Who owns the family furniture?"* *is the subject of an interesting dispute now being carried on between Mrs. Nathaniel McKay of 323 McDonough street and her husband as a side issue to the suit for divorce which Mr. McKay recently instituted. Incidental to this dispute is a lively difference of opinion regarding Mrs. McKay's age.*

Nathaniel McKay
From his 1901 book

Her husband declares she is not twenty five years younger than he and that she was 50 years old when he married her, instead of 38, as she claimed. She is emphatic in the assertion that she is not yet 50 years old. Mr. McKay is nearly 70."

The article goes into lengthy detail about all of the things that Nathaniel bought, including the house. However, he essentially says that she can have it all if she would only stop annoying him. *"If she were to take me out in the street, with a platoon of men, and ask me to live with her or have the men shoot me, I would say shoot."*

Nathaniel stopped the divorce proceedings in Washington and filed for divorce in Guthrie, Oklahoma.

February 1902 - There are several letters in the Harrison Loring Collection at the Mystic Seaport library in Mystic, Connecticut concerning Bills that Nathaniel was filing before Congress. These

Bills were for the collection of money that the government had refused to pay for ships that Harrison Loring had built for the Navy from 1861 to 1863 during the Civil War. One ship was the steamer *Winnipec* that was launched in 1863 in Massachusetts, and for which the government owed $63,715 ($1.6 million in 2009 dollars) for additional material and labor required because of changes to the specifications. Another ship was the light draught monitor *Canonicus* that Loring was also owed money for the same reasons. The contract between Nathaniel and Harrison stipulated that Nathaniel would receive 50% of whatever amount was actually paid to Harrison, and that Nathaniel would pay all expenses incurred in collecting this money.

May 1902 - There was a letter from Harrison Loring to Nathaniel's lawyer, John S. Blair, stating that Nathaniel was very sick, and not expected to live, and Harrison was very concerned as to what would happen to the Bills before congress in the event that Nathaniel died. In November of 1902, John Blair wrote to Harrison to say that the Bills were being processed but that he himself was having a terrible time trying to collect any money from the "crook" who was handling the estate.

June 27, 1902 - Washington, D. C. - "Colonel Nathaniel McKay, the proprietor of the Hotel Dewey of Washington, D. C., and Miss Mable G. Geyer, also of Washington, were married today at Crisfield, near this city. Colonel McKay, accompanied by his bride and her brother and sister, arrived at Crisfield this morning and secured apartments at the Crisfield Hotel. At 10:30 o'clock the wedding ceremony was performed by the Rev. G. W. G. Wynne of Smith's Island, an uncle of the bride.

"The bride's brother was groomsman and her sister was bridesmaid. After the ceremony the couple remained at the hotel until 12:30 o'clock, when they left for Peninsula Junction, where a palace car of the Pennsylvania Railroad awaited them to carry *them through to Atlantic City, where they will remain during the season.*

"The marriage license, which was obtained by the Rev. Mr. G. Wynne, gives the age of the groom as 71 and of the bride as 27. ... Miss Geyer and her brother and sister ... live just across the street from the Dewey ... ."

NATHANIEL McKAY DIES

July 10, 1902 - Washington, D. C. - *"It was announced here this afternoon that Nathaniel McKay, the old shipbuilder, a former resident of Brooklyn, and brother of the late Donald McKay of Boston, **died** suddenly at Atlantic City last night.*

"About two weeks ago McKay married Miss Mable G. Geyer, a young woman of this city, and they went to Atlantic City to spend their honeymoon. The marriage license gave the age of the groom as 71 years and of the bride as 27. She lived across the way from the Dewey Hotel, which was owned by McKay. ...

"Nathaniel McKay had for years been one of the picturesque figures of the capital until stricken with heart trouble about two years ago he was a man of commanding presence and splendid physique. He was the most successful claim agent in Washington, and had secured during the last few years for himself and others millions of dollars from Congress.

"He owned a great deal of real estate in this city, including the Dewey Hotel, a favorite resort for Western Senators and representatives. ...

"McKay lived until a year ago in an old fashioned house on Thirteenth street, where surrounded by art treasures gathered from every quarter of the globe, he dispensed a liberal hospitality. Every month he gave a state banquet to his congressional and other friends. These dinners were unique in their way. A canvas upon which was painted flowers, sea nymphs and bacchanalian subjects was placed around a long table, in the center of which

generally appeared the model of a United States man-of-war brilliantly illuminated by electric lights. ...

"Like all successful men, McKay made many enemies, and he has again and again been bitterly assailed in the newspapers and by means of special pamphlets in which he was arraigned as an unscrupulous and conscienceless lobbyist. McKay, however, fought back whenever he was attacked, and once his Scotch fighting blood was aroused he stopped at nothing.

"About a year ago he published and distributed extensively an artistic little pamphlet, bound in red morocco, in which he told the story of his life and incidentally paid respects to his enemies. He stated that his business was a legitimate one, and that the claims he had pushed through Congress were just. ... A few months ago Mr. McKay purchased a big granite house on K street facing Franklin Square, that belonged to the late John Sherman.

"Mrs. McKay, of Brooklyn, divorced, will contest any claim for McKay's estate that the second wife may set up. She will base her fight on the allegation that Mr. McKay's marriage two weeks ago was illegal, in that the divorce decree secured in Oklahoma last April was improperly issued."

NOTE: On one of my trips to Washington in 2004, I stopped by the Library of Congress to see the book that Nathaniel wrote. The book was titled "Nathaniel McKay" (E480.m15), was about 5" by 7", 44 pages, and about 1/2" thick, and their copy was bound in red cloth, instead of the red morocco. It contained about 50 letters, and most were written explicitly to say that Nathaniel was honest, trustworthy, and an all around great guy. The letters were written by company owners, bank presidents, governors, mayors, Secretaries of the Navy, and one by John Q. Adams. He wrote the book to counteract the personal attacks of one person who has been circulating false and malicious statements about him and the Dewey Hotel.

There were some items in the book that were very informative. All of the literature that I had read claimed that Donald

McKay was one of 18 children, yet I could only account for 16. Nathaniel wrote that two children died before they were given names. It also states that Donald was 6' 4" and was a Methodist. Nathaniel also stated that he was earning $1.00 per day when he started work in Donald's shipyard. He said that McKay & Aldus made 100 locomotives, 14 large steamships, and hundreds of boilers. He also mentioned that Donald was struck down by paralysis about July 17, 1880, then suffered from a variety of diseases before he died on September 20th.

There was one letter from the owner of the Chicago and Northwestern R.R., dated January 17, 1967, that constituted their contract for McKay & Aldus to build five switching engines for $12,000 each, and six locomotives at $15,500 each. This was followed by a letter from Nathaniel stating that they would deliver them in six months, by June 1, 1867.

July 14, 1902 - Washington, D. C. - *"The will of the late Nathaniel McKay was read at the McKay residence on L street, this city, yesterday afternoon after the family returned from the Rock Cemetery, where the remains of the deceased were deposited in a vault. The will is brief and names five persons to share in the estate. After two small bequests, the entire fortune of McKay is to be divided equally among Mrs. Mabel Geyer McKay, his widow, and Mrs. Theodore Wiedersheim and Mrs. C. C. Kneisly, his married daughters. No mention was made of Mrs. Jennie Pope McKay of Brooklyn or of his other divorced wife, who now resides in Chicago.*

"A bequest of $25,000 was made to Samuel Tatum, a San Dominican, who for many years has acted as Colonel McKay's confidential secretary, and another bequest of $1,500 was made to his colored coachman, Mitchell. The balance of the estate, which is variously estimated to be worth anywhere between $400,000 and $1,000,000, is to be divided equally between his widow and his two daughters.

"Colonel McKay's last will was made in this city about ten days before he died and was forwarded to him in Atlantic City last week, where it was signed four days before he died."

Note: Nathaniel's body was later moved from the Rock Creek Cemetery in Washington, D.C. to Nathaniel's family plot in the Woodlawn Cemetery in Everett, Massachusetts.

August 12, 1902 - Washington, D. C. - *"Fresh complications have developed in the fight over the estate of the late Nathaniel McKay ... It is declared that the actual property left to be divided between the widow and the two daughters of Colonel McKay ... will amount to practically nothing after Mrs. McKay gets together all the money and securities which she says her husband gave to her before his death.*

"It seems that the greater part of Colonel McKay's fortune consisted of bonds and securities of all kinds, and that the bulk of all this is now claimed by the young widow, exhausting practically the entire estate. ... Money to the amount of $30,000 or $40,000, which was on deposit in banks, was claimed by the young widow, who said that it was given to her. ... The will of McKay provided that his secretary, Samuel Tatum, was to have a bequest of $25,000 and his coachman $1,500. The estate is said to be insufficient to even pay the bequest to the secretary."

November 2, 1902 - Washington, D. C. - *"It is only the matter of days now before the mystery regarding the contents of the will of Nathaniel McKay, the former shipbuilder of Brooklyn, will be known. Justice Barnard has signed an order in the Probate Court directing the attorneys of Mrs. Mabel Geyer McKay to file the will in the office of the register of wills. The instrument has been in the hands of the attorneys of the widow since July 10 last ... It is expected that as soon as the will is filed for probate steps will be taken to contest it by Mrs. Jennie Pope McKay."*

November 12, 1902 - Washington, D. C. - *"Mrs. Elizabeth R. Wiedersheim and Harriet A. Kneisly, daughters and legatees of Nathaniel McKay, today instituted equity proceedings against Mrs. Mabel Grace McKay, the widow, who was to share alike with the daughters under the will, and Joseph J. F. Klein, trustee and holder of title, to real estate property in this city, for possession of the deeds to this property. This is the first step in court looking to a contest of the will."*

June 2, 1903 - The auction house of C. G. Sloan & Company published a book of items from Nathaniel's estate which were to be auctioned. There were 673 individual lots to be auctioned, containing antiques and rare items both large and small from all corners of the globe. There was rare French china, Turkish rugs, Brazilian dining room suit, a rare Japanese sword, etc. There were 125 lots of fine tableware of crystal, gold plate, silver, and even plates with Nathaniel's portrait on them. There were 27 oriental rugs, 35 oil paintings, statues and marble pedestals, and an old English hall clock carved by Grinling Gibbons about 1700. I would guess that if these items were auctioned today, they would bring several million dollars.

NOTE: The on-line version of the Brooklyn Eagle is only available to the end of 1902, and it looks like the final Will was probably settled much after that. The continuation of this soap opera will only occur if I can get a copy of the final disposition of the Will, or a later copy of the Eagle. In the mean time, this will have to remain a cliff hanger.

Did his new wife get away with all of his money?

Did his daughters get anything?

Did his ex-wife, Jennie Pope, get anything from his estate after he worked so hard to make sure that she would not get even a penny?

Did his second ex-wife, Ellen Kneisly, try to get anything from his estate?

The answer to these, and other questions, will be found in the next episode of "Nathaniel's World".

On one of my trips to Washington in 2004, I stopped by the National Archives to lookup the will. I looked at the court proceedings for 1903 through 1907 and found a lot of legal maneuvering, but no final conclusion. Perhaps on a future trip I will get the answers.

The story on Nathaniel is a bit long, but I thought that the detail would point out Nathaniel's versatility, his wide experiences, and give a clearer picture of his personality. Nathaniel certainly had his faults, but you have to admire his gusto for life.

Matilda Nancy McKay, the youngest of Hugh and Ann

McKay's children, was born October 14, 1832 in Jordan Falls, Nova Scotia. She was one year younger than Nathaniel, and 22 years younger than Donald.

She was married to Donald Dewar in Boston on September 19, 1850 by the Rev. J. D. Bridge. Matilda and Donald had one child.

- 1. Elizabeth Smith Dewar, who was born July 17, 1851.

Donald, who was originally from Prince Edward Island, was a carpenter in East Boston when he died of consumption on February 18, 1852, less than one and a half years after Matilda married him.

After Donald Dewar died, Matilda married John A.C. Geddes in East Boston. John, a native of Clyde River, Nova Scotia, was a ship joiner in East Boston. John and Matilda had two more children, Simon McKay Geddes and Mary Jane Geddes.

- 2. Simon McKay Geddes was born January 8, 1855 in East Boston. In 1880, he was still single, living with his parents at 169 Lexington Street in Boston, and working for a clothing manufacturer. Sometime after the census he married Emma Jordan, but died a few years later in 1884 at the age of 29.

- 3. Mary Jane Geddes was born on August 3, 1869 in East Boston. When she was about 23, she married Alvin George, Jr. Alvin was a druggist in Boston and they had one child named Marion Matilda Alvin. The family later moved to Northfield, Massachusetts.

  Mary Jane suffered from Anemia for a couple of years before she died on November 25, 1910 at 41.

  After Mary died, Alvin married a woman named Bessie in Northfield, Massachusetts.

Matilda Nancy (McKay) Dewar/Geddes died on May 15, 1898 in East Boston at the age of 66. Her husband John A. C. Geddes died the following year, 1899.

Donald McKay's family in front of their house in East Boston - 1868

Picture courtesy of Kate Silvernale of Seattle, Washington

I believe that this picture was taken in the summer of 1868 with Donald (57) sitting on the stairs with his son Guy Allen (1 ½). The twins, Anna Cushing McKay (4) and Nichols Litchfield McKay (4) are on the top step. The two girls standing in the grass are his daughters, Frances (14) and Mary Cressy (12). The woman sitting on the porch is Donald's wife Mary Cressy (36). The woman sitting on the top step is probably Donald's daughter, Albenia (McKay) Bodemer (22), who gave birth to her first child, Mary, on July 2, 1868. If the date of the picture is correct, Mary Cressy would be 6 or 7 months pregnant with her son Wallace who was born October 6, 1868.

CHAPTER 6
DONALD McKAY'S
CHILDREN

We tend to think of famous people in terms of what made them famous; the way everyone looks up to them, the accolades bestowed upon them, the amazing things that they have accomplished. We seldom think of them mowing their lawn, stopping by the store to pickup milk, playing with the kids, or changing diapers. Donald grew up in a large family working on a farm. Everyone had their chores to do and the family would not survive unless everyone chipped in their share of the work. I am sure that these values carried over into Donald's married life. Although Donald worked a six day week, probably from sunup to sun down, I can almost picture him playing with his children, helping them with their homework, perhaps playing the violin and teaching them music, and then tucking them into bed. At least one of his children learned to play the violin.

Donald had 17 children. Two of the children are presumed to have died as infants. The cemetery stone in the McKay family plot in Newburyport says that there are three infants buried there. One of those infants could have been his daughter Anna Cushing (McKay) Burton's infant daughter. Still births, miscarriages and deaths of day old infants were not always recorded in the 1840's. Donald's wife Albenia died in childbirth, and although there is no record of the child, or his death, it is assumed that a child must have existed. There is also another child, Cornelius, who was born in Newburyport, did not exist a couple of years later and yet there is no record of his death. The cemetery records also do not show any infants. Of the 17 children, Donald had nine children by his first wife, Albenia Martha (Boole) McKay and eight by his second wife, Mary Cressy (Litchfield) McKay. Donald married Mary Cressy on October 7, 1849, the year after Albenia died.

One of the hardest things to endure in life, besides the death of your wife, is the death of one of your children. Donald had six of his children die during his lifetime. I can not even imagine how devastating that must have been for him.

Donald was working at the Brown & Bell Shipyard on the East River in Manhattan, New York in 1833 when he married Albenia Martha Boole. Over the years he would live in Manhattan and Brooklyn, New York, Wiscasset, Maine, Newbury, Newburyport, East Boston, and Hamilton, Massachusetts. This is why his children were born in a variety of places.

Using census data, vital records, newspapers, and family history notes to gather information on the children, this is what I have found out so far about Donald's wonderful family.

ALBENIA MARTHA (BOOLE) McKAY'S CHILDREN

Cornelius Whitworth McKay was born in Manhattan, New York on February 1, 1834 where the family was living on the fashionable East Broadway. Albenia was well educated, and I am sure that she wanted her son to also have the advantage of an education. In New York in the 1830's, children's education was home schooling, private schools, or church based schools. New York was just starting to debate taxpayer financed free public schools. Although I do not know what school he attended, Cornelius was at the age where he would be in the second grade when the family moved to Newburyport, Massachusetts. When he was 10 years old the family moved again, this time to East Boston, Massachusetts.

Around 1850, two years after his mother died and when he was only around 16 years old, Cornelius married Susan Caroline Seaver, and they would have three children. Louis was born July 15, 1851, Henry on January 10, 1853, and Cornelia January 25, 1854. Susan was the daughter of Eben and Susan Seaver of Portland, Maine.

Cornelius had a very difficult life. His second son, Henry, died in 1853 when he was only two months old. His wife, Susan, died at the young age of 29 of typhoid fever in June of 1858, seven months after their three year old daughter, Cornelia, died of the same thing. His wife and two of his children died before he turned 25 years old. Their son Louis would also die young, in 1880, at the age of 29. Louis was a machinist who lived at 165 Pleasant Street in Boston, one block away from Boston University. He was single, and died at Boston City Hospital where the doctor wrote on his death certificate that the cause of death was alcoholism. Cornelius' wife, Susan, and his three children are buried in the Woodlawn Cemetery in Everett, Massachusetts in her family's cemetery plot.

Most of Donald's children grew up around ships and the shipyard, but Cornelius took a special interest in it. He was around the shipyard so often that all of the workers knew him. He studied ship building from the very best and became a naval architect with an office at 99 State Street, across the river in Boston. In 1858,

Mary B. Dyer

some Cape Cod fishermen asked Donald to design a schooner for their fishing fleet. Donald was busy building the medium clipper *Alhambra* at that time, so he asked Cornelius to design the schooner. Cornelius, at 24 years old, not only designed the schooner *R.R. Higgins*, but he also built the schooner right beside the *Alhambra* that his father was building. The fishermen were so impressed with the ship that they had him build three more. Cornelius designed and built the *Benj. S. Wright*, the *Mary B. Dyer*, and the *H. & R. Atwood*.

In the 1860 census, Cornelius, who is 26 years old and a widower, is living next door to Donald's house and he has four of the older McKay children living with him along with his seven year old son, Louis, and a domestic servant. According to the Boston city directories, he seems to be living in a different apartment almost every year up until 1872 and then he could have left Boston. 1872 was also the year of the great Boston fire that burned more than 800 buildings. Donald had run into financial problems with the *Glory of the Seas* in 1870, and this could also have impacted Cornelius' decision to move.

Cornelius was only three years younger than his father's youngest brother Nathaniel and they seemed to have been very close. Wherever I find Cornelius, Nathaniel is not far away. On March 1, 1875, Cornelius, then listed as a merchant, married his second wife Henriette (Harriet) Senecal in New Orleans, Louisiana and in 1874 Nathaniel was also in New Orleans buying some surplus navy ships.

Cornelius and Harriet's only child, Richard Cornelius McKay, was born March 23 1876 when the family was living at 288 Carondelet Street in New Orleans. Carondelet Street is an extension of the famous Bourbon Street.

Ten years after his marriage, in 1886, Cornelius is in New York and is the yachting editor for a New York Newspaper and Nathaniel is also in New York.

In April 1893, there is a story in the Brooklyn Eagle Newspaper that tells that Cornelius was fired from his position as Inspector of Steamboats for the port of New York. It seems that Nathaniel was instrumental in getting Cornelius the job and both of them were instrumental in making sure that President Cleveland was not re-elected as President for a second term. Therefore, the New York political machine figured that this was a way to pay them both back.

In August of that same year, 1893, his wife Harriet died of peritonitis in Hoboken, New Jersey at the age of 47. Hoboken is on the other side of the Hudson River from New York City, and they lived on Park Avenue, within walking distance of the ferry that went from Hoboken to Manhattan, New York.

Sometime after Harriet died, her son, Richard Cornelius, moved into the home of his cousin, Valentine Fisher, her husband George, and their son Walter, at 1005 Garden Street, one street over from Park Street in Hoboken. Valentine (Ryan) Fisher was the daughter of Harriet's sister, Elizabeth Adele (Senecal) Ryan.

Richard Cornelius McKay, my grandfather, would write a couple of books and several magazine articles about the clipper ships and Donald McKay. Unfortunately he wrote very little about his father Cornelius or his mother Harriet. Richard married Leonie Bohler at Our Lady of Grace Church in Hoboken on September 17, 1901 and they would have five children, two boys and three girls (John, Donald, Cornelia, Albenia and Grace).

Cornelius died six years after his wife on November 30, 1899 of endocarditis and pneumonia in Manhattan, New York after suffering for months with asthenia and chronic nephritis (weakness and inflammation of the kidney). He is buried with his wife in the Greenwood Cemetery in Brooklyn, New York. Also buried in the same plot with Cornelius and his wife, Harriet, is Harriet's mother, Henriette (Mathieu) Senecal/Chatry; her sister Adele (Senecal) Ryan; her sister Ernestine (Senecal) Platosz and Ernestine's daughter Regina (Platosz) Plessis (*see page 161*).

Frances Jean McKay was born two years after

Cornelius on April 3, 1836 in Manhattan, New York and died of consumption (tuberculosis) on October 31, 1851 in East Boston, Massachusetts at the age of 15. She is buried in the family plot in the Oak Hill Cemetery in Newburyport, Massachusetts.

Anne Jane McKay was born one and a half years after

Frances on November 12, 1837 in Manhattan, New York and died of scarlet fever less than five years later on October 11, 1842 in Newburyport, Massachusetts. She is buried in the family plot in the Oak Hill Cemetery in Newburyport.

Dennis Condry McKay was born three years after Anne

on October 29, 1840 in Newburyport, Massachusetts. Dennis was named after a New York merchant for whom his father had built the ship **Delia Walker** in John Currier's shipyard in Newburyport. This merchant, Dennis Condry, was the one who introduced Donald McKay to Enoch Train, who was instrumental in convincing Donald to move down to East Boston.

Dennis, like most of the McKay children, went to school in East Boston and grew up around ships. In the 1860 census, Dennis, at 19 years old, is living with his older brother, Cornelius Whitworth, in East Boston and is listed as a seaman. Unfortunately, he died the following February after enduring 3 days of convulsions. He was only 20 years old. Dennis is buried in the family plot in the Oak Hill Cemetery in Newburyport, Massachusetts.

Donald McKay Jr. was born in Newbury, Massachusetts

one and a half years after Dennis on May 3, 1842. The Town of Newbury was just east of the Town of Newburyport. Newburyport broke off from the Town of Newbury in 1764 and later became a City in 1851, so even today the Town of Newbury and the City of Newburyport are two distinct municipalities.

Donald Jr. married Emilie Pieniger about 1865 and they had one son on July 27, 1866 who they named Donald McKay. That son would later get married and have a son who they also named Donald. Therefore I will refer to them as Donald Jr., Donald II, and Donald III.

Although I do not know the exact timing of events, at some point Donald Jr. and Emilie divorced and at some point they moved to Europe. From 1881 to 1883, their son is enrolled in the Harrow School in Harrow, England - about 20 miles northwest of London. At that time Emilie is living at 46 Avenue D'Eylau in Paris and her 15 year old son is not living at the School. Although the school records do not show his name, it is possible that he is living with his father in England. Their son, Donald II, received a gold medal for his knowledge of French in 1886. In 1887, he joined the Royal Artillery and retired as a Major in 1907. In 1911, he was living at 49 Avenmore Road in London.

The Brooklyn Eagle newspaper lists a Donald McKay and his wife as guests at Nathaniel McKay's wedding to his third wife, Jenney Wilson Pope, in Brooklyn, New York. This wedding was

140

Donald McKay II
at the Harrow School in England
Courtesy of the Harrow School

in January of 1889, and since it occurred a little over eight years after Donald Sr. had died, there is a good chance that it was Donald Jr., then 46 years old. It is possible that he was accompanied at the wedding by Emilie, but it is more likely that it was his future second wife, Mary F. Willoughby.

Donald Jr. married his second wife, Mary F Willoughby, on January 7, 1891 in Chicago, Illinois.

In the 1910 census, I found that Donald Jr. was a book salesman living in Baltimore, Maryland with wife, Mary and they did not have any children.

Donald Jr. died on December 1, 1919 in Baltimore, Maryland at the age of 77.

Cornelius McKay was born August 23, 1843. According to the Newburyport vital records, Cornelius was born in Newburyport, Massachusetts to Donald and Alvenia McKay. It is hard to imagine that Donald and Alvenia McKay are not really Donald and Albenia McKay. Donald was in Newburyport from 1840 to 1844. Cornelius is not listed with the family in the 1850 Boston census when he would be six years old. He is not listed in the vital records under deaths, although it was common not to report infants who died within a day or two. He is not listed on the tombstone in the family plot in Newburyport, unless he is one of the three infants mentioned anonymously on the stone. He is not listed in the cemetery records, but non of the infants are mentioned in the cemetery records. He is not listed in William Kean's McKay genealogy. It also seems strange

that Donald and Albenia would name a second son Cornelius when the first Cornelius Whitworth was still alive unless he had died right away. There is a slight possibility that there was a Donald and Alvenia McKay living in Newburyport at the same time as Donald and Albenia, but it is much more likely that Cornelius was Donald's son.

John Boole McKay was born two and a half years after

Donald, and almost one and a half years after Cornelius, on December 11, 1844 in East Boston, Massachusetts. John is named after Albenia's father who was a shipwright in a New York shipyard, but had come up to Boston in the mid 1840's.

John is listed in the 1860 census, when he was 15 years old, living with his brother Cornelius Whitworth next door to his father's house in East Boston.

At the start of the Civil War, John enlisted in the 1st Regiment Massachusetts Volunteer Infantry on May 23, 1861, claiming to be 18 years old when he was only 16. He was assigned to Company B. After some very brief training, the 1st Regiment left Massachusetts by train on June 15th, and arrived in Washington on the 17th when it was assigned to the Richardson Brigade. They remained in camp in the Washington area until the Regiment started to advance to Manassas, Virginia where it took part in the battle of Blackburn's Ford on July 18, three days before the main battle of Bull Run. In August they became part of the famous Hooker Brigade. During the fall of 1861, they camped in Bladensburg, did duty on the Potomac above Washington, built Fort Lincoln, moved to Budd's Ferry, and was variously engaged until spring 1862 when they became part of Grover's Brigade. On April 6th, they were in action before Yorktown, and on May 5th they suffered heavy losses at Williamsburg. The regiment was encamped in the White Oak

Swamp region until June 25, 1862 when they fought at Fair Oaks. This was the battle in which John was wounded. Although the 1st Regiment went on to fight in most of the heavy battles of the Civil War, this was John's last battle. He was discharged because of his wounds on April 3, 1863 at 18 years of age.

John appears in the 1870 census as a ship painter in East Boston, and he is living in a rooming house. He does not appear on the 1880 census, but he is mentioned in his father's Will that year. He did not receive anything from the estate because "*He had received as much of my property as is just*". Then in 1892 he was admitted to the US National Home for Disabled Soldiers in Sawtell, Los Angeles, CA. I have not found a death notice for him.

Albenia McKay was born almost two years after John on September 20, 1846 in East Boston, Massachusetts. Albenia married J. G. Bodemer about 1867 and they would have five children, all girls. Their children are:

- 1. Mary Bodemer was born July 2, 1868. She married Woldemer Bretschneider and had two children of her own, Marianne and Moritz.
- 2. Johannes Bodemer was born August 8, 1870 but she died before the age of four in April of 1874.
- 3. Margareta Bodemer was born June 12, 1873.
- 4. Friederike Bodemer was born May 15, 1875.
- 5. Else Bodemer was born August 3, 1876.

Albenia might be the woman on the top step in the picture at the beginning of this chapter.

Unknown Child born on December 10, 1848 and presumed to be stillborn. Although there is no record of his birth or death, his

mother, Albenia, died in childbirth and it is assumed that he, or she, must have existed.

MARY CRESSY (LITCHFIELD) McKAY'S CHILDREN

Lauchlan McKay was born on October 31, 1850 in East Boston, Massachusetts. Unfortunately Lauchlan only lived two and a half years and died in Boston, on April 10, 1853 of "congestion of the brain" (probably meningitis). He is buried in the family plot in the Oak Hill Cemetery in Newburyport, Massachusetts.

Frances McKay was born on April 12, 1854 in East Boston, Massachusetts. Frances was a very talented woman. She played the violin like her father. In October of 1869, at the age of 15, she christened her father's last clipper ship, the *Glory of the Seas*. She also must have been very smart because Donald sent her to Switzerland to study. While she was at school in Bulle, Switzerland, she met her husband, August Clavel. According to the Michel family history written by Elsie Michel, August was from a prominent Swiss banking family. Frances married August and they had three children. They were Louise Clavel born October 28, 1879, Mary Cressy Clavel on August 27, 1883, and François Henri August Clavel on March 31, 1893.

The family lived for a time in a section of the La Part Dieu Monastery in Bulle, Switzerland. This monastery was one of two that the Carthusian monks owned, and they abandoned this one in favor of consolidating their living quarters in the other one. La Part Dieu was then divided up and sold. Family legend has it that

144

Jules Jerome Michel and Mary Cressy (Clavel) Michel
Picture courtesy of Kate Silvernale

August's father, François Clavel, helped a member of the Russian Royal family get out of Russia in the 1840's and she was the one who bought the monastery and then she left part of it to the Clavels after she died. August and Frances would later use this as a summer retreat. This "Royal" might have been Catherine Schakowski who was thought to be part of the Rumine Royal family in Russia and who owned the Rumine Palace in Lausanne that is today used as a museum. The Clavels also owned the "Estate Florimont" in Lausanne where they raised their family.

Frances' second daughter, Mary Cressy Clavel, learned to play the violin from her mother, and played with the Lausanne Symphony Orchestra. She married Jules Jerome (Jerry) Michel. Jerry had a very interesting life. He was born in Lyon France in 1884. He came from a long line of military men and at the age of 14 the family wanted him to enter the French Military Academy, but he had other ideas. He ran off to Paris, to the Paris Conservatory of Music, to study the cello. He graduated with honors at 18 and taught cello and toured the US and Europe with an orchestra, giving concerts. He even went to Calcutta, India where he taught cello and became the head of their Conservatory of Music. At the start of WWI Jerry returned to France and joined the French army. He was wounded in the battle of Somme, and was sent to Switzerland to recuperate. There he was hospitalized with a paralyzed leg. It was here that he met Mary Cressy Clavel.

Jerry noticed that the new electric radios were getting very popular, so he started importing them from America. This financial boon allowed he and his wife to live on the Clavel estate in Lausanne, Switzerland where their only child, Jean Claude Donald Michel was born.

After Frances and August Clavel died, their estate was divided among their three children. Their son, François, was left the Clavel estate in Lausanne; Louise was left the monastery grounds which the family had used as a summer retreat; and Mary Cressy was left all of the cash. However, there was not very much cash left in the estate, so Jerry Michel sued to break the terms of the Will asking that all assets be divided equally among the three children. This caused such a rift in the Clavel family that around 1943 Jerry and Mary immigrated to the United States. They moved to Pierce Hill Road in Lincoln, Massachusetts. Jerry and Mary's son, Jean Claude Donald Michel, became a doctor, married Elsie Jeanette Charman, and settled in Seattle, Washington. Mary Cressy Clavel suffered with lung cancer for two to eight years, and it had spread to other parts of her body in her last year. She died in Lincoln, Massachusetts on March 27, 1948 at the age of 64 and is buried in the Lincoln Cemetery.

There was a note in Dr. Donald McKay's copy of William Kean's McKay genealogy that said that Frances (McKay) Clavel died in 1943 in France when she would have been 89. I tend to believe that it is more likely that she died in Switzerland.

Mary Cressy McKay was born on January 4, 1856 in East Boston, Massachusetts. Mary Cressy married Edward Penniman Bliss about 1885 and they lived in Lexington, Massachusetts. Edward was a partner with his brother Henry in the firm of Cushing & Bliss at 65 Franklin St. in Boston. After

1892, they started the Massachusetts Mohair Plush Company. Edward had a B.A. and an M.A. from Harvard University. He served twice on the Lexington School Committee. He was president of the Lexington Historical Society in 1905, and was a Selectman for the Town of Lexington in 1912.

In 1885, Mary wrote a cook book which she called "The Practical Cook Book" which was published by David McKay. In 1887, Edward Bliss wrote a history book called "Old Taverns of Lexington", which has been quoted by many authors.

Edward was also the executor of Donald McKay's estate and he was fighting the government, in addition to Nathaniel's fight, to have the government pay what they still owed for the ships that Donald had built for the Civil War.

Mary and Edward did not have any children.

In 1920, Mary's mother, Mary Cressy McKay, was living with her widowed daughter in Mary Cressy Bliss' home at 19 Oakland Street in Lexington, and that is where her mother died in February of 1923. Mary Bliss apparently did not die in Lexington, and I have not been able to find her death notice, nor where she is buried.

Lawrence Litchfield McKay was born on January 25, 1860 in East Boston, Massachusetts. He is named after his mother's brother Lawrence. In 1880, at 20 years old, he was working on the family farm in Hamilton, Massachusetts along with two farm hands. Around 1890, after the family farm had been sold, he married Anne Newbold Bispham. In 1910, Lawrence was a manager on a farm in Brewster, New York. Lawrence and Anne did not have any children.

Anna Cushing McKay was born on June 17, 1864, along with her twin brother Nichols, in East Boston, Massachusetts.

Anna was named after her grandmother, Anna (Cushing) Litchfield, Mary Cressy's mother.

When she was 19 years old, Anna married a 31 year old teacher from Rochester, named Henry F. Burton, on June 28, 1883. They were married by the Congregational Minister, the Rev. Temple Cutler, and they made their home in a house on Richards Street in Hamilton, Massachusetts. She died of consumption one and a half years later on January 6, 1885 when she was only 20 years old. Since her gravestone indicates that she had a daughter, and there is no record of the daughter's birth or death in the Hamilton Town Records, it is possible that she might have been pregnant when she died. Both she and her daughter are buried in the McKay family plot in the Oak Hill Cemetery in Newburyport, Massachusetts.

Nichols Litchfield McKay was born on June 17, 1864 in East Boston, Massachusetts. Nichols is named after his mother's father, Nichols Litchfield. Nichols married Grace A. Russell about 1888 and they would have three children, all girls and all born in Arlington, Massachusetts. They are:

- 1. Frances Clavel McKay was born October 19, 1889. Frances Clavel is named after Nichols' sister Frances who was over in Switzerland at that time.
- 2. Mildred McKay was born April 2, 1892.
- 3. Anna Cushing McKay was born January 12, 1895. Anna Cushing is named after her father's twin sister Anna who had died ten years before his daughter was born.

In 1910, the family was living at 73 Jason Street in Arlington, Massachusetts and Nichols is a sales manager for a leather company. When his mother, Mary Cressy, sold her house in Hamilton, Massachusetts in 1888, she lived with Nichols and his family for many years.

Nichols died on April 14, 1947 in Arlington at 82.

There is a note in Dr. Donald McKay's copy of William Kean's McKay genealogy that says that Nichols was connected in some way with the Hotel Vendome in Boston, but I have not found out what that connection is. The Hotel Vendome burned down in a spectacular fire in 1972.

Guy Allen McKay was born on October 4, 1866 in East Boston, Massachusetts. Guy married Allie Pierson on March 2, 1889. Allie was born on May 30, 1870 and was the daughter of Alan Samuel Pierson and Anna M. Slusser. Guy and Allie had three children, all born in Texas. They are:

Guy Allen McKay(60)
Hugh Robert McKay(37)
by the charred remains of the *Glory of the Seas* a half mile south of Brace Point, Seattle, WA April 1926.

- 1. Donald McKay was born May 9, 1891. He married Eleanor Hamlin in Hutchinson, Kansas sometime before 1920.

  In 1910, when he was still single, he was a driver for an express company.

  There was a note in Dr. Donald McKays copy of Kean's book that said that Donald was shot, but I have not been able to substantiate this.

- 2. Hugh Robert McKay was born December 23, 1893.

  He married an Hawaiian girl named Agasta about 1901.

  In 1920, Hugh was a boat broker living in Seattle, WA.

- 3. Albenia McKay was born in June of 1897.

In 1900, Guy Allen was a farmer and a stockman in Hansford, Texas. His brother, Wallace, also had a ranch in the same town.

In 1910, Guy Allen is living in Hutchinson, Kansas and is divorced living alone. His wife and children are also in Hutchinson at a different address. By 1920 Guy has married a woman named Ellie and they are living in St. Louis, Missouri and he is a clerk in an office in that city.

Wallace McKay was born on October 6, 1868 in East Boston, Massachusetts. Wallace married Mary C. (maiden name unknown) and they would have three children. They are:

- 1. Margaret McKay was born in Oklahoma in February of 1897.
- 2. Guy Allen McKay born in Kansas in November of 1898.
- 3. Roscoe McKay born in Texas in 1901.

In 1900, Wallace is a stockman in Hansford, Texas, in the same town as his brother Guy Allen. By 1910, Wallace is a clerk in a lumber company in Wichita, Kansas and is married to a different woman named Cassie (or Carrie), who he married about 1904. The children are still with them and they have another four year old son, Gordon,

- 4. Gordon McKay was born in Oklahoma around 1906.

Because all of the children are living with Wallace in 1910, and Wallace has remarried, I tend to believe that his first wife, Mary, had died.

If all of this census information is correct, Wallace sure did like to move around. He went from Massachusetts, to Oklahoma, to Kansas, to Texas, to Oklahoma, and then back to Kansas.

150

McKay Family burial plot

Oak Hill Cemetery
Newburyport, Mass
2004

151

In
Memory of

Frances J. McKay
Born April 3, 1836
Died Oct 31, 1851

———

Lauchlan McKay
Born Oct 31, 1850
Died April 10, 1853

———

Dennis C. McKay
Born Oct 29, 1840
Died Feb 2, 1861

In
Memory of
Anne Jane

Daughter of Albenia Martha
& D. McKay

———

Who departed this life
Oct 11th 1842
Aged 4 years 11 months

Also their three
Infant Children

ANNA CUSHING McKAY

Wife of Henry F. Burton
June 17,1864 - Jan 6, 1885
and infant daughter

APPENDIX 1
REFERENCE DOCUMENTATION
DONALD McKAY

DEATH CERTIFICATE

The Commonwealth of Massachusetts
UNITED STATES OF AMERICA.
COPY OF RECORD OF DEATH

Town of Hamilton

I, the undersigned, hereby certify that I am clerk of the Town of Hamilton that as such I have custody of the records of deaths required by law to be kept in my office; that among such records is one relating to the death of

Donald McKay

and that the following is a true copy of so much of said record as relates to said death, namely:

Date of death........ September 20, 1880

Place of death........ Hamilton

Name .... Donald McKay
If deceased is a married, widowed or divorced woman, give also maiden name and name of husband.

Sex .... Male .... Color .... N/A

Single, Married, Widowed or Divorced .... Married

Age .... 70 .... Years .... -- .... Months .... 16 .... Days

Residence .... Hamilton

Occupation .... Farmer and Ship Builder

U. S. War Veteran .... N/A
Specify War

Place of Birth .... Shelburne, N.S.

FATHER	MOTHER
Name .... Hugh McKay	Maiden Name .... Ann McKay
Place of Birth .... N.S	Place of Birth .... N.S

Cause of Death .... Consumption

Place of Burial .... Newburyport .... Name of Cemetery .... N/A

Date of Record .... January 10, 1881

SEAL

And I do hereby certify that the foregoing is a true copy from said records.

Witness my hand and seal of said Town of Hamilton on this 18th day of January 2006

Jane M. Stetson
Clerk

Year........ 1880
Vol........ Death
Page........ 110-111
No........ N/A

FORM 431 HOBBS & WARREN, INC. PUBLISHERS

APPENDIX 1
REFERENCE DOCUMENTATION
ALBENIA MARTHA (BOOLE) McKAY

DEATH CERTIFICATE

Certificate
No. 012425

REGISTRY DIVISION, CITY OF BOSTON

COUNTY OF SUFFOLK, COMMONWEALTH OF MASSACHUSETTS, UNITED STATES OF AMERICA

CERTIFIED COPY OF RECORD OF DEATH IN OFFICE OF THE CITY REGISTRAR

I, the undersigned, hereby certify that I hold the office of .... City Registrar of the City of Boston and I certify the following facts appear on the records of Births, Marriages and Deaths kept in said City as required by law.

Date of Death DECEMBER 10, 1848

BOOK 1847
No.

Name and surname of Deceased albina McKAY
(If Married, Widowed or Divorced, Maiden Name)

Sex and Color	
Condition (Single, Married, Widowed or Divorced)	
Supposed Age: Years 33, Months –, Days –	
Name and Surname of Husband or Maiden Name or Wife of Deceased: FAMILY OF DONLAND McKAY	Residence (Street and Number): BOSTON MA.
Occupation	
Place of Death: BOSTON	Place of Birth
Disease or Cause of Death (Primary or Secondary): CHILD BED	Names and Birthplaces of Parents (Maiden Name of Mother)
Place of Burial (Name of Cemetery): NEWBURY PORT	Date of Record
DECEMBER 13, UNDERTAKER	
JOHN WHITE	

I further certify that by annexation, the Record of the following named cities and towns are in the custody of the City Registrar of Boston:—

	Annexed
Charlestown	1874
Brighton	
West Roxbury	
Hyde Park	1912

Annexed	
East Boston	1637
South Boston	1804
Roxbury	1868
Dorchester	1870

WITNESS my hand and the SEAL of the CITY REGISTRAR

.... on this .... Day of MAR 2 7 2006 A. D. 10 ......

Judith A Doherty

By Chapter 214 of the Acts of 1852, "the certificate or attestation of either Assistant City Registrar shall have the same force and effect as that of the City Registrar."

.... City Registrar

APPENDIX 1
REFERENCE DOCUMENTATION
MARY CRESSY (LITCHFIELD) McKAY

DEATH CERTIFICATE

Town of Lexington
Commonwealth of Massachusetts

I hereby certify that I hold the Office of Town Clerk of the Town of Lexington, in the County of Middlesex, and the Commonwealth of Massachusetts, and that the Records of Births, Marriages and Deaths are in my custody, and that the following is a true copy from the records as certified by me.

OFFICE OF THE SECRETARY
DIVISION OF VITAL STATISTICS

The Commonwealth of Massachusetts

STANDARD CERTIFICATE OF DEATH   Lexington
(City or town)

1 PLACE OF DEATH
County Middlesex   State   Mass.   Registered No. 10

City or Town Lexington,   No. 19 Oakland Street   St.   Ward
(If death occurred in a hospital or institution, give its NAME instead of street and number)

2 FULL NAME   Mary Cressy McKay

(a) Residence. No.   St.,   Ward   Arlington
Length of residence in city or town where death occurred 35 years months days.   How long in U.S., if of foreign birth? years weeks days

PERSONAL AND STATISTICAL PARTICULARS			MEDICAL CERTIFICATE OF DEATH
3 SEX	4 COLOR OR RACE	5 SINGLE, MARRIED, WIDOWED, OR DIVORCED (WRITE THE WORD)	16 DATE OF DEATH February 6th. 1923

Female   White   Widow

5a If married, widowed, or divorced
HUSBAND of
(or) WIFE of   Donald McKay

16 I HEREBY CERTIFY, That I attended deceased from

6 AGE Years 91 Months 4 Days 8   If LESS than 1 day, hrs. or min.

7 OCCUPATION OF DECEASED
(a) Trade, profession, or particular kind of work   at home
(b) Name of employer

8 BIRTHPLACE (City)   Hingham, Mass.
(State or country)

9 NAME OF FATHER   Nichols Litchfield

10 BIRTHPLACE (City) of FATHER   Scituate, Mass.
(State or country)

11 MAIDEN NAME OF MOTHER   Anna Cushing

12 BIRTHPLACE (City) OF MOTHER   Scituate Mass.
(State or country)

13 Informant   Mrs Mary C. Bliss
(Address)   Lexington, Mass.

The CAUSE OF DEATH was as follows:

CONTRIBUTORY
(secondary)

17 Where was disease contracted
if not at place of death?
Did an operation precede death?   Date of
Was there an autopsy?
What test confirmed diagnosis?

18 PLACE OF BURIAL, CREMATION, OR REMOVAL   Oak Hill Cem. Newburyport

DATE OF BURIAL   Feb.9,23

19 UNDERTAKER   ADDRESS

APPENDIX 1
REFERENCE DOCUMENTATION
MARY CRESSY (CLAVEL) MICHEL
Frances McKay's daughter

DEATH CERTIFICATE

The Commonwealth of Massachusetts
OFFICE OF THE SECRETARY
DIVISION OF VITAL STATISTICS
STANDARD
CERTIFICATE OF DEATH

To be filed for burial permit with Board of Health or its Agent

white

Registered No. 6

PLACE OF DEATH

Middlesex (County)

Lincoln (City or Town)

No. Pierce Hill Road

St. (If death occurred in a hospital or institution, give its NAME instead of street and number)

2 FULL NAME MARY CRESSY (Clavel) MICHEL
(If deceased is a married, widowed or divorced woman, give also maiden name.)

PHYSICIAN - IMPORTANT
Was deceased a U. S. War Veteran, if so specify WAR)

(a) Residence. No. Pierce Hill Road St.
(Usual place of abode)
(If nonresident, give city or town and State)

Length of stay: In hospital or institution _____ years _____ months _____ days.
(Before death) (Specify whether)
In this community 13 yrs. _____ mos. _____ days.

PERSONAL AND STATISTICAL PARTICULARS

3 SEX Female

4 COLOR OR RACE White

5 SINGLE (write the word) MARRIED WIDOWED or DIVORCED Married

5a If married, widowed, or divorced HUSBAND of
(or) WIFE of Jules J. Michel
(Husband's name in full)

6 Age of husband or wife if alive 64 years

7 IF STILLBORN, enter that fact here.

8 AGE 64 Years 7 Months _____ Days _____ | If less than 1 day _____ Hours _____ Minutes

9 Usual Occupation: Housework

10 Industry or Business: At Home

11 Social Security No. None

12 BIRTHPLACE of Lausanne
(State or country) Switzerland

13 NAME OF FATHER Auguste Clavel

14 BIRTHPLACE OF FATHER (City) Lausanne
(State or country) Switzerland

15 MAIDEN NAME OF MOTHER Frances McKay

16 BIRTHPLACE OF MOTHER (City) Boston
(State or country) Massachusetts

17 Informant Jules J. Michel (Husband)
(Address) Pierce Hill Road, Lincoln, Mass

MEDICAL CERTIFICATE OF DEATH

18 DATE OF DEATH March 22 1948
(Month) (Da.) (Year)

19 I HEREBY CERTIFY, That I attended deceased from November, 1947, to Mar. 27, 1948
I last saw her alive on Mar. 27, 1948, death is said to have occurred on the date stated above, at 4.30 P. m.

Immediate cause of death Carcinoma of lung
Duration 2.5.8 years

Due to _____

Due to _____

Other conditions carcinomatosis
(Include pregnancy within 3 months of death)
12.7.19 mo.

Major findings: Of operations _____

Of autopsy _____ Date of _____

What test confirmed diagnosis? clinical

20 Was disease or injury in any way related to occupation of deceased? no
If so, specify _____

(Signed) F. Van Bugh M. D.
(Address) Weston, Mass. Date Mar. 29 1948

21 Place of Burial, Lincoln Cemetery-Lincoln, Mass.
(City or Town)

DATE OF BURIAL March 29 1948

22 NAME OF FUNERAL DIRECTOR Rothwell N. MacRae
ADDRESS Concord, Mass.

I HEREBY CERTIFY that a satisfactory standard certificate of death was filed with me BEFORE the burial or transit permit was issued:

Signature of Agent of Board of Health or other
(Official Designation) (Date of Issue of Permit)

Received and filed MAR _____ 19 _____
(Registrar)

APPENDIX 1
REFERENCE DOCUMENTATION
ANNA CUSHING (McKAY) BURTON
Donald and Mary's daughter

DEATH CERTIFICATE

The Commonwealth of Massachusetts
UNITED STATES OF AMERICA.
COPY OF RECORD OF DEATH

Town .... of .... Hamilton

I, the undersigned, hereby certify that I am clerk of the ...Town.........of.......Hamilton.........
that as such I have custody of the records of deaths required by law to be kept in my office;
that among such records is one relating to the death of
Anna McKay Burton

and that the following is a true copy of so much of said record as relates to said death, namely:

Date of death.............. January 6, 1885
Place of death.............. Hamilton

Name .... Anna McKay Burton
If deceased is a married, widowed or divorced woman, give also maiden name and name of husband.
Sex .... Female .... Color .... N/A

Single, Married, Widowed or Divorced .... Married

Age .... 20 .... Years .... 1 .... Months .... N/A .... Days

Residence .... Hamilton

Occupation .... N/A

U. S. War Veteran .... N/A
Specify War
Place of Birth .... East Boston

FATHER	MOTHER
Name ...... Donald McKay	Maiden Name...... Mary McKay
Place of Birth........ N/A	Place of Birth...... N/A

Cause of Death .... Consumption
Place of Burial ...... Newburyport .... Name of Cemetery .... N/A
Date of Record.............. January 26, 1886

And I do hereby certify that the foregoing is a true copy from said records.
Witness my hand and seal of said ...Town..... of ....Hamilton
on this....... 18th .... day of ...... January 19 2006

SEAL

Jane M. Thetson
Clerk

Year.... 1884
Vol..... Death
Page... 120-121
No....... N/A

FORM 431 HOBBS & WARREN, INC. PUBLISHERS

APPENDIX 1
REFERENCE DOCUMENTATION

CORNELIUS WHITWORTH McKAY
Donald and Albenia's son

DEATH CERTIFICATE

APPENDIX 1
REFERENCE DOCUMENTATION
HARRIET (SENECAL) McKAY
Cornelius McKay's second wife

DEATH CERTIFICATE

State of New Jersey
OFFICE OF THE REGISTRAR OF VITAL STATISTICS
City of Hoboken, County of Hudson

This is to Certify that the following is correctly copied from a record of Death in my office.

NAME OF DECEASED: HARRIET McKAY
SEX: FEMALE COLOR: WHITE MARITAL CONDITION: MARRIED
SOCIAL SECURITY NUMBER: 000-00-0000
PLACE OF DEATH: HOBOKEN, NEW JERSEY
DATE OF BIRTH: / /1846
AGE: YRS. 47 MON. DAYS
DATE OF DEATH: 08/27/1893
PLACE OF BIRTH: UNITED STATES
CAUSE OF DEATH: PERITONITIS

SUPPLEMENTAL INFORMATION IF DEATH WAS DUE TO EXTERNAL CAUSES
☐ ACCIDENT ☐ SUICIDE ☐ HOMICIDE ☐ HOW INJURY OCCURRED.
TIME OF INJURY: HOUR, MONTH, DAY, YEAR   ☐ A.M. ☐ P.M.
INJURY OCCURRED: WHILE AT WORK ☐ NOT WHILE AT WORK ☐
PLACE OF INJURY
CITY, TOWN, OR LOCATION   COUNTY   STATE
NOT STATED

NAME OF PERSON WHO CERTIFIED CAUSE OF DEATH: W.T. KUDLICH, M.D.

FOR INFORMATIONAL PURPOSES ONLY
NOT TO BE USED FOR IDENTIFICATION
OR LEGAL PURPOSES.

18938001   07/10/2003
Date of Issue

Registrar of Vital Statistics
ADDRESS

THIS CERTIFICATE NOT VALID UNLESS THE RAISED SEAL OF THE
HOBOKEN BOARD OF HEALTH IS AFFIXED HEREON.

Information included with the death certificate from the City Clerk of Hoboken, NJ

Residence: 503 Park Avenue Hoboken, NJ
Father: Amable Senecal
Mother: Henrietta Senecal
Buried: Greenwood Cemetery Brooklyn, NY

APPENDIX 1
REFERENCE DOCUMENTATION
McKAY FAMILY PLOT - OAK HILL CEMETERY, Newburyport, MA

MOTHER
[Albenia Martha
(Boole) McKay]

DENNIS

FATHER
[Donald McKay]

Anna Cushing McKay
Wife of Henry F. Burton
JUNE 17, 1864
JAN 6, 1885

And Infant daughter

In Memory of
Albenia Martha
Wife of Donald McKay
Who departed this life
Dec 10, 1848 aged 33 years

All her toils on earth are done
Jesus owns her for his own

Wouldst thou know her virtues
They are registered in heaven

APPENDIX 1
REFERENCE DOCUMENTATION
CORNELIUS AND HENRIETTE (HARRIET) McKAY
Donald and Albenia McKay's son

Cornelius Whitworth McKay and his second wife, Harriet Senecal, are both buried in an unmarked grave at the Greenwood Cemetery in Brooklyn, New York (Section 162 Lot 14941). Unmarked except for a small stone, lying flat on the ground half buried, that has the inscription "Ernestine Platosz". Harriet died on August 27, 1893 in Hoboken, NJ and Cornelius died on November 30, 1899 in Manhattan.

The Senecal Stone
Ernestine (Senecal) Platosz and her daughter Regina Plessis

The grave is to the left of the Harding plot and to the right of the green hedge. The Cemetery is very well marked and laid out with Avenues to drive on and marked Paths to walk on. Lot 14941 is on the west side of Saffron Path that runs between Sassafras Avenue and Grape Avenue, if you ever decide to visit the cemetery.

The grave site is behind the green hedge behind the angel

There are 6 people buried in this Senecal plot. Besides Cornelius and Harriet, there is Henrietta (Mathieu) Senecal/Chatry (Harriet's mother), and two of Harriet's sisters: Adele (Senecal) Ryan and Ernestine (Senecal) Platosz, and Ernestine's daughter Regina H. Plessis.

APPENDIX 1
REFERENCE DOCUMENTATION
East Boston, Massachusetts 1858

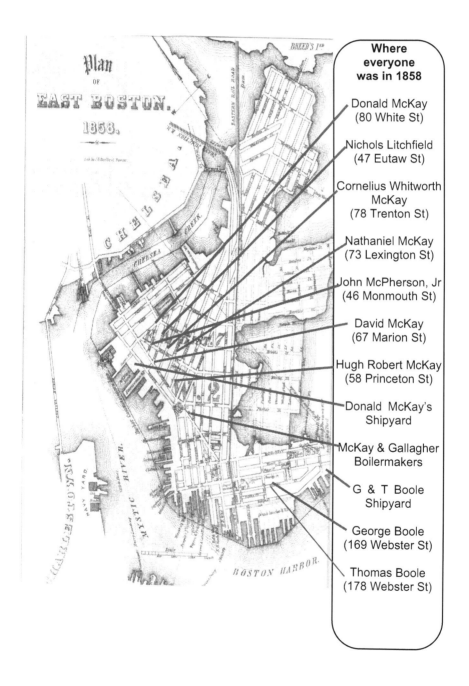

Where everyone was in 1858

Donald McKay
(80 White St)

Nichols Litchfield
(47 Eutaw St)

Cornelius Whitworth
McKay
(78 Trenton St)

Nathaniel McKay
(73 Lexington St)

John McPherson, Jr
(46 Monmouth St)

David McKay
(67 Marion St)

Hugh Robert McKay
(58 Princeton St)

Donald McKay's
Shipyard

McKay & Gallagher
Boilermakers

G & T Boole
Shipyard

George Boole
(169 Webster St)

Thomas Boole
(178 Webster St)

163

APPENDIX 1
REFERENCE DOCUMENTATION
Newburyport, Massachusetts

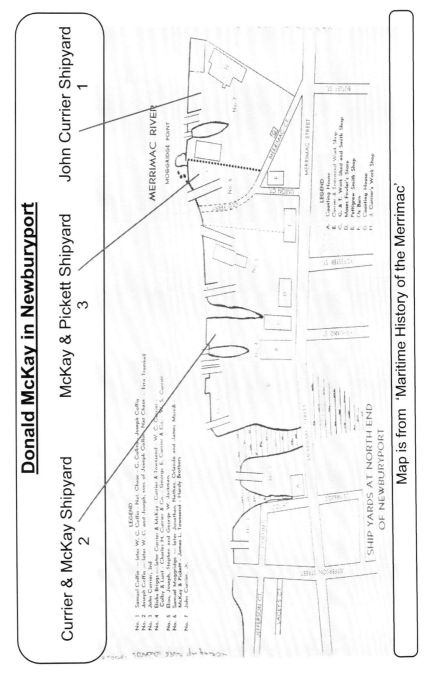

Donald McKay in Newburyport

Currier & McKay Shipyard
2

McKay & Pickett Shipyard
3

John Currier Shipyard
1

LEGEND

No. 1 Samuel Coffin — later W. C. Coffin - Nat Chase - G. Collins, Joseph Coffin
No. 2 Joseph Coffin — later W. C. and Joseph, son of Joseph Coffin. Nat Chase - Ezra Trumbull
No. 3 John Currier, 3rd
No. 4 Elisha Briggs — later Currier & McKay. Currier & Townsend . W. C. Currier.
       Colby & Lunt : Charles H. Currier & Co. . George E. Currier & Co. . Wm S. Currier
No. 5 Elias, Joseph, Stephen and George W. Jackman.
No. 6 Samuel Maggridge — later Jonathan, Nathan, Orlando and James Merrill
       McKay & Pickett - James L. Townsend - Hardy Brothers
No. 7 John Currier, Jr.

MERRIMAC RIVER

MOGGRIDGE POINT

MERRIMAC STREET

LEGEND

A. Counting House
B. Currier & Townsend Work Shop
C. C. & T. Work Shed and Smith Shop
D. Moses Fowler's Store
E. Pettigrew Smith Shop
F. Ox Barn
G. Counting House
H. J. Currier's Work Shop

SHIP YARDS AT NORTH END
OF NEWBURYPORT

Map is from 'Maritime History of the Merrimac'

164

APPENDIX 1
REFERENCE DOCUMENTATION
Verona Island, Maine

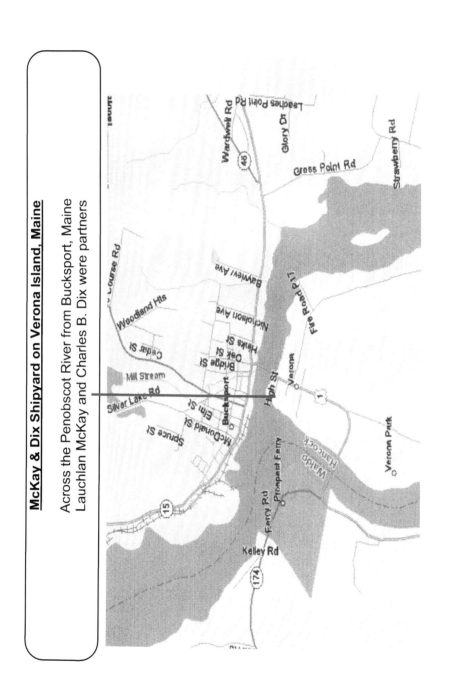

McKay & Dix Shipyard on Verona Island, Maine

Across the Penobscot River from Bucksport, Maine
Lauchlan McKay and Charles B. Dix were partners

APPENDIX 2
BOOLE FAMILY GENEALOGY

Information for the Boole Family genealogy was graciously supplied by Robin Ogilvie through multiple e-mails. All of the following information was supplied by her except for the information that is in *Italics. This is information, from various sources, that has come out of my research.*

....1 Francis Boole (Francis' Regiment fought at Bunker Hill, Boston in 1775, after which the regiment was sent to Halifax for two months for R&R prior to returning to the Revolutionary War)
Francis Boole married Catherine Dieffendorf while stationed in Halifax, NS in 1776

........2 Samuel Boole born Jan 26, 1784 died 1827

........2 Elizabeth Boole christened Aug 13, 1786
Elizabeth Boole married Ebenezer Locke on Dec 18, 1806 in Christ Church Shelburne NS
Ebenezer Locke was the son of Jacob Locke and Viss Vernan [16]
In 1860, at 74, Elizabeth was living with her niece, Catherine (Boole) Sproule in East Boston, MA [3]

............3. *John Berry Locke baptized Nov 15, 1807 in Shelburne, NS* [11]
John Berry Locke married Margaret R. Hammond on Dec 20, 1836 [11]
...............4. *Margaret Hammond Locke born Nov 28, 1837 in Shelburne, NS* [11]
3. *2nd marriage John Berry Locke marries Ann Holden on Feb 28, 1842* [11]
...............4. *Lemuel Berry Locke born May 9, 1843* [11]
Lemuel Berry Locke married Catherine McKay Jun 16, 1871 [11]
....................5. *John Locke* [11]
....................5. *Ann Locke* [11]
....................5. *Josephine Locke* [11]
...............4. *George Locke* [11]
George Locke married Jerusha Thornburne [11]
....................5. Frederick Locke [11]
....................5. William Locke [11]

APPENDIX 2 - BOOLE FAMILY GENEALOGY

.................5. Lillian Locke [11]

..............4. *John Locke* [11]

       John Locke married Mary Mahoney [11]

..............4. *Samuel Locke* [11]

..............4. *Colin Locke* [11]

..............4. *Jacob Locke* [11]

..............4. *Mary Locke* [11]

       Mary Locke married John Anderson [11]

.................5. *Frederick Anderson* [11]

..........3. *Eleanor Jane Lock baptized Jul 16, 1809 in*
            Shelburne, NS [11] *- died Aug 31, 1896 in*
            Green Bay Harbor, Shelburne, NS at 87 [16]
      Eleanor Jane Locke married Joseph Williams on
            Jan 23, 1833 in Shelburne, NS [11]
         Joseph C. Williams was baptized Aug 16, 1808
         died Dec 19, 1880 at 72 [16]

..............4. *John Collin Williams was born Nov 1, 1833 - died*
         May 22, 1883 in Green Harbor, Shelburne
         at 49 [16]

      John Collin Williams married ___ [16]
      John Collin Williams was a master mariner [16]

.................5. *Frederick Gibson Williams adopted* [16]

.................5. *May Dunlop Williams adopted* [16]

.................5. *Effie Peterson Williams adopted* [16]

.................5. *Elizabeth Chymist Williams adopted* [16]

..............4. *Catherine Mary Williams was born Jan 11, 1836 -*
         died 1895 [16]

      Catherine Mary Williams married Michael Ringer on
         Jan 11, 1836 [11]

.................5. George Williams Edgar Ringer was born
         Dec 2, 1855 [11]

.................5. Jolin Colin Williams Ringer was born Apr 29, 1857 [11]

.................5. William Herbert Ringer was born Jan 16, 1859 [11]
      William Herbert Ringer married Emily E. abt 1865 [11]

..............4. *George Francis Williams was born Sep 13, 1837 -*
         died about 1856 at sea at 19 [16]

..............4. *Jane Stuart Williams was born Mar 27, 1841 in*
         Christ Church, Shelburne, NS [16]

      Jane Stuart Williams married William Morris Doleman
         on Feb 3, 1865 [11]

..............4. *William Henry Williams was born Jul 11, 1842 -*
         died Apr 30, 1909 at 66 [16]

..............4. *Elizabeth Locke Williams was born Apr 13, 1843*
         in Green Harbor - died 1924 [16]

...............4. Thomas Perry Williams was born Mar 11, 1845
in East Green Harbor, NS - died Apr 1, 1906 at
61 in Osborne,NS
Thomas was a Captain [16]
Thomas Perry Williams married Eliza Harding on
Mar 19, 1873 [11]
..................5. Lewis Harding Williams was born Oct 27, 1881[11]
Lewis Harding Williams Married Helen Maud Wiley [11]
5. 2nd marriage Lewis Harding Williams married
Elizabeth Carroll on Sep 28, 1909[11]
..................5. **Victor Williams** [16]
...............4. **Arthur Wellington Williams was born Jan 19, 1847**
He was a mariner [16]
...............4. **Tryphena Churchill Williams was born Nov 12, 1849**
He died Mar 18, 1938 at 88 in Barrington,
Shelburne [16]
Tryphena Churchill Williams married Seth B. Ciffin
on Dec 17, 1874 [11]
3. **2nd marriage Eleanor Jane (Locke) Williams married**
David Eisenhaur on Dec 4, 1841 in Shelburne,
NS [11]
...........3. **Jacob Locke baptized Oct 27, 1811 in Shelburne, NS** [11]
Jacob Locke married Melinda Williams [16]
...............4. **Albert Locke was born Oct 1840** [11]
...............4. **John Fader Locke was born 1842 - died 1905 at abt**
63 in Lockeport, NS [16]
John Fader Locke married Letitia Harding [11]
...............4. **George Locke** [11]
...............4. **James Locke** [11]
...............4. **Ebenezer Locke** [11]
Ebenezer Locke married Caroline Hewitt [11]
...............4. **Bethia Locke** [11]
...............4. **Olivia Locke** [11]
Olivia Locke married Walt Dunn [11]
3. **2nd marriage - Jacob Locke married Emmeline**
Marion Jamieson on Sep 2, 1852 in Shelburne,
NS [11]
...............4. **Marion Locke born Dec 3, 1853 in Shelburne, NS** [11]
...............4. **Frederick Dore Locke born Jun 19, 1855 in**
Shelburne, NS [11]
...............4. **Sophia Clarissa Locke born Nov 10, 1857 in**
Shelburne, NS [11]
...............4. **George Snyder Locke born Nov 18, 1859 in**
Shelburne, NS [11]
...............4. **Janet Stalker Locke born Oct 13, 1862 in**
Shelburne, NS [11]

APPENDIX 2 - BOOLE FAMILY GENEALOGY

.................4. *Margaret Weiser Locke born Jul 27, 1864 in Shelburne, NS* [11]

.................4. *Harriet McDowell Locke born Dec 14, 1866 in Shelburne, NS* [11]

...........3. *George Frederick Augustus Locke born Jan 16, 1812 in Shelburne, NS* [11]

...........3. *Catherine Ann Locke born Jul 4, 1815 in Shelburne, NS* [11] *- died Jan 26, 1903 at 87 in Shelburne, NS she is buried in Pine Grove Cemetery* [16]
Catherine Ann Locke married William Graham Swineberg on May 3, 1841 in Shelburne, NS [11]
William Graham Swineberg was born Mar 9, 1815 - died Dec 15, 1907 at 92 in Shelburne [16]
William later changed his name to Swansburg [16]
William was a cooper and they lived on Locke's Island in Jordan Bay, NS.

.................4. *Harple Luke Swansburg was born Jul 7, 1841 - died Sep 24, 1919 at 78* [16]
Harple was a master mariner and often Captain of the "Annie Dee" [16]

.................4. *Elizabeth Bess Swansburg was born Apr 1, 1842 died Jul 1934 at 92 in Somerville, MA* [16]

.................4. *Guion Locke Swansburg was born Sep 9, 1846 - died May 27, 1861 at 14 while aboard a fishing vessel that was <u>lost at sea</u> during a thunder storm.* [16]

.................4. *William Albert Swansburg was born Dec 5, 1847 in Christ Church, Shelburne* [16]

.................4. *Thomas Jones "Doane" Swansburg was born May 12, 1852 in Jordan Bay, NS - died Jul 8, 1907 at 55 of <u>acute meningitis</u> in East Boston, MA. He is buried in Bennington St. Cemetery in East Boston, MA.* [16]
Thomas Jones Swansburg married ___ Grovestine in Jordan Falls, NS. [16]
She was the daughter of Peter and Deborah Grovestine [16]

.................4. *Manus Swansburg was born abt 1854 in Shelburne, NS. He died Oct 9, 1940 at 86 in Quincy, MA. Manus could possibly be a twin of James and was adopted* [16]
Manus Swansburg married Mary H. ___ abt 1892 [7]
Manus came to this country in 1875 -

In 1910, he was a fisherman [7]

................5. *Albert Swansburg was born abt 1901 in MA* [7]

............4. *James Swansburg was born abt 1854 - died Mar 1890 at 36 when the fishing schooner "William St. Rice" was <u>lost at sea</u> on a trip to Iceland. James was a resident of Gloucester, MA at the time of his death.* [16] *James could possibly be a twin of Manus and was adopted* [16]

............4. *Margaret Swansburg was born Aug 10, 1859 - died Mar 7, 1923 at 63 in Jordan Branch, NS - she is buried in the Pine Grove Cemetery in Shelburne, NS* [16]

............4. *Alexander Swansburg was born abt 1864 - died Oct 15, 1928 at 64 and is buried in Pine Grove Cemetery in Shelburne, NS. He was a truckman.* [16]

............4. *Jasper N. Swansburg was born in 1877 - died Aug 3. 1905 at 28 in New Bedford, MA* [16] *Jasper N. Swansburg married Emeline Caufield in 1904* [16] *Emeline Caufield was from Wallace, NS* [16]

........3. *2nd marriage of Catherine Anne Locke to Daniel E. Brooks about 1884* [7] *Daniel E. Brooks came to this country from Wales in 1880* [7] *In 1910, Daniel was a machinist in a foundry* [7]

............4. *Albert A. Brooks born abt 1886 in Boston, MA - In 1910, he was a laborer* [7]

............4. *Ellsworth Brooks born abt 1889 in Boston, MA in 1910, he was a box maker* [7]

............4. *Bessie Brooks born abt 1891 in Boston - in 1910 she was a nurse in a hospital* [7]

............4. *Ernest L. Brooks born abt 1896 in Boston, MA in 1910, he sold vegetables* [7]

........3. *Thomas Perry Locke born Jan 9, 1820 in Shelburne, NS* [11] *Thomas Perry Locke married Elizabeth McKay* [11]

........3. *William Locke* [11]

........3. *James Locke* [11]

........3. *Samuel Locke* [11]

........3. *Ebenezer Locke* [11] *Ebenezer Locke married Sarah Ryer* [11]

............4. *Robert Locke* [11]

............4. *George Locke* [11]

APPENDIX 2 - BOOLE FAMILY GENEALOGY

........2 Eleanor Boole was christened Jun 1, 1788 and died 1789 in Jordan, NS at 1 year old.

........2 George Boole born Nov 2, 1789 - died Nov 16, 1852 at 63 *of __consumption__* (Tuberculosis) in Bent Point, Shelburne, NS
George Boole married Elizabeth Perry on Feb 7, 1816 at Christ Church Shelburne,NS
> **Elizabeth Perry was the daughter of Thomas and Margaret Perry**
> **Elizabeth died of __Bronchitis__ on Apr 9, 1868 at 75 in East Boston, MA** [15]

............3 Margaret Perry Boole born Jan 1817 - died Mar 18, 1895 at 78 in Boston, MA
Margaret Perry Boole married James Sprague Bent on Jun 26, 1838
James Sprague Bent born abt 1807 [4]

................4. *Elizabeth Bent born abt 1840 in Nova Scotia* [3,4]
In 1860, she was a milliner [3]

................4. *James H. Bent born abt 1841 in Nova Scotia* [3]
James H. Bent married Kate M. ___ [4]
Kate M, ___ born abt 1850 [4]
In 1860, he was a daguerreotypist in East Boston, MA [3]
In 1870, he was a clerk in a clothing store in East Boston, MA [4]

....................5. *Hattie M. Bent born abt 1864 in MA*

................4. *Margaret Bent born abt 1843 in Nova Scotia* [3]

................4. *William Melbourne Bent born abt 1845 in Nova Scotia* [3]
William M. Bent married Emma C. ___ [6]
Emma C. born Jan 30, 1853 [6]
In 1870, he was a journeyman machinist [4]
In 1900, he was a conservator of books in Chicago, IL [6]

....................5. *Alanson Bent born Dec 22, 1876 in MA* [6]

....................5. *Rena Bent born Feb 21, 1878 in MA* [6]

....................5. *Lillian Bent born Dec 30, 1880 in IL* [6]

....................5. *George B. Bent born Feb 19, 1883 in IL* [6]

....................5. *Nettie E Bent born Feb 23, 1887 in IL* [6]

....................5. *Williford Bent born Sep 6, 1892 in MI* [6]

................4. *Hattie J. Bent born abt 1847 in Nova Scotia* [3]

................4. *George B. Bent born abt 1849 in Nova Scotia* [3]
In 1870, he was a clerk in a store [4]

APPENDIX 2 - BOOLE FAMILY GENEALOGY

...............4. *Charles T. Bent born abt 1853 in MA* [3]
...............4. *Ida J. Bent born abt 1857 in MA* [3]

...........3 Catherine Dieffendorf Boole was born Aug 24, 1818 - died
Aug 16, 1913 at 94 in Everett, MA. She is buried in
the Woodlawn Cemetery in Everett, MA
Catherine Dieffendorf Boole married Andreas Sproule
Andreas Sproule born abt 1808 in Nova Scotia [3]
*In 1860, Andreas was a ship joiner in East Boston,
MA.* [3]
...............4. *Charles E. Sproule born abt 1843 in Nova Scotia* [3]
*In 1860, he was a daguerreotypist and in 1870,
he was a photographer in Cambridge, MA* [4]
...............4. *Mehitable Sproule born abt 1845 in Nova Scotia* [3]
...............4. *Mathew Sproule born abt 1846 in Nova Scotia* [3]
*In 1860, he was an apprentice to a tailor in
East Boston, MA* [3]
...............4. *William A. Sproule born abt 1848 in Nova Scotia* [3]
*In 1870, he was a clerk in a dry goods store in
Cambridge, MA* [4]
...............4. *Ann L. Sproule born abt 1851 in Nova Scotia* [3]
...............4. *Thomas Sproule born abt 1855 in Nova Scotia* [3]
...............4. *Catherine Sproule born abt 1859 in MA* [3]

...........3 Elizabeth Ann Boole born Jun 10, 1820 - died Jul 21, 1899
at 79 and is buried In Woodlawn Cemetery in
Everett, MA
Elizabeth Ann Boole married Isaiah Sproule
...............4. *Agnes Sproule was born - died Jul 22, 1899* [16]

...........3 George William Boole christened May 10, 1822 in Nova
Scotia - died *after the 1900 census in
San Francisco, CA* [3, 6]
George William Boole married Eleanor D'Arcy
Eleanor D'Arcy born abt 1832 in MA [3,4]
*From 1855 to 1868, he was a partner with his
brother Thomas in the G & T Boole Shipyard
at Jeffries Point in East Boston, MA* [10]
*From 1870 to 1900, George was a Ship builder in
San Francisco, CA* [4, 6]

...............4. *Emma J. Boole born abt 1853 in MA - she never
married* [3]
*In 1880, she is living with her family in San
Francisco, CA* [5]

APPENDIX 2 - BOOLE FAMILY GENEALOGY

> In 1920, she is still in San Francisco in the same boarding house as John and Robert McPherson [8]

..................4. *Frank A. Boole born Jun 1855 in MA* [6] - died prior to the 1920 census [8]

> *Frank A. Boole married __ after the 1880 census* [14]

....................5. *George Boole born Aug 1881* - died in 1954[14]

> *George Boole married Eo ___ in 1905 in Seattle, WA* [14]

> > *In 1910, George is working in a hardware store in Seattle, WA* [7]

> > *In 1920, George is a manager in an iron and steel company. In Seattle, WA* [8]

........................6. *George Warren Boole born abt 1908 in Seattle, WA* [14]

> 4. *2nd Marriage -Frank A. Boole married Rhoda Potts abt 1889 in San Francisco CA*

> > *Rhoda Potts born Feb 1866 in CA - daughter of Margaret Potts* [3]

> > *In 1880, Frank is the superintendent in a pencil factory in San Francisco* [5]

> > *In 1900 and 1910, Frank was a manager of a saw mill and lumber camp in Placerville, CA* [6,7]

> > *In 1920, Rhoda is a widow living with her daughter's family in Ducor, CA* [8]

....................5. *Margaret Boole born Dec 1889 in CA* [6]

> > *Margaret Boole married James R. Baird in CA* [8]

> > *James R. Baird was born abt 1888 in Chile*

> > > *In 1920, he was a farmer on a fruit farm* [8]

........................6. *James B. Baird was born Oct 1918 in CA* [8]

..................4. *George Boole born abt 1859 in MA* [4]

> *George Boole married Margaret T. ___ abt 1907* [7]

> > *Margaret T. Born abt 1862 in Scotland* [7]

> > *In 1880, George is a clerk in a hardware store in San Francisco, CA* [5]

> > *In 1910, George is a merchant in a hardware store in Seattle, WA* [7]

..................4. *Frederick W. Boole born abt 1861 in MA* [4]

> *Frederick W. Boole married Dee B. ___ abt 1896* [6]

> > *Dee B. was born Mar 1871 in CA* [6]

> > *In 1880, Frederick is a clerk for a coal company in San Francisco, CA* [5]

> > *In 1900, Frederick is a solicitor for an insurance company in Belvedere, CA* [6]

> > *In 1910, Frederick is a broker for an insurance company in San Francisco, CA* [7]

...................5. *Frederick W. Boole Jr. born Jan 1897 in CA* [6]
...................5. *Ruth Boole was born abt 1904 in CA* [6]
.................4. *Stella M Boole born Mar 1870 in CA* [4]
   Stella M Boole married William B. Hunt abt 1890
      William B. Hunt was born Feb 1869 in NJ [6]
      In the 1900 Census, they are living with
         Stella's father in San Francisco, CA and
         William is a secretary for a coal company.
      In 1910, William is a clerk living alone in
         Seattle, WA.
      In the 1920 Census, he is divorced, living in
         Seattle, and is a purchasing agent for a
         hardware company. [6,7,8]
...................5. *Unknown child born after 1890 - died prior to*
   1900 [6]

...........3. Thomas Perry Boole christened Apr 4, 1824 in Nova
   Scotia- *died Mar 16, 1897 at 72 of heart*
      disease. He was living at 600 Tremont St. in
      Boston at the time of his death. [15]
   Thomas P. Boole married Ann Miles on Aug 2, 1852 in
      East Boston , MA [10a]
      Ann born abt 1829 in Maine [3]
      In 1853, he is a shipwright in East Boston, MA.
      From 1855 to 1863, he is listed as a partner in the
         G & T Boole Shipyard with his brother George
         on Jeffries Point in East Boston, MA.
      From 1868 to 1870, he is listed in East Boston as a
         Captain. [10]
.................4. *Ella Boole born abt 1855 in MA* [3]
.................4. *Moses D. Boole born Jan 1859 in MA* [3]
   Moses D. Boole married Lana L. Shorley abt 1887 [6]
      Lana L. Shorley born Nov 1864 [6] *They did not*
         have any children [6]
      Moses was a hardware salesman in Malden, MA[6,7]
.................4. *Maria Boole born Mar 1860 in Boston, MA* [3]

............3 Jacob Boole

............3 Lucretia Boole born Jun 16, 1826 - died Jun 18, 1900
   at 74 in Everett, MA
   Boston vital records shows that she died
      Jun 16, 1901 at 75 of Cerebral Hemorrhage at her
      home at 12 Central Sq. in East Boston, MA [10a]
   She is buried In Woodlawn Cemetery in Everett, MA

APPENDIX 2 - BOOLE FAMILY GENEALOGY

Lucretia Boole married Dr. John B. Fulton on Mar 8, 1865
in Boston
Dr. John B. Fulton *born abt 1834* in Londonderry, NS [4]
**He died Mar 19, 1887 at 52 of <u>Disease</u> <u>of the brain</u>
<u>and spinal cord</u> and is buried in the Woodlawn
Cemetery in Everett, MA [2]**
John was the son of Daniel and Margaret Fulton [10a]
John and Lucretia did not have any children.
**In 1856 and 1857, she is in the millinery business in
East Boston. [10]**
**In 1860, she is a milliner living with her brother
Thomas in East Boston, MA [3]**
**In the 1900 Census, at 76, she is living at 12 Central
Square in East Boston with a nurse and a
servant [6]**

............3 William August Boole born Sep 1830 - died Feb 26, 1902
at 71 in Oakland, CA
William August Boole married Barbara Ann Bent in 1853 in
Nova Scotia
**In 1870, William is a ship carpenter in San Francisco,
CA [4]**
**In 1900, William is a sea captain living in San Rafael,
CA [6]**
................4. **Annette Boole born abt 1862 in CA [4]**
................4. **Clara Boole born abt 1863 in CA [4]**
................4. **Annie Boole born abt 1871 in San Francisco, CA [5,6]**
................4. **William A. Boole born May 1872 in San Francisco,
CA [6]**
**William A. Boole married Catherine L. ___ abt 1904
in CA [7]**
**In 1900, William is a shipbuilder in San Rafael,
CA [6]**
....................5. **Katherine L. Boole born abt 1907 in CA [7]**
....................5. **Gordon H. Boole born Mar 1908 in CA [7]**
................4. **Lillie Boole born Feb 1879 in CA [6]**
................4. **Unknown child born and died prior to 1900 [6]**
................4. **Unknown child born and died prior to 1900 [6]**

........2 Judah Boole born Aug 1, 1791 - died 1792

........2 John Boole christened Jun 8, 1793 - died **May 5,1875 at 82
in Brooklyn, NY [19]** - He is buried in the Cypress Hill
Cemetery, Brooklyn, NY

APPENDIX 2 - BOOLE FAMILY GENEALOGY

John Boole married Magdalene (Laney) Jane Ackerman
 Dec 18, 1814 in Shelburne, NS by Rev. James Mann
 Laney Jane Ackerman was born Jul 27, 1796 in
  Barrington, NS - died *Oct 31, 1881 at 85 of*
  Bronchitis *at the home of her daughter, Dr. Alice*
  (Boole) Campbell, in Brooklyn, NY. [17]
 She is buried in Cypress Hill Cemetery, Brooklyn, NY[2]
 Laney was the daughter of Johannes Ackerman
  and Mary Arents [16]
 John moved from Shelburne, NS to Manhattan, NY
  on October 21, 1831 and worked as a shipwright
  in one of the shipyards there.
 From 1846 to 1849, he is working in East Boston,
  presumably in Donald McKay's shipyard, before
  moving back to New York. [10]
 In 1869, he was a Customs Inspector at the NY
  Customs House. [20]
 In 1870, at 77 years old, John is a City Sealer in
  Brooklyn, NY and they are living with his
  daughter Alice at 114 South 3rd St. *in Brooklyn* [4]

............3 **Albenia Martha Boole** born Sep 8, 1815 in Jordan
  Falls, Shelburne - *died in* ***childbirth*** *Dec 10, 1848*
  in East Boston, MA and is buried in the Oak Hill
  Cemetery, Newburyport, MA [17]
 Albenia Martha Boole married Donald McKay in 1833
  in New York City
................4 *Cornelius Whitworth McKay born Feb 1, 1834 in*
  Manhattan, NY - died Nov 30, 1899 in
  Manhattan, NY buried in Greenwood
  Cemetery, Brooklyn, NY
 Cornelius Whitworth McKay married Susan
  Caroline Seaver in Boston, MA
......................5 *Louis McKay born Jul 15, 1851 in Boston, MA*
  He died Apr 28, 1880 at 29
......................5 *Henry McKay born Jan 10, 1853 in Boston, MA*
  He died Mar 11, 1853 at 2 months
......................5 *Cornelia McKay born Jan 25, 1854 in Boston,*
  MA - died Nov 9, 1857 at 3
 4. *2nd marriage Cornelius Whitworth McKay*
  married Henriette (Harriet) Senecal on
  Mar 1, 1875 in New Orleans, LA
......................5 *Richard Cornelius McKay born Mar 23, 1876*
  in New Orleans, LA - died Aug 15, 1957 in
  Brentwood, NY

APPENDIX 2 - BOOLE FAMILY GENEALOGY

..................4 *Frances Jean McKay born Apr 3, 1836 in NY*
   She died Oct 31, 1851 at 14 in Boston, MA
..................4 *Anne Jane McKay born Nov 12, 1837 in NY*
   She died Oct 11, 1842 in Newburyport, MA of
   <u>scarlet</u> <u>fever</u> *at 4 yr 11 mo*
..................4 *Dennis Condry McKay born Oct 29, 1840 in*
   Newbury, MA - died Feb 2, 1861 at 20
..................4 *Donald McKay born May 3, 1842 in Newburyport, MA*
   Donald McKay married Emilie Pieniger
......................5 *Donald McKay born Jul 27, 1866*
   Donald McKay married Ethel Margaret Matterson
..................4 *Cornelius McKay born Aug 23, 1843 in*
   Newburyport, MA - died same month
..................4 *John Boole McKay born Dec 11, 1844 in Boston,*
   MA
..................4 *Albenia McKay born Sep 20, 1846 in Boston, MA*
   Albenia McKay married J. G. Bodemer
......................5 *Mary Bodemer born Jul 2, 1868*
   Mary Bodemer married Woldemer Bretschneider
.........................6 *Marianne Pauline Albenia Bretschneider*
   born Feb 24, 1890
.........................6 *Moritz Bretschneider born May 20, 1892*
......................5 *Johannes Bodemer born Aug 8, 1870 - died*
   Apr 1874 at 4 years old
......................5 *Margareta Bodemer born Jun 12, 1873*
......................5 *Friederike Bodemer born May 15, 1875*
......................5 *Else Bodemer born Aug 3, 1876*

(See APPENDIX 4 - "McKay Family Genealogy" for more detail on Albenia Martha Boole and Donald McKay)

...........3 Mary Ann Catherine Boole born Jan 25, 1817 in Shelburne,
   NS. She lived as a spinster In Brooklyn, NY until her
   death.
   In the 1880 Brooklyn, NY census, at 62, she is living
   with her sister Alice's family, her mother, and
   she is listed as a cripple.

...........3 Charlotte Jane Boole born Nov 23, 1819 in Shelburne, NS.
   Charlotte Jane Boole married Cornelius Clark
   Cornelius Clark was born abt 1808 in CT [4]
   Charlotte and Cornelius Clark are buried in the
   Cypress Hills Cemetery Brooklyn, NY
   (Section 2 Plot 255) [2]

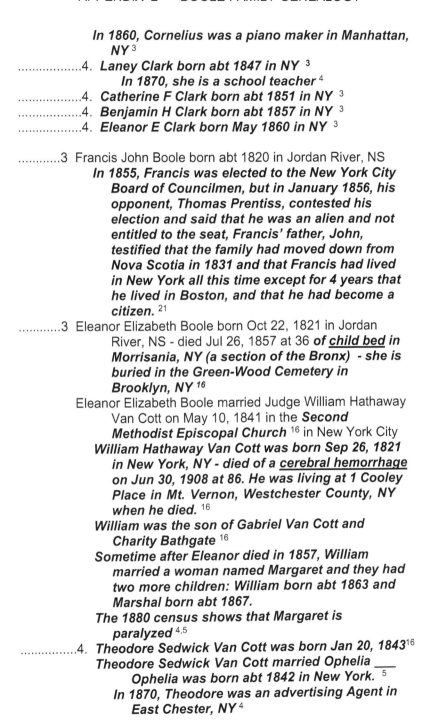

In 1860, Cornelius was a piano maker in Manhattan, NY[3]

.................4. **Laney Clark born abt 1847 in NY** [3]
In 1870, she is a school teacher[4]

.................4. **Catherine F Clark born abt 1851 in NY** [3]

.................4. **Benjamin H Clark born abt 1857 in NY** [3]

.................4. **Eleanor E Clark born May 1860 in NY** [3]

............3 Francis John Boole born abt 1820 in Jordan River, NS
In 1855, Francis was elected to the New York City Board of Councilmen, but in January 1856, his opponent, Thomas Prentiss, contested his election and said that he was an alien and not entitled to the seat, Francis' father, John, testified that the family had moved down from Nova Scotia in 1831 and that Francis had lived in New York all this time except for 4 years that he lived in Boston, and that he had become a citizen. [21]

............3 Eleanor Elizabeth Boole born Oct 22, 1821 in Jordan River, NS - died Jul 26, 1857 at 36 *of <u>child bed</u> in Morrisania, NY (a section of the Bronx) - she is buried in the Green-Wood Cemetery in Brooklyn, NY* [16]

Eleanor Elizabeth Boole married Judge William Hathaway Van Cott on May 10, 1841 in the **Second Methodist Episcopal Church** [16] in New York City

William Hathaway Van Cott was born Sep 26, 1821 in New York, NY - died of a <u>cerebral hemorrhage</u> on Jun 30, 1908 at 86. He was living at 1 Cooley Place in Mt. Vernon, Westchester County, NY when he died. [16]

William was the son of Gabriel Van Cott and Charity Bathgate [16]

Sometime after Eleanor died in 1857, William married a woman named Margaret and they had two more children: William born abt 1863 and Marshal born abt 1867.

The 1880 census shows that Margaret is paralyzed [4,5]

..............4. **Theodore Sedwick Van Cott was born Jan 20, 1843**[16]
Theodore Sedwick Van Cott married Ophelia ___
Ophelia was born abt 1842 in New York. [5]
In 1870, Theodore was an advertising Agent in East Chester, NY[4]

In 1880, Theodore was a public school teacher living in Manhattan, NY [5]

.....................5. *William S. Van Cott was born abt 1864 in NY [5]*

.....................5. *Marshall B. Van Cott was born abt 1867 in NY [5]*

.....................5. *Walter W. Van Cott was born abt 1875 in NY. [5]*

................4. *William Hathaway Van Cott Jr. was born Nov 19, 1844 - died of* chronic endocarditis *on May 1, 1923 at 78 in the Manhattan State Hospital . He is buried in the Green-Wood Cemetery in Brooklyn, NY [16]*

William Hathaway Van Cott Jr. married Janet or Jennett Crawford McGowan on Dec 24, 1873[16] Janet or Jennet was born Nov 30, 1838 in NY and died Aug 10, 1923 at 84 of a cerebral hemorrhage *at 251 Fiske Ave. in Staten Island, NY. [16]*

Janet was the daughter of Charles McGowan and Elizabeth Ann Crawford. [16]

In 1880 William was a school teacher in East Chester, NY [5]

.....................5. *Eleanor Elizabeth "Bessie [5]" Van Cott was born Dec 20, 1878 in New York, NY She died May 9, 1955 at 76 of* uremia and arteriosclerosis cardiovascular disease *in Tonawanda, NY. She is buried in the Moravian Cemetery in Staten Island, NY. [16]*

Eleanor Elizabeth Van Cott married Orrin Lawrence Brodie on Oct 3, 1905 in Mt Vernon, Westchester, NY [16]

Orrin Lawrence Brodie was born Jul 5, 1879 in Pittsburgh, PA - died Oct 5, 1943 at 64 in Westerleigh, Staten Island, NY and is buried in the Moravian Cemetery on Staten Island, NY. [16]

Orrin was the son of Henry Tregerthen Brodie and Agnes Augusta Barthberger.

Eleanor is a graduate of Barnard College and Orrin graduated from Columbia University in 1901 [16]

In 1910, Orrin was a civil engineer for the City of New York, living on Staten Island. He also wrote a technical book on "High masonry dam design" [16]

> *In 1920, he was a civil engineer working for the State of New York still living on Staten Island* [16, 8]

........................6. *Janet Crawford "Janie" Brodie was born Mar 25, 1907* [16]

........................6. *Agnes Althea "Aggie" Brodie was born Sep 15, 1910* [16]

........................6. *Margaret Elizabeth "Miggie"Brodie was born Feb 21, 1912* [16]

........................6. *Eleanor Van Cott "Lovie" Brodie was born Apr 25, 1915* [16]

.................4. *Leonard Boole Van Cott was born Dec 20, 1845 - died Dec 2, 1862 at almost 17 in Centerville, VA - he is buried in the Green-Wood Cemetery in Brooklyn, NY* [16]

.................4. *Daniel Tuttle Mac Farland Van Cott was born Nov 23, 1848 - died Dec 26, 1903 at 55* [16]
In 1880, Daniel is a lawyer living at 105 Third Ave in East Chester, NY with his son and daughter, but no wife. [5]

....................5. *Harman Van Cott was born abt 1873 in NY* [5]

....................5. *Adele Van Cott was born abt 1875 in NY* [5]
In 1900, Adele is living at home and is a clerk in an office. [6]
In 1920, Adele is the director of a broker's office and she is living with her mother and sister Emily [8]

4. *2nd marriage Daniel Tuttle Mac Farland Van Cott married Elizabeth ___ abt 1880 in NY* [6]
In the 1900 census, Daniel is a lawyer and the family is living at 41 West 128th St. in Manhattan, NY, and Daniel's father William is living with them. [6]

....................5. *Emily Van Cott was born Sep 1881 in NY* [6]
In 1920, she was still single and was a public school teacher [8]

....................5. *Helen Van Cott was born Mar 1891 in NY* [6]

....................5. *Merrill Van Cott was born 1895 in NY* [6]

.................4. *Frank Lindsay Van Cott was born Jan 26, 1851 - died Jan 16, 1855 at 4 years old. He is buried in the Green-Wood Cemetery in Brooklyn, NY* [16]

.................4. *Jessie Bathgate Van Cott was born Dec 8, 1855 - died in 1858 at 2 years old* [16]

............3 James Mann Boole *born May 13, 1823* [16] - died young

APPENDIX 2 - BOOLE FAMILY GENEALOGY

............3 Leonard Hoffman Boole born *Jun 9, 1825* [16] in
           Barrington, NS - died before the 1880 Census.
           Leonard Hoffman Boole married Nancy F. ___ (Canadian)
              in New York abt 1846
              Nancy F. was born Sep 1825
              In 1900, she had nine children five living [6]
              Leonard was an engineer, accountant, and a Lt
                Engineer during Civil War.
              *In 1858, he published his book "The shipwright's
                handbook and draghtsman's guide"* [18]
              In 1860, he was a ship inspector in Milwaukee, WI [3]
              In 1870, he was a shipwright in New York. [4]
.................4. *Caroline Boole born abt 1847 in NY* [4]
.................4. *Leonard H. Boole born Aug 1849 in NY* [4]
              Leonard H. Boole married Celeste C. ___ abt 1902 [7]
                Celeste C. Born abt 1884 in New York [7]
              *In 1900, Leonard is an accountant in a
                shipyard, living at 2524 29th St.
                Philadelphia with his widowed mother* [6]
              *In 1910, Leonard is living with wife and two
                children and is still at the shipyard.*
              *In 1920, Leonard's son Celnard has joined
                him at the shipyard* [8]
.....................5. *Celnard B. Boole born abt 1903 in Philadelphia,
              PA* [7]
              *In 1920, he is a clerk in a shipyard in
                Philadelphia, PA* [8]
.....................5. *Winifred D. Boole born abt 1908 in Philadelphia,
              PA* [7]
.................4. *Agnes Boole born abt 1852 in NY* [4]
.................4. *Grace Boole born abt 1854 in NY* [4]
.................4. *Clara Boole born abt 1856 in NY* [4]
.................4. *Unnamed Child born May 1860* [3] *died before
              the 1870 census.* [4]
.................4. *Francis Boole born abt 1863 in Wisconsin* [4]
.................4. *Adrienne Boole born abt 1865 in NY* [4]
.................4. *Dewitt Boole born abt 1867 in NY* [4]

............3 William H. Boole born Apr 24, 1827 in Shelburne, NS -
           died Feb 24, 1896 at 68 on Staten Island, NY.
           He was a Methodist Minister, joined Sickle's
              Brigade during the Civil War. He had a very
              interesting career (available on the Internet)
           William H. Boole married Eunice C. ___ [3]

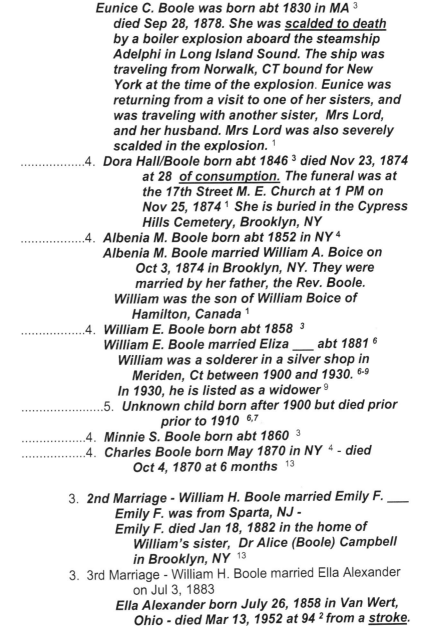

Eunice C. Boole was born abt 1830 in MA [3]
*died Sep 28, 1878. She was <u>scalded to death</u>
by a boiler explosion aboard the steamship
Adelphi in Long Island Sound. The ship was
traveling from Norwalk, CT bound for New
York at the time of the explosion. Eunice was
returning from a visit to one of her sisters, and
was traveling with another sister, Mrs Lord,
and her husband. Mrs Lord was also severely
scalded in the explosion.* [1]

.................4. *Dora Hall/Boole born abt 1846* [3] *died Nov 23, 1874
at 28 <u>of consumption.</u> The funeral was at
the 17th Street M. E. Church at 1 PM on
Nov 25, 1874* [1] *She is buried in the Cypress
Hills Cemetery, Brooklyn, NY*

.................4. *Albenia M. Boole born abt 1852 in NY* [4]
*Albenia M. Boole married William A. Boice on
Oct 3, 1874 in Brooklyn, NY. They were
married by her father, the Rev. Boole.
William was the son of William Boice of
Hamilton, Canada* [1]

.................4. *William E. Boole born abt 1858* [3]
William E. Boole married Eliza ___ abt 1881 [6]
*William was a solderer in a silver shop in
Meriden, Ct between 1900 and 1930.* [6-9]
In 1930, he is listed as a widower [9]

.....................5. *Unknown child born after 1900 but died prior
prior to 1910* [6,7]

.................4. *Minnie S. Boole born abt 1860* [3]

.................4. *Charles Boole born May 1870 in NY* [4] *- died
Oct 4, 1870 at 6 months* [13]

3. *2nd Marriage - William H. Boole married Emily F. ___
Emily F. was from Sparta, NJ -
Emily F. died Jan 18, 1882 in the home of
William's sister, Dr Alice (Boole) Campbell
in Brooklyn, NY* [13]

3. 3rd Marriage - William H. Boole married Ella Alexander
on Jul 3, 1883
*Ella Alexander born July 26, 1858 in Van Wert,
Ohio - died Mar 13, 1952 at 94* [2] *from a <u>stroke</u>.
She was the daughter of Isaac Newton
Alexander (a Lawyer) and Rebecca Alban*

APPENDIX 2 - BOOLE FAMILY GENEALOGY

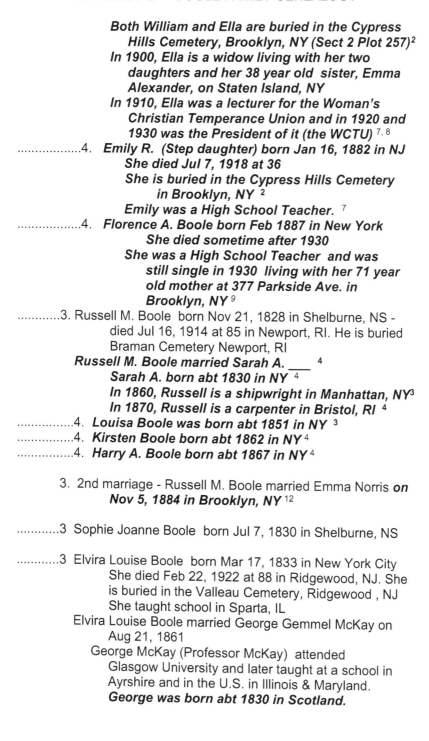

Both William and Ella are buried in the Cypress Hills Cemetery, Brooklyn, NY (Sect 2 Plot 257)[2]
In 1900, Ella is a widow living with her two daughters and her 38 year old sister, Emma Alexander, on Staten Island, NY
In 1910, Ella was a lecturer for the Woman's Christian Temperance Union and in 1920 and 1930 was the President of it (the WCTU) [7, 8]

.................4. *Emily R. (Step daughter) born Jan 16, 1882 in NJ*
She died Jul 7, 1918 at 36
She is buried in the Cypress Hills Cemetery in Brooklyn, NY [2]
Emily was a High School Teacher. [7]

.................4. *Florence A. Boole born Feb 1887 in New York*
She died sometime after 1930
She was a High School Teacher and was still single in 1930 living with her 71 year old mother at 377 Parkside Ave. in Brooklyn, NY [9]

............3. Russell M. Boole born Nov 21, 1828 in Shelburne, NS - died Jul 16, 1914 at 85 in Newport, RI. He is buried Braman Cemetery Newport, RI
Russell M. Boole married Sarah A. ___ [4]
Sarah A. born abt 1830 in NY [4]
In 1860, Russell is a shipwright in Manhattan, NY[3]
In 1870, Russell is a carpenter in Bristol, RI [4]

...............4. *Louisa Boole was born abt 1851 in NY* [3]
...............4. *Kirsten Boole born abt 1862 in NY* [4]
...............4. *Harry A. Boole born abt 1867 in NY* [4]

3. 2nd marriage - Russell M. Boole married Emma Norris *on Nov 5, 1884 in Brooklyn, NY* [12]

............3 Sophie Joanne Boole born Jul 7, 1830 in Shelburne, NS

............3 Elvira Louise Boole born Mar 17, 1833 in New York City
She died Feb 22, 1922 at 88 in Ridgewood, NJ. She is buried in the Valleau Cemetery, Ridgewood , NJ
She taught school in Sparta, IL
Elvira Louise Boole married George Gemmel McKay on Aug 21, 1861
George McKay (Professor McKay) attended Glasgow University and later taught at a school in Ayrshire and in the U.S. in Illinois & Maryland.
George was born abt 1830 in Scotland.

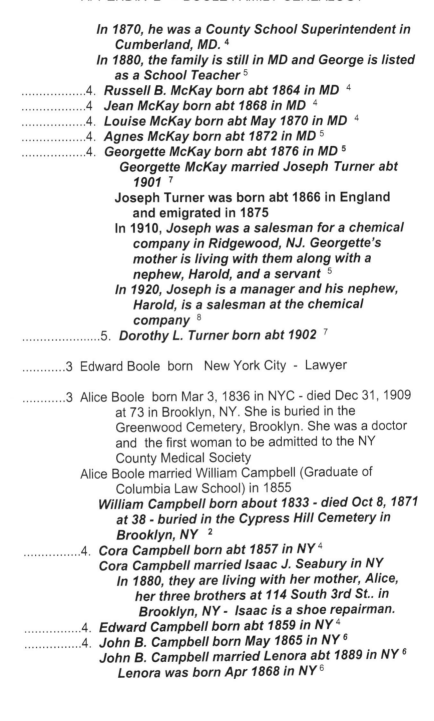

In 1870, he was a County School Superintendent in Cumberland, MD. [4]

In 1880, the family is still in MD and George is listed as a School Teacher [5]

.................4. *Russell B. McKay born abt 1864 in MD* [4]

.................4 *Jean McKay born abt 1868 in MD* [4]

.................4. *Louise McKay born abt May 1870 in MD* [4]

.................4. *Agnes McKay born abt 1872 in MD* [5]

.................4. *Georgette McKay born abt 1876 in MD* [5]

Georgette McKay married Joseph Turner abt 1901 [7]

Joseph Turner was born abt 1866 in England and emigrated in 1875

In 1910, Joseph was a salesman for a chemical company in Ridgewood, NJ. Georgette's mother is living with them along with a nephew, Harold, and a servant [5]

In 1920, Joseph is a manager and his nephew, Harold, is a salesman at the chemical company [8]

.....................5. *Dorothy L. Turner born abt 1902* [7]

............3 Edward Boole born   New York City - Lawyer

............3 Alice Boole born Mar 3, 1836 in NYC - died Dec 31, 1909 at 73 in Brooklyn, NY. She is buried in the Greenwood Cemetery, Brooklyn. She was a doctor and the first woman to be admitted to the NY County Medical Society

Alice Boole married William Campbell (Graduate of Columbia Law School) in 1855

William Campbell born about 1833 - died Oct 8, 1871 at 38 - buried in the Cypress Hill Cemetery in Brooklyn, NY [2]

.................4. *Cora Campbell born abt 1857 in NY* [4]

Cora Campbell married Isaac J. Seabury in NY

In 1880, they are living with her mother, Alice, her three brothers at 114 South 3rd St.. in Brooklyn, NY - Isaac is a shoe repairman.

.................4. *Edward Campbell born abt 1859 in NY* [4]

.................4. *John B. Campbell born May 1865 in NY* [6]

John B. Campbell married Lenora abt 1889 in NY [6]

Lenora was born Apr 1868 in NY [6]

>> *In 1900, John was a doctor living at 552
>> McDonough St. in Brooklyn, NY and his 64
>> year old mother, Alice, was living with them* [6]

...................5. *Carleton Campbell born Nov 1895 in NY* [6]

...................5. *Alice Campbell born abt 1906 in NY* [8]

...............4. *Joseph F. Campbell born abt 1868 in NY* [4]

...........3 Ambrose Boole born NYC

........2 Ann Nancy Boole born Nov 3, 1796 - died 1824 at 28 in
Nova Scotia
Ann Nancy Boole married William Ryer Dec 22, 1818
>> *William Ryer christened Sep 18, 1796 in Christ
>> Church, Shelburne - died Mar 30, 1843 at 46 in
>> Ohio, Shelburne, NS* [16]
>> *William Ryer was the son of Conrad Ryer and Abigail
>> Hater* [16]

...........3. *John Thomas Ryer was born Aug 13, 1820* [16]
*John Thomas Ryer married Jane Firth on Nov 28, 1855
in Christ Church* [16]

...............4. *Emma Jane Ryer was born Aug 27, 1856 in
Shelburne - was buried May 5, 1872 at 15 in
Pine Grove Cemetery in Shelburne, NS* [16]

...............4. *Cecilia Annie Ryer was born Jun 26, 1858 in
Shelburne - died May 23, 1910 at 51 in
Bridgewater. She is buried in Brookside
Cemetery in Bridgewater, NS* [16]

...............4. *Lewis John Ryer was born Jul 19, 1859 in Shelburne
He died Feb 7, 1918 at 58 and is buried in the
Pine Grove Cemetery in Shelburne, NS* [16]

...............4. *Melissa Isabelle Ryer was born May 6, 1861 in
Shelburne - died at 4 years old - buried
May 9, 1865 in Pine Grove Cemetery in
Shelburne, NS* [16]

...............4. *Charles W. Ryer was born Aug 1863 in Shelburne* [7]
Charles W. Ryer married Maggie ___ in 1892 [7]
>> *Maggie was born Nov 1867 in MA* [7]
>> *In 1900 and 1910, they were living at 210 Medford
>> St. in Somerville, MA and Charles is a cutter
>> for a paper company* [7,8]

...................5. *Unknown child died before the 1900 census* [7]

...............4. *Alberta Louise Ryer was born Mar 5, 1868 in
Shelburne,NS* [16]

...............4. *Eleanor Ryer was born ___ - died 1870* [16]

...............4. *Frederick K. Ryer was born in 1870* [16]

APPENDIX 2 - BOOLE FAMILY GENEALOGY

................4. *Leslie W. Ryer was born in 1874* [16]

............3. *Sarah Ann Ryer* [16]
           Sarah Ann Ryer married Ebenezer Locke - on
                Oct 28, 1846 [10a]
           Ebenezer was the son of Ebenezer Locke and
                Elizabeth Boole [16]

........2 William Boole born Nov 7, 1798 died May 24, 1828 at 29
        in Nova Scotia
        William Boole married Sarah Charlotte Ackerman (Sister of
        Laney)

........2 Hannah Boole born Jan 29, 1801 - died Jun or Jul 15, 1829
        at 28 *In Shelburne, NS* [16]
        (Laura Hobbs record shows burial Jul 25, 1839 [16] *)*

........2 Thomas Benjamin Patrick Boole born May 27, 1803 died
        Mar 29, 1880 at 77 in Eatontown, NJ
        Thomas Boole married Mary Ann Roxby on Nov 28, 1834
        in St. Paul's Anglican Church [16]
        In the 1870 census, Thomas was 67, a gardener, living
        in Monmouth, NJ [4]

APPENDIX 2 - BOOLE FAMILY GENEALOGY

FOOTNOTES

1. Brooklyn Eagle Newspaper, Brooklyn, NY Oct 5, 1875
      Nov 23,1874, Sep 29, 1878
2. Cemetery Records
3. 1860 US Census
4. 1870 US Census
5. 1880 US Census
6. 1900 US Census
7. 1910 US Census
8. 1920 US Census
9. 1930 US Census
10. City Directory
10a City Vital Records
11. "Lockport & the Lockes of Shelburne County" on
       Rootsweb.com
12. Marriage Index
13. New York Evening Post
14. Diane Daly's genealogy for Boole
15. New England Historic Genealogical Society
16. Laura Hobbs - Descendants of Francis Boole
17. Death Certificate
18. Mystic Seaport research library - Mystic, CT
19. Obituary in the New York Daily Tribune
       May 6, 1875 pg 7
20. New York Daily Tribune Jul 20, 1869 pg 5
21. New York Daily Tribune Jan 15, 1856 pg 6

ABBREVIATIONS

AZ -	Arizona		MI -	Michigan
CA -	California		MO -	Missouri
CT -	Connecticut		NJ -	New Jersey
DE -	Delaware		NS -	Nova Scotia, Canada
FL -	Florida		NY -	New York
IA -	Iowa		OH -	Ohio
IL -	Illinois		PA -	Pennsylvania
KS -	Kansas		RI -	Rhode Island
LA -	Louisiana		TX -	Texas
MA -	Massachusetts		VA -	Virginia
MD -	Maryland		WA -	Washington
ME -	Maine		WI -	Wisconsin

APPENDIX 3
LITCHFIELD FAMILY GENEALOGY

....1 Nichols Litchfield born Jul 18, 1805 - died Apr 23, 1879 at
73 of *gangrene* in Holliston, MA. Nichols was the son
of Lawrence and Rebecca (Wiltirub ?) [13]
Nichols was a Shipwright in East Boston and, for a time,
was Donald McKay's next door neighbor on White St.
His brother, Davis Litchfield, from Scituate, MA, was a
shipwright who also lived on White St.
Nichols Litchfield married Anna Cushing on Dec 10, 1828 in
Scituate, MA [8]
Anna Cushing was born Jan 20, 1809 in Scituate, MA [10]
She was the Daughter of Joseph (born Mar 12, 1765
in Scituate, MA) and Desire (Barker) Cushing (born
Oct 12, 1769 in Scituate, MA) [10]
In various documents, Anna's name is spelled Ann,
Anne, and Anna.
In the 1900 census, Anna had 5 children, only 4 still living

........2. Lawrence Litchfield born Dec 26, 1829 in Hingham, MA
died on Mar 8, 1915 at 85 of *Cancer of ascending
colon* at 315 Harvard St. in Cambridge, MA [13]
He is buried in the Forest Hills Cemetery in
Boston [13]
Lawrence Litchfield married Sarah Minot Lincoln abt
1853 [5]
Sarah Minot Lincoln born Oct 9, 1828 in
Charlestown, MA [11] - died sometime after the
1910 census [5]
In 1870, Lawrence was living in East Boston next
door to Donald McKay on White St. He was a
store clerk [2]
In 1900, at 71, Lawrence is retired living with Sarah
and Mary at 56 W. Cedar St. in the Beacon Hill
section of Boston, MA [4]
In 1910, Lawrence, Sarah and Mary are living at
353 Harvard St. in Cambridge,MA [5]

...........3. Abbie S. Litchfield born abt 1846
In 1870, she was a seamstress in East Boston,
MA [2]

APPENDIX 3 - LITCHFIELD FAMILY GENEALOGY

............3. Mary E. Litchfield born Mar 1854
>   In 1910, she was still single and was a teacher in a
>   private school in Cambridge, MA [5]
>   In 1920, she is retired and still living in Cambridge,
>   MA [6]

........2. **Mary Cressy Litchfield** born Sep 30, 1831 in
>   Hingham, MA -died Feb 6, 1923 at 92 in Lexington,
>   MA
>   Mary Cressy Litchfield married Donald McKay on
>   Oct 7, 1849 in East Boston, MA
>   This was Mary's first marriage and Donald's second.
>   Donald's first wife, Albenia Martha Boole died
>   Dec 10, 1848.
>   Mary was Donald's secretary at the shipyard

............3. Lauchlan McKay
............3. Frances McKay
............3. Mary Cressy McKay
............3. Lawrence Litchfield McKay
............3. Anna Cushing McKay
............3. Nichols Litchfield McKay
............3. Guy Allen McKay
............3. Wallace McKay

(See Appendix 4, "McKay Family Genealogy" for the details on Mary Cressy's children)

........2. Allyne Cushing Litchfield born Jul 15, 1835 in Hingham,
>   MA [9] - died sometime after the 1910 Census [5]
>   In 1860, Allyne, at age 25, is a lumberman in
>   Georgetown, MI [1]

   At the start of the Civil War (1861), Allyne was living in Michigan. In 1862 he raised a company for the Union's 5th Michigan Cavalry. His superiors were so impressed with his organizational skills that he made the rank of Captain. Before the regiment left the state, he was transferred to the 7th Michigan Cavalry with the rank of Lieutenant Colonel. Between April and November of 1863, his regiment was in 16 battles and skirmishes in Maryland and Virginia. In July of that year he was in the battle of Gettysburg, had his horse shot out from under him, and was nearly captured, but he continued firing his Spencer carbine.

   At Falling Waters, Allyne, then a full Colonel, with a single battalion, captured a full rebel regiment of 400 men. Later, in the

APPENDIX 3 - LITCHFIELD FAMILY GENEALOGY

famous Kilpatrick-Dahlgren raid on Richmond, VA, Allyne was captured by the enemy and sent to Libby Prison for 4 ½ months. From Richmond he was taken to Macon, GA and then to Charleston, SC. At the end of the year he was exchanged for rebel prisoners. On his return from prison he was made a brigadier general. [9,11]

Allyne Cushing Litchfield married Susan ___ abt 1858[4]
   Susan was born Nov 1835 in MA [2] - died sometime after the 1910 Census [5]
   In 1870, Allyne was a shipping clerk in Northport, MI [2]
   In 1871, he was consul-general in Calcutta [9]
   In 1880, he is still US Consul for Calcutta and the family (Susan, Lawrence, Lucius and Almira) are living in East Boston, MA [3]
   In 1900, Allyne (64), Susan (64), and their daughter Almira (24) are living in Oakmont, PA
   In 1910, Allyne and Susan, at 74, are living with their son Lawrence and his family in Pittsburgh, PA [5]

............3. Lawrence Litchfield born Nov 1860 in Michigan [4]
   Lawrence Litchfield married Ethel H. Jones abt 1898 [4]
      Ethel H. Jones born Apr 1876 in PA - is the daughter of David & Sarah Jones [4]
      In 1900 and 1910, Lawrence is a physician in general practice living at 5431 5th Ave. in Pittsburgh, PA [4,5]
      The 1910 and 1920 Census show Ethel as a pianist [5,6]
...............4. Ethel C. Litchfield born May 1899 in Pittsburgh, PA [4]
...............4. Lawrence J. Litchfield born abt 1901 in Pittsburgh, PA [5]
      In 1920, Lawrence is a cadet at the US Naval Academy in Annapolis, MD [6]
...............4. Margaret Litchfield born abt 1904 in Pittsburgh, PA [5]
...............4. Unknown child died prior to 1910 census [5]

............3. Lucius Litchfield born abt 1866 in MA [2]
      In 1910, Lucius is the manager of a lumber company, living alone in a rooming house in

APPENDIX 3 - LITCHFIELD FAMILY GENEALOGY

Philadelphia, PA and has been married 18
years [5]
In 1920, he is a lumber merchant living in New
York, NY married to Kate L. ___.
...............4. Allyne C. Litchfield born abt 1894 in PA [5]
Allyne C. Litchfield married Dorothy B. ___ [6]
In 1920, Allyne is a statistician for a rubber Co.
in Hartford, CT [6]
In 1930, Allyne is divorced and his former wife,
Dorothea B., is living with her daughter,
Jesse in Hartford, CT [7]
..................5. Jesse Litchfield born abt 1922 in Hartford, CT [7]
...............4. Catherine Litchfield born abt 1896 in NY [5]

.............3. Almira Litchfield born Nov 1875 in British East Indies [4]

.............3. Unknown child - on 1900 census, Susan is listed as
having four children, three living [4]

........2. Almira Howe Litchfield born Dec 1843 [4] in Hingham, MA [9]
She died prior to the 1910 census [5]
Almira Howe Litchfield married George S. Merrill abt
1862 [4]
George Merrill born Feb 1832 in NH [4] - died prior to
the 1910 census [5]
In 1870, George is a shoe dealer in Cambridge,
MA [2]
In 1900, Almira had four children, all living, only
Maud was at home
In 1910, Almira is a widow living with her daughter,
Maud, in Cambridge, MA [5]
In 1920, Almira is a widow living with her daughter,
Maud, in Newton, MA [6]

............3. Allyne L. Merrill born abt 1864 in MA [2]
Allyne L. Merrill married Mary ___ abt 1897 [5]
Mary born abt 1866 in MA [5]
In 1910, they are living in Belmont, MA- Allyne
is a University professor
In 1920, they are living in Arlington, MA - Allyne
is a professor [6]
...............4. Albenia Merrill born abt 1898 in MA [5]
...............4. Eleanor Merrill born abt 1904 in MA [5]

APPENDIX 3 - LITCHFIELD FAMILY GENEALOGY

............3. George H. Merrill born abt 1868 in MA [2] died prior
to the 1920 census [6]
George H. Merrill married Clara B. ___ abt 1889 [5]
In 1910, both George and Clara are telegraphers
living at 12 Bay State Ave. in Somerville, MA.
George works for a telegraph company and
Clara works for a stock broker [5]
In 1920, Clara is a widow living at same address
with the same job. [6]
..............4. Walter E. Merrill born abt 1890 in Massachusetts [5]
Walter E. Merrill married Dignent ___ a clothes
model from Finland [6]
Dignent born abt 1897 in Finland [6]
In 1920 they are living in Medford, MA and
Walter is an engineer at Tufts College [6]

............3. Albenia Merrill born Jan 1870 in Cambridge, MA [2]

............3. Maud Merrill born Oct 1878 in MA [4]
Maud Merrill married Harry F. Sawtelle abt 1906 [5]
Harry F Sawtelle born abt 1876 in MA
In 1900, Maud is a bookkeeper
In 1910, they are in Cambridge, MA. Harry is a
civil engineer for a railroad [5]
In 1920, Harry is a civil engineer in Newton, MA
and they do not have any Children [6]

........2. Abigail S. Litchfield - birth unknown - died prior to 1900 [12]

FOOTNOTES

1. 1860 US Census
2. 1870 US Census
3. 1880 US Census
4. 1900 US Census
5. 1910 US Census
6. 1920 US Census
7. 1930 US Census
8. City or Town Vital Records
9. "History of the Town of Hingham" published by the Town in 1893
10. "Genealogy of the Cushing Family" by James Cushing - 1905 Perrault Printing
11. Ancestry.Com on-line - Family and Military Records
12. "The Genealogy of the Cushing family" by James Stevens - 1905
13. Death Certificate

ABBREVIATIONS

AZ -	Arizona	MI -	Michigan
CA -	California	MO -	Missouri
CT -	Connecticut	NJ -	New Jersey
DE -	Delaware	NS -	Nova Scotia, Canada
FL -	Florida	NY -	New York
IA -	Iowa	OH -	Ohio
IL -	Illinois	PA -	Pennsylvania
KS -	Kansas	RI -	Rhode Island
LA -	Louisiana	TX -	Texas
MA -	Massachusetts	VA -	Virginia
MD -	Maryland	WA -	Washington
ME -	Maine	WI -	Wisconsin

APPENDIX 4
McKAY FAMILY GENEALOGY
Edited by Paul D. Hamilton

The following genealogy of the McKay family is largely taken from "The Genealogy of Hugh McKay and his lineal descendants" by William Lawrence Kean, republished in 1976. This 39 page document is available at the central library of the Boston Public Library in Copley Square, Boston, MA. This book also contains a supplement by Ida May Ashworth, Lottie Alice Thurston Wilford and Robert Barnes McKay. My thanks to all of these wonderful people for their enormous research effort. The only reason that I have decided to rewrite it is to be able to add to it and to change the format to a genealogical format that will incorporate the dates with the names within the family group and, hopefully, make it a little more readable.

All of the following information is from this book except the information that is in *Italics. This is information, from various sources, that has come out of my research.*

Information in script is what I am still in the process of documenting.

__Information underlined is the cause of death & any known diseases, to help those tracing their family's health history.__

....1. Donald McKay born in Tain, Ross County, Scotland **about 1751 (*His grandson Nathaniel says that he came from Edinburgh [9]) - died sometime between Dec 7, 1826, when he wrote his will, and Mar 5, 1827 when his will was probated. Donald was a Sergeant in the Scottish 76th Regiment, and* settled in Shelburne, Nova Scotia at the close of the American revolution.**
Donald McKay married Margaret ___ in Shelburne, NS in 1787. She died shortly after the twins where born in 1790.
........2. Hugh McKay born in Shelburne, NS May 12,1788 - died Dec **30**,1871 *at 83 in the home of daughter-in-law Adeline McKay (Nathaniel's wife) East Boston, MA.* [14, 6]

See page 199 for Hugh McKay's descendent

........2. Simon Fraser McKay born in Shelburne in 1790 *and died
Oct 1867 in Mill Village, NS*. [27]
*Simon was named after Lord Lovat who was Donald
McKay's Commander.* [27] *He lived on the east side
of the Jordan river on 50 acres of land willed to
him by his father.* [1] *Later he moved to Mill Village
and was a painte*r. [27]
*Simon Fraser McKay married Elizabeth Anne Mauser in
1828 in Port Medway, NS* [27]
*Elizabeth Anne was born in 1800 and died on
Feb 22, 1893 in Clyde River, NS at 93. She is
buried in the Presbyterian Churchyard there.
She is the daughter of Captain John Conrad
Mauser and Mary Fehder.* [27]
............3. *Sophia McKay was born 1830 and died 1840 at 10 years
old* [27]
............3. *Elizabeth McKay was born 1832 and died in 1916 at abt
84 in NY* [27]
............3. *Gordon McKay was born in 1838 and died in 1921 at abt
83 in Jordan Falls, NS.* [27]
............3. *Annie Sophia McKay was born 1841 and died in 1922 at
abt 81 in Auburn, NS and is buried in the Union
Cemetery in Aylesford, NS.* [27]
*Annie Sophia McKay married Josiah McClare in 1860 in
Shelburne* [27]
Josiah was born May 1, 1831. [17] *and died in Mar of
1901 at 69 in Arlington, MA and is buried in the
Mt. Pleasant Cemetery* [27]
*Josiah was the son of Joseph McClare and Isabel
Barron.*
Annie and Josiah had nine children.
................4. *Charles Herbert McClare born Feb 15, 1861 in NS* [17]
*Charles Herbert McClare married Ella Gertrude
Johnston Oct 22, 1890 in Willimantic, CT* [17]
*In 1900, Charles is an architect living at
9 Brentwood Rd. in Arlington and his mother,
father, and sister Thora are also living with
them.* [17]
*In 1910, Charles owns his architectural firm and is
living at 211 Pleasant St. in Arlington and his
parents are no longer living with him.* [18]
....................5. *Herbert Gordon McClare born May 8, 1892 in
Cambridge MA - died Jul 25, 1892 at 2
months.*

.................5. *Donald Roy McClare born Jul 30, 1894 in Arlington MA - died Dec 30, 1928 at age 34 in Needham, MA*

.................5. *Edythe Victoria McClare born Dec 25, 1895 in Arlington, MA* [27]
Edythe Victoria McClare married Donald Gunn Ross on Jul 13, 1918 in Princeton, NJ
Donald Gunn Ross born in Arlington, MA - died Feb 27, 1938 in Rye, NY [27]

.....................6. *Donald Gunn Ross Jr. born Jul 11, 1919 in Halifax, NS* [27]

.....................6. *Madeline Virginia Ross born Jan 8, 1921 in Waltham, MA* [27]

.....................6. *Barbara Louise Ross born Sep 12, 1923 in New Haven, Ct* [27]

.....................6. *Richard Alan Ross born Jan 26, 1927 in Needham, MA* [27]

.................5. *Enid Elizabeth McClare born Nov 30, 1899 in Arlington, MA* [27]
Enid Elizabeth McClare married Warren McLeod on Oct 15, 1929 in Needham, MA

.....................6. *Anne McLeod born Nov 2, 1930 in Needham, MA* [27]

.....................6. *Marcia McLeod born Nov 26, 1933 in Needham, MA* [27]

.....................6. *Ellen McLeod born Nov 26, 1933 in Needham, MA*

.................5. *Muriel Gertrude McClare born Jan 16, 1905 in Arlington, MA* [18]

.............4. *Helen Minerva McClare born Mar 15, 1863* [27]
Helen Minerva McClare married Philip Andrew Freeman on Jun 2, 1896 in Cambridge, MA. Philip was a native of Newcastle, England - he died on May 21, 1934 in Halifax NS. [27]

.................5. *Philip Andrew Freeman Jr. born 1887 - died 1922* [27]

.................5. *Mildred Freeman born 1889* [27]

.................5. *Percy Freeman born 1892* [27]

.................5. *Herbert Freeman born 1894 - died 1936* [27]

.................5. *Sophie Freeman born 1895* [27]

.................5. *Kathleen Freeman born 1898* [27]

.................5. *Thora Freeman born 1901* [27]

.................5. *Betty Freeman born 1904* [27]

.................5. *Harry Weller Freeman born 1906* [27]

.................5. *David Mitchell Freeman born 1908* [27]

.............4. *Milledge S. McClare born Jan 30, 1865 - died Apr 6, 1938 at 73* [27]
Milledge S. McClare married Mable Ward [27]

          Milledge was a painter in Boston, MA, living at 42 Lawrence St. when he died.

          They did not have any children.

..............4. *Ernest DeWelton McClare born Mar 19, 1867 - died Dec 9, 1944 at 77* [27]

          Ernest DeWelton McClare married Ethel Mason in June 1893 in Boston [27]

          Ethel was the daughter of Isaac Conrad Mason and Matilda Musgrave, both from Halifax. Ethel died sometime in the 1940's. [27]

          Ernest was an engineer for Boston Electric Co. [27]

          In 1918, they moved to Lakelands NS and took up farming. [27]

          In Jan 1944, he was seriously ill and they moved in with their daughter Bernice in Hantsport, NS[27]

...................5. *Carlyle Somerset McClare born May 29, 1894* [27]

...................5. *Gladys Vivian McClare born Feb 10, 1896* [27]

...................5. *Ethelbert Ernest McClare born Jun I, 1899 - was seriously wounded in WWI and died in England. He is also buried there.* [27]

...................5. *Vera May McClare born Oct 10, 1902 - died in infancy* [27]

...................5. *Mazie Ethelyn McClare born Oct 3, 1905* [27]

...................5. *Bernice Musgrave McClare born Apr 9. 1910* [27]

...................5. *Ruth Harrington McClare born Apr 9, 1910* [27]

..............4. *Percy Lamont McClare born May 2, 1869* [27]

          Percy Lamont McClare married Gertrude Winthrop in Mar 1897 in Boston

          Gertrude Winthrop was the daughter of William and Mary Ellen Winthrop of Ottawa, Canada.

          Percy was employed in construction in the Boston area until Sep 1908 when he moved to Lakelands, NS to manage a large farm there[27]

...................5. *Percy Winthrop McClare born Mar 1898 - died in WWI* [27]

...................5. *Helen Gertrude McClare born May 2, 1900* [27]

...................5. *Herbert Fredrick McClare born Oct 23, 1902* [27]

...................5. *Dorothy Christena McClare born Dec 17, 1904* [27]

...................5. *Robert Josiah McClare born May 2, 1908* [27]

...................5. *Edwin Andrew McClare born Dec 23, 1909* [27]

...................5. *Malcolm Reid McClare born Jul 26, 1914* [27]

..............4. *Martin Luther McClare born Jan 13, 1872* [27]

          Martin Luther McClare married Cora Lillian Freeman[27]

          Cora was the daughter of John Freeman and Charlotte Claverly of Cambridge

Martin and Cora did not have any children [27]
Martin attended schools in Cambridge, MA and
held various jobs there.
In the fall of 1887, he and a friend started for the
Klondike and arrived in Dawson City in the
spring of 1889. When they did not find the gold
that they hoped for, they returned to Cambridge
in 1900. [27]

................4. *Coralinda Elizabeth McClare born Jul 12, 1874 -*
died Aug 8, 1945 at 71 [27]
Coralinda Elizabeth McClare married Malcolm
Edmond Rideout, Jr. on Jun 28, 1899 [27]
Malcolm died Nov 29, 1921

....................5. *Malcolm Edmund Rideout III born 1900* [27]
....................5. *Dorothy Rideout born 1902* [27]
....................5. *Louise Rideout born 1906* [27]
....................5. *Frances Rideout born 1910* [27]
....................5. *Eleanor Rideout born 1912* [27]
....................5. *Hugh McKay Rideout born 1914 - died in the*
1940's [27]
....................5. *Edith Rideout born 1921* [27]

................4. *Bernice McClare born Jul 1877 - died Aug 1880 at*
3 years old [27]

................4. *Thora Christena McClare was born Feb 27, 1881*
in NS - died Oct 24, 1967 at 88 [27]
Thora Christena McClare married John Wesley
Jacques in Jun 1908
Thora and John lived on the Jacques homestead
in Auburn, NS and this is where Thora's
mother, Annie S. (McKay) McClare spent her
last years.

....................5. *Thora Louise Jacques born 1909* [27]
Thora Louise Jacques married Farnsworth ___ [27]
....................5. *John Wesley Jacques, Jr. was born 1911*
John Wesley Jacques, Jr. married Violet M. Bligh.

........2. Margaret McKay born in Shelburne in 1790. *She probably*
died prior to Dec 7, 1826 because she is not
mentioned in her father's will. [1]

1. 2nd Wife - Donald McKay married Sarah Ketland in Shelburne,
NS on April 21, 1793
Sarah was born in Dumfries, Scotland. [9]

APPENDIX 4 - McKAY FAMILY GENEALOGY

........2. Robert George Gordon McKay born in Shelburne - *baptized Jan 1801*

> *Robert George Gordon McKay married Mary Robertson of Port Joli, NS. She was a daughter of Corporal John Robertson, who served with Donald in the 76th Regiment, and wife Margaret (Hupman) Robertson.* [1]

............3. *Sarah McKay born 1825* [1]

............3. *Elizabeth McKay born 1827 -*

> *Elizabeth McKay married John McNulty on Sep 8, 1848 in Lawrence, MA (although the dates are similar, this could possibly be a different Elizabeth McKay)* [2]

............3. *Catherine Jane McKay born Apr 16, 1829* [1]

............3. *Allen McKay born 1830 in Nova Scotia, later moved to Boothbay, ME* [1]

> *Allen McKay married Sarah Young in Maine*
> > *In 1870, the family is in Boothbay, ME with Sarah's mother, Betsy, and Allen is a fisherman* [14]

................4. *Mary E. McKay born abt 1860 in ME* [14]

................4. *Sumner O. McKay born abt Oct 1869* [14]

> *Sumner O. McKay married Marie ___* [19]
> > *In 1920, Sumner worked for an ice company in Boothbay Harbor, ME* [19]

3. *2nd marriage Allen McKay married Margaret A ___ in Boothbay, ME* [15]

................4. *John McKay born abt 1873 in Boothbay Harbor, ME*[15]

................4. *Maggie McKay was born abt Aug 1879 in Boothbay Harbor, ME* [15]

............3. *Desiah Greeves McKay born Jul 18,1831* [1]

........2. Elizabeth McKay born in Shelburne

> *Elizabeth McKay married Patrick Wall on Jul 12, 1823* [1]

........2. *Donald McKay Jr. Although he is not listed in William Kean's book, there is a good possibility that he did exist. In 1826 when Sergeant Donald McKay made a statement for the justices investigating illegal voting in the election of that year, he stated that when he made a survey of the back country along the Jordan in 1819 he was assisted by Donald McKay Jr. The bill that he presented for the survey included an account of 2.10 Pounds paid to Donald McKay Jr. If there was a son Donald, he must have died prior to 1826 since Sergeant Donald McKay did not mention him in his will. [1] Considering the survey in 1819, it would be logical to assume that he was born before Robert George Gordon McKay. [1]*

APPENDIX 4 - McKAY FAMILY GENEALOGY

The following are the descendants of HUGH McKAY

........2. Hugh McKay born May 12, 1788 - died Dec 30, 1871 at 83
of **"Old age"** in East Boston, MA. *He was living with his son Nathaniel's ex-wife, Adeline, on Princeton St. when he died.*

Hugh McKay married Ann McPherson in St. John's Kirk in Shelburne on Oct 15, 1808 by the Rev. Matthew Dripps

Ann McPherson was born in Shelburne, NS on Nov 4, 1789 - died in East Boston on Nov 14,1856 at 67.

Ann McPherson was the daughter of Lauchlan and Elizabeth (Urquhart) McPherson. Lauchlan was from Glasgow and Elizabeth from Edinburgh.

See Appendix 5 for more information on the McPherson family.

............3. Elizabeth Ann McKay born in Shelburne Oct 14, 1809 - died Feb 18,1869 at 60

Elizabeth Ann McKay married John Crocheron *on Aug 23, 1827*

John was the son of Abraham and Penniah Crocheron [1]

...............4. Thomas Jones Crocheron born May 8,1829 - died Jun 18,1874 at 45

Thomas Jones Crocheron married Catherine S. Bowers *on Jan 1, 1850* [1]

Catherine S. Bowers was born Sep 29, 1825 in Jordan Bay, Nova Scotia [16]

...................5. John Crocheron born Dec 18,1850

John Crocheron married Ellen Purney

John Crocheron married Mary E. ___ [16]

Mary E. ___ was born Jan 16, 1843 [16]

...................5. Annie McPherson Crocheron born Sep 9,1852

Annie McPherson Crocheron married Robert Major Jr.

.......................6. Mary Eva Major born Aug 24,1870 - died Jun 21, 1891 at 20

.......................6. Alonzo William Major born Dec 1,1872 - died Nov 30,1877 at 4

.......................6. Lonie Alice Major born Nov 3,1874 - died Nov 24,1877 at 3

.......................6. Robert Everett Major born Apr 20,1876

Robert Everett Major married Mary McKay

.......................6. Kate Luella Major born Dec 18,1878

.......................6. Helen Peabody Major born Oct 20,1882

..................6. Inez Annie Major born Nov 9,1885
................5. Angeline Crocheron born Dec 18,1853 - died
      Oct 23,1894 at 40
      Angeline Crocheron married Thomas Simpson
..................6. Frank Crocheron Simpson born Feb 26,1886
..................6. Ethel Nettie Simpson born Apr 6,1888
................5. Antoinette Elizabeth Crocheron born Nov 8,1855 -
      died Jun 26,1894 at 38
      Antoinette Elizabeth Crocheron married Frederick
      Thompson
..................6. Roland Clifford Thompson born Feb 8,1890
................5. Alma Kate Crocheron born Jul 7,1857
      Alma Kate Crocheron married William Thornburn
..................6. Stanley Berton Thornburn born Dec 16,1878
..................6. Howard Liston Thornburn born May 24,1880
................5. Agnes Catherine Crocheron born May 3,1864
      Agnes Catherine Crocheron married John O'Connell
................5. Helen Marr Crocheron born Sep 1,1866
      Helen Marr Crocheron married Lewis Thornburn
      Lewis Thornburn was born May 16, 1864 [16]
..................6. Lionel Chester Thornburn born Oct 26,1887 -
      Canadian Census shows Oct 26, 1886[16]
..................6. Merton Leroy Thornburn born Nov 4,1889   -
      Canadian Census shows Nov 5, 1888 [16]
..................6. Edgar St. Clair Thornburn born Sep 8,1891 -
      Canadian Census shows Sep 7, 1891 [16]
..................6. **Lewis Thornburn born Jul 19, 1894** [16]
..................6. **Nettie Thornburn born Oct 13, 1896** [16]
..................6. **Kattie Thornburn born Nov 16, 1898** [16]

   3. 2nd husband Elizabeth Ann (McKay) Crocheron married
      Robert Major
      Robert Major was born abt 1816 in Nova Scotia [3a]
      **In the 1860 census, Robert and his son John are
      ship carpenters in East Boston.** [13a]
............4. **Eliza Major born abt 1836 in Nova Scotia** [13a]
............4. **John Major born abt 1838 in Nova Scotia** [13a]
............4. **William Major born abt 1843 in Nova Scotia** [13a]
      In 1860, he is an apprentice to a boiler Maker [13a]
............4. **Robert Major born abt 1844 in Nova Scotia** [13a]
............4. **Mary Major born abt 1849 in Maine** [13a]
..........3. **Donald McKay** born in Shelburne born Sep 4, 1810 - died
      Sep 20,1880 at 70 **of _consumption after having
      suffered a paralytic stroke 2 months before_** [6]

Donald was one of the most famous clipper ship builders

Donald McKay married Albenia Martha Boole in NY in 1833. *Albenia Martha Boole born Sep 8, 1815 in Jordan Falls, Shelburne, NS - died Dec 10, 1848 at 33 of Child Bed (died in childbirth) in East Boston, MA and is buried in the Oak Hill Cemetery, Newburyport,MA* [6]

Albenia was the daughter of John and Magdalene [Laney] (Ackerman) Boole. [5]

...............4. Cornelius Whitworth McKay born in *Manhattan*, NY Feb 1, 1834 - *died Nov 30, 1899 at 65 in Manhattan, NY of asthenia, chronic nephritis, endocarditis, and pneumonia . He is buried in Greenwood Cemetery, Brooklyn, NY* [4]

Cornelius Whitworth McKay married Susan Caroline Seaver

Susan Caroline Seaver born abt 1829 in Portland, ME - died on Jun 17, 1858 at 29 in Boston of typhoid fever and is buried in the Woodlawn Cemetery in Everett, MA in her family's plot 495[4]

Susan was the daughter of Eben and Susan Seaver of Portland, ME [6]

...................5. Louis McKay born Jul 15,1851 - died Apr 28,1880 at 29 of *alcoholism*. [6] *He was single when he died. He is buried in the Woodlawn Cemetery in Everett, MA*

...................5. *Henry McKay born Jan 10, 1853 in East Boston, MA He died on Mar 11, 1853 at 2 months old* [6]

...................5. Cornelia McKay born Jan 25,1854 - died Nov 9,1857 at 3 of *typhoid fever* [6]

4. 2nd marriage - Cornelius Whitworth McKay married Henriette [Harriet] Senecal *on March 1, 1875 in New Orleans, LA.*

Harriet born 1846 -died August 27, 1893 at 47 in Hoboken, NJ of Peritonitis. [4] *She is buried in Greenwood Cemetery, Brooklyn, NY*

Harriet was the daughter of Amable and Henriette Senecal

...................5. Richard Cornelius McKay *born in New Orleans, LA on Mar 23,1876 - died Aug 15, 1957 at 81 in Brentwood, NY of arteriosclerosis heart disease.*

APPENDIX   4 - McKAY FAMILY GENEALOGY

Richard Cornelius McKay married Leonie Bohler in Hoboken, NJ on Sep 17, 1901.
Leonie born in Hoboken, NJ Dec 25, 1875
died in Hempstead, NY Sep 17, 1958 at 82
of bronchopneumonia [4]
Both are buried in the St. Charles Cemetery, Farmington, NY
.......................6. *Cornelia McKay born Mar 1903 in Brooklyn, NY*
She died Aug 1903 at 5 months of scarlet fever [8] She is buried in the New York Bay Cemetery in Jersey City, NJ.
.......................6. *John Richard McKay born Jan 23, 1905 in Brooklyn, NY - died Jun 06, 1970 at 65 in Madeira Beach, FL*
John Richard McKay married Grace Mae (Raynor) Moore
Grace Mae was born Oct 17, 1908 in Freeport, NY - died Oct 24, 1981 in Fort Pierce, FL at 73
...........................7. *Gordon Wells Moore (stepson) born May 20, 1928 in Mineola, NY*
Gordon Wells Moore married Corinne Louise Siebert on Jul 11, 1953 in Floral Park, NY [37]
Corinne Louise Sirbert born Sep 6, 1933 in Brooklyn, NY. She is the daughter of Henry Anthony Seibert and Louise Kirschenheuter [37]
...........................7. *Leonie McKay*
Leonie McKay married Charles Bailey Kelley
.......................6. *Donald Gregory McKay born Oct 24, 1906 in Brooklyn, NY - died Apr 11, 1996 at 89 in Morton, PA*
Donald Gregory McKay married Eleanor Theresa Kuck
...........................7. *Donald Francis McKay born Dec 20, 1931*
Donald Francis McKay married Elizabeth Crewalk
Elizabeth Crewalk born Mar 07, 1936
...........................7. *Elaine McKay born Jan 31, 1933*
Elaine McKay married Ralph Pagano Jan 17, 1953 in Brooklyn, NY
Ralph Pagano born Jun 20, 1933 in Brooklyn, NY - died Mar 12, 1999 at 66, in Media, PA

APPENDIX 4 - McKAY FAMILY GENEALOGY

..........................7. *Grace McKay born Sep 02, 1935*
Grace McKay married Bill Wasch on
Sep 17, 1955 in Eddystone, PA
6. *2nd marriage Donald Gregory Pius McKay*
married Marie Reagan on Jan 26, 1952 in
Philadelphia, PA
Marie Reagan born May 20, 1912 in
Philadelphia, PA - died Nov 07, 1994 at 82
in Morton, PA
..........................7. *Living McKay*
.......................6. *Albenia Leonie McKay born Brooklyn, NY*
Oct 9, 1908 - died May 17, 1991 at 82 in
Fredericksburg, VA
Albenia Leonie McKay married Andrew Kane
in Brooklyn, NY on Sep 11, 1932
Andrew born Jan 8, 1905 in Brooklyn, NY
He died Feb 23, 1992 in Fredericksburg,
VA at 86
..........................7. *Richard Kane born Aug 28, 1933*
..........................7. *Grace Leonie Kane born Jun 02, 1937*
Grace Leonie Kane married William Ferrall
..........................7. *Edward Kane born Apr 28, 1939*
Edward Kane married Maureen ___
.......................6. *Grace Harriet McKay born Dec 12, 1910 in*
Brooklyn, NY - died Nov 22, 2000 at 90 of
<u>*cardiopulmonary arrest, bowel*</u>
<u>*obstruction, also suffered from*</u>
<u>*Rheumatoid arthritis*</u> [4]
Grace Harriet McKay married Paul Sebastian
Hamilton Aug 27, 1933 in Brooklyn, NY
Paul born Jun 30, 1901 - died Nov 29,1984
at 83 in Dunedin, FL of <u>*cardio-respiratory*</u>
<u>*insufficiency, chronic obstructive*</u>
<u>*Pulmonary disease, emphysema*</u> [4]
..........................7. *Dorothy Leonie Hamilton born Aug 14, 1934 in*
Chicago, IL
..........................7. *Paul Donald Hamilton born Nov 5, 1935 in*
Chicago, IL
Paul Donald Hamilton married Frances
Elizabeth LaPalme Jul 10, 1965 in
Seekonk, MA
Frances Elizabeth was born Aug 4, 1937 in
Attleboro, MA
..........................7. *Robert Ernest Hamilton born Apr 1, 1941 in*
Chicago, IL - died Sep 12, 2007 In

*Portland, ME of <u>adenocarcinoma of
the esophagus that spread to the
back.</u>*
*Robert Ernest Hamilton married Rhondalyn
Joan Hicks Jun 28, 1966 in Cape Ann,
ME*
..............................7. *Living Hamilton*
...............4. Frances Jean McKay born Apr 3, 1836 in *New York* -
died Oct 31,1851 *at 15 in Boston of
<u>Consumption (Tuberculosis).</u> [6] She is buried
in the Oak Hill Cemetery in Newburyport, MA*
...............4. Anne Jane McKay born Nov 12, 1837 in NY - died
*Oct 11,1842 In Newburyport, MA at 4 yr 11 mo
of <u>scarlet fever</u>* [6]
...............4. Dennis Condry McKay born born Oct 29, 1840 in
Newburyport,MA - died Feb 2,1861 *at 20 after
3 days of <u>convulsions</u> - He is buried in the Oak
Hill Cemetery in Newburyport, MA.*
*He is named after a business associate, Dennis
Condry, who was instrumental in having Enoch
Train convince Donald to open his own
shipyard in East Boston in 1844.*
...............4. Donald McKay born May 3, 1842 in *Newbury, MA* [6] -
died Dec 01, 1919 at 77 in Baltimore, MD [6]
Donald McKay married Emilie Pieniger
*Donald divorced Emilie sometime prior to 1891
In 1881, according to Harrow School records,
Emilie is living at 46 Avenue D'Eylau in Paris,
France and Donald's name is not mentioned.* [28]
....................5. Donald McKay born Jul 27,1866
Donald McKay married Ethel Margaret Matterson
*According to the school records, Donald was
enrolled in the Harrow School in Harrow
England, about 20 miles outside of
London, from 1881 to 1883.* [28]
*Donald joined the Royal Artillery in 1887 and
retired as a Major in 1907.*[28]
*In 1911, he was living at 49 Avonmore Rd. in
London.* [36]
......................6. *Donald Angus McKay born in 1904* [29]
Donald Angus McKay married Gladys Moxey [29]
..........................7. *June Elizabeth McKay born 1930* [31]
..........................7. *Donald James Reay McKay born 1932* [31]
*Donald James Reay McKay married Heather
Ann Reaves* [31]

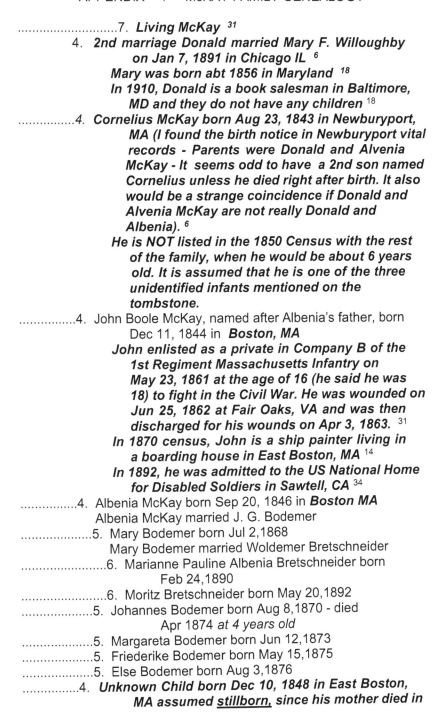

..............................7. *Living McKay* [31]

4. *2nd marriage Donald married Mary F. Willoughby on Jan 7, 1891 in Chicago IL* [6]
Mary was born abt 1856 in Maryland [18]
In 1910, Donald is a book salesman in Baltimore, MD and they do not have any children [18]

...............4. *Cornelius McKay born Aug 23, 1843 in Newburyport, MA (I found the birth notice in Newburyport vital records - Parents were Donald and Alvenia McKay - It seems odd to have a 2nd son named Cornelius unless he died right after birth. It also would be a strange coincidence if Donald and Alvenia McKay are not really Donald and Albenia).* [6]
He is NOT listed in the 1850 Census with the rest of the family, when he would be about 6 years old. It is assumed that he is one of the three unidentified infants mentioned on the tombstone.

...............4. John Boole McKay, named after Albenia's father, born Dec 11, 1844 in **Boston, MA**
John enlisted as a private in Company B of the 1st Regiment Massachusetts Infantry on May 23, 1861 at the age of 16 (he said he was 18) to fight in the Civil War. He was wounded on Jun 25, 1862 at Fair Oaks, VA and was then discharged for his wounds on Apr 3, 1863. [31]
In 1870 census, John is a ship painter living in a boarding house in East Boston, MA [14]
In 1892, he was admitted to the US National Home for Disabled Soldiers in Sawtell, CA [34]

...............4. Albenia McKay born Sep 20, 1846 in **Boston MA**
Albenia McKay married J. G. Bodemer

...................5. Mary Bodemer born Jul 2,1868
Mary Bodemer married Woldemer Bretschneider

.....................6. Marianne Pauline Albenia Bretschneider born Feb 24,1890

.....................6. Moritz Bretschneider born May 20,1892

...................5. Johannes Bodemer born Aug 8,1870 - died Apr 1874 *at 4 years old*

...................5. Margareta Bodemer born Jun 12,1873

...................5. Friederike Bodemer born May 15,1875

...................5. Else Bodemer born Aug 3,1876

...............4. *Unknown Child born Dec 10, 1848 in East Boston, MA assumed <u>stillborn,</u> since his mother died in* *childbirth it is assumed that he, or she, must have existed.*

3. 2nd marriage - Donald McKay marries Mary Cressy
Litchfield *in East Boston, MA on Oct 7, 1849 by the Rev. M. Langford*
Mary was born Sep 30, 1831 In Hingham, MA - died Feb 6, 1923 at 92 of <u>arteriosclerosis</u> *in Lexington, MA. She was the daughter of Nichols and Anna Cushing Litchfield* [22]
Mary was Donald's secretary at the shipyard.

See Appendix 3 for more information on the Litchfield family.

..............4. Lauchlan McKay born Oct 31, 1850 in *Boston, MA* -
died Apr 10,1853 at 2 ½ of <u>*congestion of the brain*</u> (probably meningitis) [6] He is buried in the Oak Hill Cemetery in Newburyport, MA
..............4. Frances McKay born Apr 12, 1854 in *Boston, MA* -
died in Switzerland in 1943 at the age of 89 [12]
Frances McKay went to school in Switzerland where she met August [10]
Frances McKay married August Clavel
Frances, August and the children lived in a section of the La Part Dieu monastery in Lausanne, Switzerland which August Clavel had acquired. This monastery was one of two that the Carthusian monks owned and they abandoned this one in favor of living in the other. La Part Dieu was then divided up and sold in pieces, which is how the Clavels came to live there. [10]
..............5, Louise Clavel born Oct 28,1879 in Switzerland
..............5. Mary Cressy Clavel born Aug 27,1883 in Switzerland -
died Mar 27, 1948 at 64 in Lincoln, MA of <u>*Carcinoma of the lung*</u>. She is buried in the Lincoln Cemetery in Lincoln, MA [6]
Mary Cressy Clavel married Jules Jerome Michel [10]
Jules Jerome Michel born in 1884 in Lyon, France - died of <u>cancer</u> abt 1961 while visiting his son in Seattle, WA [10]
..............6. *Jean Claude Donald Michel born Mar 10, 1927 in Lausanne, Switzerland - died Dec 1, 1996 at 69* [10]

Jean Claude Donald Michel married Elsie
Jeanette Charman Oct 30, 1950[10]
Elsie Jeanette was born Jun 2, 1917 in
Portland, OR - died Nov 17, 2006 at 89 in
Seattle, WA [26]

................................7. *Donald Cochran Michel born Jul 26, 1956*
died Dec 14, 2003 at 47 [10]

......................5. François Henri August Clavel born Mar 31,1893

..................4. Mary Cressy McKay born in *Boston, MA* Jan 4, 1856
Mary Cressy McKay married Edward P. Bliss *abt 1885* [18]
Edward P. Bliss was born abt 1851 and died
prior to 1920 -
In 1880, he was a dealer in dry goods [15]
In 1910, he worked in a brush factory. They
lived in Lexington, MA and did not have
any children [18, 19]

..................4. Lawrence Litchfield McKay born in *Boston, MA*
Jan 25, 1860
Lawrence Litchfield McKay married Anne Newbold
Bispham *abt 1890* [18]
Anne Newbold Bispham was born Apr 1860 in
Virginia [17]
In 1900, Lawrence was a farmer in Charlottesville,
VA [17]
In 1910, Lawrence was a manager on a farm on
Guina Rd. In Brewster, NY. They did not
have any children [18]

..................4. Anna Cushing McKay born Jun 17, 1864 in *Boston,*
MA - died Jan 6, 1885 *at 20 in Hamilton, MA*
of <u>*consumption*</u>. [6] *She is buried with her*
infant daughter in the Oak Hill Cemetery
in Newburyport, MA
Anna Cushing McKay married Henry F. Burton *on*
Jun 28, 1883 in Hamilton, MA by the Rev.
Temple Cutler - Congregational Minister -
when Henry was 31 and Anna was 19 [6]
Henry F. Burton born abt 1852 in Elmira, NY
was a teacher in Rochester [6]

......................5. *Unnamed infant daughter - mentioned on Anna's*
grave stone.

..................4. Nichols Litchfield McKay born Jun 17, 1864 in *Boston,*
MA - died on Apr 14, 1947 in Arlington, MA
at 82 [6] *Nichols is named after his*
grandfather, Mary Cressy's father

APPENDIX 4 - McKAY FAMILY GENEALOGY

Nichols Litchfield McKay married Grace A. Russell
abt 1888 [17]
Grace A Russell was born Feb 1863 in MA [17]
In 1900, the family is living at 146 Jason St.
Arlington, MA and Nichols is a leather
merchant
In the 1910 and 1920 Census, they are living at 73
Jason St. Arlington, MA and he is a Sales Mgr
for a leather Co Possible connection with the
Hotel Vendome in Boston, MA [12]
...................5. Frances Clavel McKay born Oct 19,1889
Frances Clavel McKay married Wentworth Caleb
Carr [32]
........................6. *Barbara Carr*
Barbara Carr married Glen Pride Woodbury [32]
...................5. Mildred McKay born Apr 2,1892
...................5. *Anna Cushing McKay born Jan 12,1895* [12],[17]
New England Historic Genealogical Society has
birth date as Jan 31, 1896 in Arlington, MA [30]
...............4. Guy Allen McKay *born* Oct 4, 1866 *in Boston, MA*
Guy Allen McKay married Almira (Allie) Pierson
Mar 2, 1889 in Texas [25]
Allie Pierson was born May 30, 1870 in
Connersville, IN - died Nov 7, 1937 in Tacoma,
WA at 66. [25] *She was the daughter of Alan*
Samuel Pierson and Anna M Slusser. [25]
In 1900 Census, Guy Allen is a farmer & stockman
in Hansford, TX.
In 1910 Census, Guy and Allie are divorced and
living in Hutchinson, KS [18]
...................5. Donald McKay born May 9,1891 *in Texas* [17]
Donald McKay married Eleanor Hamlin
Eleanor Hamlin born abt 1894 in Kansas is the
daughter of Mortimer and Annie Hamlin [19]
In 1910 Census, Donald, living with his mother
and is a driver for an express Company
In 1920 Census, Donald is living with the
Hamlin family in Hutchinson, KS. [19]
In 1930, Donald is divorced living at 7401 Texas
Ave. in Houston, TX and working as an
operator for an oil refinery [20]
(a note in Dr. Donald McKay's book says
Donald was shot [12])
...................5. *Hugh Robert McKay born Dec 23,1893* [12] *in Texas* [17]
Hugh Robert McKay married Agasta ___

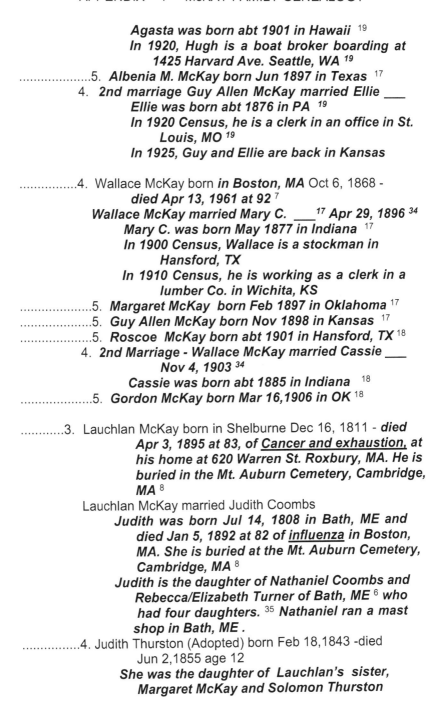

Agasta was born abt 1901 in Hawaii [19]
In 1920, Hugh is a boat broker boarding at 1425 Harvard Ave. Seattle, WA [19]
..................5. *Albenia M. McKay born Jun 1897 in Texas* [17]
    4. *2nd marriage Guy Allen McKay married Ellie* ___
        Ellie was born abt 1876 in PA [19]
        In 1920 Census, he is a clerk in an office in St. Louis, MO [19]
        In 1925, Guy and Ellie are back in Kansas

...............4. Wallace McKay born *in Boston, MA* Oct 6, 1868 - *died Apr 13, 1961 at 92* [7]
    Wallace McKay married Mary C. ___[17] *Apr 29, 1896* [34]
    Mary C. was born May 1877 in Indiana [17]
    In 1900 Census, Wallace is a stockman in Hansford, TX
    In 1910 Census, he is working as a clerk in a lumber Co. in Wichita, KS
..................5. *Margaret McKay born Feb 1897 in Oklahoma* [17]
..................5. *Guy Allen McKay born Nov 1898 in Kansas* [17]
..................5. *Roscoe McKay born abt 1901 in Hansford, TX* [18]
    4. *2nd Marriage - Wallace McKay married Cassie* ___ *Nov 4, 1903* [34]
    Cassie was born abt 1885 in Indiana [18]
..................5. *Gordon McKay born Mar 16,1906 in OK* [18]

............3. Lauchlan McKay born in Shelburne Dec 16, 1811 - *died Apr 3, 1895 at 83, of <u>Cancer and exhaustion,</u> at his home at 620 Warren St. Roxbury, MA. He is buried in the Mt. Auburn Cemetery, Cambridge, MA* [8]
Lauchlan McKay married Judith Coombs
    Judith was born Jul 14, 1808 in Bath, ME and died Jan 5, 1892 at 82 of <u>influenza</u> in Boston, MA. She is buried at the Mt. Auburn Cemetery, Cambridge, MA [8]
    Judith is the daughter of Nathaniel Coombs and Rebecca/Elizabeth Turner of Bath, ME [6] *who had four daughters.* [35] *Nathaniel ran a mast shop in Bath, ME .*
...............4. Judith Thurston (Adopted) born Feb 18,1843 -died Jun 2,1855 age 12
    She was the daughter of Lauchlan's sister, Margaret McKay and Solomon Thurston

...............4. William Lawrence Kean (Adopted) born Sep 23,1854 -
died Jun 15, 1923 at 68.
**He is the son of Lauchlan's sister Mary Ann and
second husband John Kean** [8]
William Lawrence Kean married Eliza Jane Hacker in
Boston Feb 11,1895
Eliza Jane Hacker **born Oct 12, 1846 in
Bridgewater, MA - died May 25, 1924 at 78, is
buried in Mt. Auburn Cemetery, Cambridge,MA**[8]
**She was the daughter of Captain William and
Mary (Coombs) Hacker**
**Note: William and Eliza were adopted much later in life on
Jan 18, 1892, when they were 37 and 45 respectively, and
Lauchlan was 80 years old.** [6]

..............3. Sarah McKay born in Shelburne Feb 26, 1813 - died
Sep 22,1868 at 55 *of disease of the spine 16
years and dysentery for 6 weeks* [6]
Sarah McKay married George **Washington** Thurston in
Feb 1837 [6]
**George was the son of William and Nancy
(Foster) Thurston** [1]
...............4. Emma Louisa Thurston born Jan 19,1842
Emma Louisa Thurston married John R. Major
..................5. Elizabeth Lucretia Major born Jun 22, 1869
..................5. Ralph Thurston Major born Dec 14, 1873
..................5. Sarah Theresa Major born Sep 23, 1875
..................5. Reginald Ewing Major born Nov 12, 1877
**Reginald Ewing Major married Louise M. ___ abt
1904 in California
In 1910, Reginald is a farmer in Merced
County, CA** [18]
**In 1920, the family is in Oakland, CA and
Reginald is a carpenter** [19]
......................6. *Alice E Major born abt 1906 in CA* [18]
......................6. *Evelyn born abt 1913 in CA* [19]
..................5. Mabel Emma Major born Jan 20, 1880
..................5. Donald Henry Major born Aug 19, 1883 - *died
Oct 4, 1895 at 12* [12]
...............4. Susan Alice Thurston born Nov 1, 1843 *in Bristol, ME*
She died Jan 15,1866 at 22 *in East Boston
of* Phthisis *(probably tuberculosis).*
**She was living with her parents at 20 Eutaw St.
when she died. She is buried in the East
Boston Cemetery.** [6]

APPENDIX   4 - McKAY FAMILY GENEALOGY

...............4. Henry William Thurston born Oct 19, 1846 - *died prior*
to 1920 Census
Henry William Thurston married Margretta Gilmore on
Oct 9, 1867 [32]
Henry learned the machinist trade in Donald
McKay's shipyard.
In 1875, he was a foreman of the American Net
& Twine Co. in East Cambridge, MA [32]
...................5. Donald Henry Thurston born Oct 13, 1868 - died
May 27,1869 at 7 months
...................5. Lottie Elizabeth Thurston born Mar 24, 1870 - died
May 14,1876 at 5 years old
...................5. Alice Emma Thurston born Apr 4, 1872 - died
Apr 2,1876 at 4 years old
...................5. Ida May Thurston born Sep 17, 1874 - died 1951 at
abt 77 years old
Ida May Thurston married Fred W. Ashworth on
Jun 29, 1893
Fred W. Ashworth was born Jan 1865 in England
In 1900, they are living at 409 Courtland St. in
Belleville, NJ. Fred is a weaver. [17]
In 1910, Fred is a superintendent at Weir Works
in Belleville, NJ. [18]
......................6. Ruth T. Ashworth born Aug 6,1898 - died 1974
at the age of 76
Ruth T. Ashworth married Melvin Mundy Hunt in
1916
...........................7. Douglas Melvin Hunt born Nov 6,1918
Douglas Melvin Hunt married Eleanor Babcock
...........................7. *Living* Hunt
......................6. Paul W. Ashworth born Nov 11, 1900 - died 1950
Paul W. Ashworth married Ethyl Maitlant Amann on
Sep 03, 1927
...........................7. Phylis Ashworth born Nov 25, 1934
Phylis Ashworth married Joseph Peter Peltack on
Jan 13, 1958
......................6. Alice M. Ashworth born Jun 1,1902 - died 1972
at abt 70
Alice M. Ashworth married Ralph Prugh in Jun 1928
...........................7. Betsy Prugh born Aug 14, 1931
Betsy Prugh married Robert David Conover on
Jul 08, 1956
6. 2nd marriage - Alice M. (Ashworth) Prugh married
Walter Apostolik on Apr 19, 1940
......................6. John Henry Ashworth born Mar 06, 1904

John Henry Ashworth married Gertrude Wharmby
on Jan 07, 1928
...........................7. Jean Thurston Ashworth born Jan 20, 1929
Jean Thurston Ashworth married Robert David
Mundellaon Jun 12, 1948
...........................7. Fredric William Ashworth born Jan 08, 1932
...........................7. Virginia Aldred Ashworth born Dec 19, 1935
Virginia Aldred Ashworth married Louis Parete on
Sep 04, 1954
........................6. Frederick William Ashworth (1908 - 1918)
Frederick William Ashworth married Donis Drake on
Sep 11, 1952
...........................7. Mark Ashworth born May 30, 1953
...................5. Lottie Alice Thurston born Apr 17, 1877 - died
Nov 10, 1955 at 78
Lottie Alice Thurston married Edgar Marshall
Wilford in Jun 1903
**Edgar Wilford was born Sep 1872 and died
prior to the 1920 census** [19]
**In 1900, Lottie was single, living with her
sister Ida in Belleville, NJ and Edgar was
her next door neighbor** [17]
**In 1910, Edgar and Lottie are living in Cedar
Grove, NJ and he is a color artist at NY
World** [18]
**In 1920, Lottie is a widow living in the same
house and is a secretary for a railroad** [19]
........................6. Rowland Henry Wilford born Mar 17, 1904
Rowland Henry Wilford married Eleanor Meeks in
1929
...........................7. Edgar Marshall Wilford born Apr 1, 1930
Edgar Marshall Wilford married Dorothea Hardy
on Oct 30, 1954
...........................7. Donald McKay Wilford born Feb 16, 1932
Donald McKay Wilford married Mary Jeannette
Perry on Jun 05, 1954
...........................7. Constance Meeks Wilford born Nov 24, 1936
....................6. Edgar Marshall Wilford born Jan 4, 1906 - died
1910 at 4
....................6. Elizabeth Alice Wilford born Dec 9, 1908 - died
1956 at 48
....................6. Donald Thurston Wilford born Dec 1, 1910
Donald Thurston Wilford married Ruth Hickman on
Jul 05, 1937
....................6. Charlotte May Wilford born Jan 31, 1913

Charlotte May Wilford married Leroy Osborne in
Feb 1944
.............................7. *Living* Osborne
.......................6. Margaret Louise Wilford born Apr 23, 1915 -
died 1958 at abt 43
Margaret Louise Wilford married Lloyd Sigurd
Anderson in 1935
.............................7. Elizabeth Thurston Anderson born Jul 04, 1939
.............................7. *Living* Anderson

            4. 2nd marriage - Henry William Thurston married Sarah
J. Dove *abt 1882*
*They lived in Saddle River, NJ and Henry was
a hosiery manufacturer* [17]
...................5. Susan Andrews Thurston born Jun 26,1883 *in MA* [17] -
She died Jul 12,1948 at 65
...................5. Henry Nathaniel Thurston born Jul 8,1889 *in CT* [17]
Henry Nathaniel Thurston married Meta ___ [19]
*In the 1920 Census, Henry was a manager of
an auto garage in Allendale, NJ* [19]
.......................6. *Frederick H. Thurston born abt 1915 in NJ* [19]
.......................6. *Louis E. Thurston born Feb 1916 in NJ* [19]
................4. Donald Thurston born Oct 19,1846 *in Bristol, ME* [6] -
died Sep 3,1862 at 15 *of <u>Bil Int Fever for 3
weeks and convulsions for 1 day</u>* [6]
................4. Lucretia McClure Thurston born Mar 19,1848 - died
Apr 19, 1869 at 20
Lucretia McClure Thurston married Francis O. Stevens
...................5. Sarah Emma Stevens born Oct 7,1868 - died
May 19,1870 at 2
................4. Margaret Thurston born Nov 30,1850 - died Dec 25,1870
at 20
................4. Annie Thurston born Aug 31,1852 - died Jan 19,1868
at 15
................4. Harriet Ellen Thurston born Feb 25,1858 - died
Mar 13,1870 at 12

............3. Margaret McKay born in Shelburne, NS born May 2, 1814
She died Aug 29,1867 at 53 in Weymouth, MA of
<u>cancer</u> [6]
Margaret McKay married Solomon Thurston *on
Jan 14, 1833*
*Solomon was a sea captain from Bristol, Maine
He was the son of William and Nancy (Foster)
Thurston*

*He fell off of the Welles Wharf in East Boston
and <u>drowned</u> in Boston Harbor [1] on
Nov 8, 1849.* [6]

...............4. Ann Elizabeth Thurston born Sep 22,1836 - *died
May 30, 1896 at 59* [12]

Ann Elizabeth Thurston married Montague Burke

...................5. Lauchlan McKay Burke born May 25,1856 - died
Sep 20,1861 at 5

...................5. Walter Edward Burke born Sep 20,1857 - died
Mar 21,1859 at 1 1/2.

4. 2nd marriage - Ann Elizabeth (Thurston) Burke married
Joseph F. Taylor

...................5. Fannie May Taylor born Jan 28,1873

Fannie May Taylor married George W. Bates

...................5. Frank Thurston Taylor born Aug 6,1874 *in
Weymouth, MA - died in 1954 in Malden,
MA at abt 80* [23]

*Frank Thurston Taylor married Marian Brookshaw
in Boston, MA* [23]

.........................6. *Linda Elizabeth Taylor born Jan 27, 1901* [23]

Linda Elizabeth Taylor married John A. Bossi [23]

...........................7. *Joanne Bossi*

Joanne Bossi married James True [23]

...........................7. *Carolyn Bossi* [23]

.....................6. *Henry B. Taylor born 1902* [23]

Henry B. Taylor married Muriel Gates [23]

.....................6. *Joseph Franklin Taylor born Jan 12, 1903 in
Malden, MA - died Jul 19, 1965 at 62 in
Chicago, IL* [23]

*Joseph Franklin Taylor married Bernice Muriel
Keyser on Aug 26, 1923 in Boston, MA.
Bernice was the daughter of William & Clara
(Hartley) Keyser* [23]

.............................7. *Franklin Taylor born June 08, 1923 in Boston,
MA* [23]

*Franklin Taylor married Charlyne Rae
Lympany on Nov 28, 1947 in Cuyahoga
Falls, OH* [23]

............................7. *Bernice Mae Taylor born in Revere, MA* [23]

*Bernice Mae Taylor married James Wells in
Cuyahoga Falls, OH in the First
Congregational Church* [23]

............................7. *Barbara Ann Taylor born May 17, 1927 in
Niagara Falls, NY* [23]

Barbara Ann Taylor married Arthur
Cunnington on Nov 14, 1952 in Silver
Lake (Akron), OH [23]
Arthur Cunnington born 1926 - died 2001
at 75 years old [23]
..........................6. *Franklin Thurston Taylor born 1904 - died 1914*
at 10 years old [23]
....................5. Annie Gertrude Taylor born Feb 13,1876
................4. Franklin Thurston born Feb 14,1837 *in Bristol, ME* [13a]
died Dec 31,1869 at 32
Franklin Thurston married Mary Major
................4. Eugene Thurston born Jan 13,1841
Eugene Thurston married Elnora Roff *abt 1890* [17]
In 1900 Census, Eugene is a janitor living at
107 East 27th St. Manhattan, NY living in
the same house as John Salisbury 32, his
wife Anna and son Jean
....................5. Linda Judith Thurston born Jun 15,1891
................4. Judith Thurston born *Feb 18,* 1843 *in Bristol, ME* [13a] -
died Jun 2, 1855 at 12 [1]
................4. Albenia Thurston born Nov 8,1844 *in Bristol, ME -*
died after 1900 Census [17]
Albenia Thurston married George A. Wadleigh
George A. Wadleigh was born abt 1840 - died
before the 1900 Census.
In 1870, he was a clerk in the County Clerk's
Office in Jersey City, NJ [14]
In 1900, Albenia is widowed and a dressmaker
in Weymouth, MA
....................5. Jennie Buxton Wadleigh born Sep 8,1865 -
In 1900, at 34, was living with mother in
Weymouth, MA [17]
................4. Oscar Thurston born Jul 14,1846 in Boston, MA - died
Jul 11,1880 at almost 34
Oscar Thurston married Addie White
In 1870, Oscar was married, living in Weymouth,
MA and working in a boot factory [14]
In 1880, Oscar was working in a book store in
Weymouth, MA
....................5. Albenia Thurston born Apr 7,1872
....................5. Eugene Thurston born. Mar 10,1875 - died
Dec 23,1875 at 9 months
....................5. Ernest Thurston born Aug 4,1876 -
In 1900, at 23, he is single selling shoes in
Weymouth, MA [17]

APPENDIX 4 - McKAY FAMILY GENEALOGY

..................5. Oscar Byron Thurston born Jan 5,1880 - died
Aug 1,1880 at 7 months

3. 2nd marriage - Margaret (McKay) Thurston married
Ambrose Salisbury
*Ambrose Salisbury was born Oct 1808 in
Weymouth, MA and was the son of Abiah
Whitman Salisbury and Patience Pratt* [21]
*In the 1860 Census, Ambrose and Margaret are
living in East Boston, MA with their 2 children
along with Margaret's children Frank 21 (a
marine), Albenia 16, Oscar 14, and Ambrose's
children Sarah F. 16 and Ella J. 13.*
.................4. Ambrose Salisbury born Apr 28,1854
Ambrose Salisbury married Estella Meyer
*In the 1920 Census, Ambrose 65 and Estella 59
are living at 294 East 8th St. Brooklyn, NY* [19]
..................5. Lauchlan McKay Salisbury born Nov 25,1888
.................4. Nathaniel McKay Salisbury born Dec 22,1855 - died
Oct 22,1872 at 16
*After his mother died in 1867, Nathaniel is living
with his 1/2 sister Ann Elizabeth (Thurston)
Burke in Weymouth, MA in 1870 when he was
14 years old.* [14]

............3. Jennett McKay born in Shelburne born May 4, 1815 -
died May 20, 1817 at 2

............3. Ann McKay born in Shelburne born Jan 27, 1817 - died
Feb 10, 1824 at 7

............3. Hugh Robert McKay born Mar 21, 1818 in Shelburne -
died Apr 23,1886 at 68
Hugh Robert McKay married Margaret McKay -
*Margaret was the eldest daughter of Robert and
Janet (Murray) McKay* [1]
.................4. Gurden McKay born Feb 22,1844 - died Dec 15,1888
at 44
*In Marion Robert's book, the birth is given as
Feb 2, 1842 in Jordan Falls, NS* [1]
1850 Census indicates birth abt 1842 [13]
*1870 and 1880 Census indicates birth in 1843 -
(pick your own year).*
*Gurden enlisted in Company B of the 5th
Regiment Massachusetts Infantry on*

*Apr 16, 1861 at 17 to fight in the Civil War. On
Jul 31, 1861 he was transferred to Company G
of the 22nd Regiment Massachusetts Infantry,
and then on Sep 4, 1861 was commissioned a
2nd Lieutenant. He was wounded on May 4, 1862
near Yorktown, VA. and was dismissed by
special orders of the War Dept on Aug 3, 1863* [31]
In 1870, he is a carpenter in Baltimore, MD.
*In 1880, he is a widowed Doctor in Philadelphia,
PA.*

...............4. Anna Jane McKay born Mar 16,1846 in Jordan Falls,
NS.
*In Marion Robert's book, the birth is given as
Feb 20, 1844 in Jordan Falls* [1] *The 1850
Census indicates birth abt 1844* [13] *The 1900
census gives birth date as Mar 1850* [17]
(Pick whichever you like)
Anna Jane McKay married Edmund White *abt 1871*
Edmund White was born Mar 1842 [17] *and was a
Methodist Minister in Mahoning, PA* [15]
...............5. Lorenda McKay White born May 26,1872 *in PA* [15]
*Lorenda McKay White married ___ Davis. This is
an assumption from 1900 Census where her
children are named Davis and they are living
with their grand-parents Anna and Edmund* [17]
...............6. *Harry Davis born Aug 1896 in PA* [17]
...............6. *Leinnie? Davis born Jan 1898 in PA (she is
female but her first name is not clear in
the Census)*[17]
...............5. Eliza Jane White born Jul 4,1874 *in PA* [15]
In 1900, she is a music instructor [17]
...............5. Edmund White born Jul 7,1883 *in PA* - died
Jan 14,1888 at 4
...............4. Sarah Margaret McKay born Apr 16,1847 in Jordan
Falls, NS
Sarah Margaret McKay married William R. Gwinn
*William R. Gwinn was born abt 1843 in MD -
he was a minister* [15]
...............5. William McKay Gwinn born Jun 26,1869 *in MD* [15]
...............5. Margaret McKay Gwinn born Sep 1,1870 *in MD* [15]
...............5. Hugh Gwinn born Sep 8,1873 *in MD* [15]
*Hugh Gwinn married Georgie M. Richards abt 1898
Georgie is the daughter of George and Annie
Richards* [17]

> *In 1910, he was a traveling salesman for a Bakery Co. and they were living at 202 Prospect Ave. in Baltimore, MD* [18]

.......................6. **Edith M Gwinn born abt 1905 in Baltimore, MD** [18]

.......................6. **George R Gwinn born abt 1906 in Baltimore, MD** [18]

...................5. Georgia Shure Gwinn born Feb 3,1875 *in MD* [15] - died Jul 6,1886 at 11

...................5. Sarah Gwinn born. Aug 26,1882 - died Nov 18,1886 at 4 years old

...................5. Charlton Baker Gwinn born Nov 10,1888

................4. **Margaret Elizabeth McKay born Apr 16, 1847 in Jordan Falls, NS** [1] **- died before the 1860 census. Margaret shows up on the 1850 census as 3 years old** [18]

................4. Albenia McKay born Oct 10,1849 in Jordan Falls, NS. -
> *Marion Robertson gives birth as Oct 1848 In Jordan Falls, NS* [1] *The 1850 Census shows her as 1 yr. The 1870 Census shows her as 20 yr, so the 1849 date is more likely. However, the 1900 Census shows birth date as Oct 1851.*

Albenia McKay married William E. Davis
> *William E. Davis born Mar 1848 in MD, was an insurance agent in Baltimore, MD living at 1922 East Pratt St.* [17, 19]

...................5. Lorenda Davis born Jul 3,1873 - *she was still single in 1920 at 47 years old and was a public school teacher in Baltimore, MD* [17, 19]

...................5. *Unknown child - 1900 census shows Albenia had 2 children, one living*

................4. Lorenda McKay born Feb 4, 1854 in Boston, MA - died 1934 - at 80

Lorenda McKay married Vincent McKim
> *Vincent McKim was born Nov 1857 in PA*
> *In 1880, he was a medical student in Concord, PA* [15]
> *In 1900, he was a physician in Derry, PA, and was still practicing in 1930 when he was 73 years old* [17 to 20]

...................5. Vincent **L.** McKim born Jul 7, 1883 - died Apr 1939 at 55
> *In 1910, he was a traveling salesman in Derry, PA*

In 1930, he was still single - an Insurance Agent in Charles City, IA

...................5. Margaret McKay McKim born Nov 17, 1891
Margaret McKay McKim married Ray E. White [20]
Ray E. White was born abt 1893 in PA [20]
In 1930, he was a draftsman for a steel mill [20]

...................6. *Vincent McKay White born abt 1917 in PA* [20]
...................6. *John M. White born abt 1923 in PA* [20]
...................6. *Ray E. White Jr born abt 1927 in PA* [20]
...................6. *Robert White born abt 1927 in PA* [20]

...............4. Eliza McKay born Feb 4, 1854 in Boston, MA - died May 23, 1929 - at 75
Eliza McKay married Joseph G. McGill
Joseph G. McGill born Nov 27, 1864 in Canada [7]

...................5. Josephine McGill born Dec 8, 1890 *in Philadelphia, PA -died Sep 1949 at 59* [7]
Josephine McGill married Arthur Sykes on Dec 20, 1911 in Philadelphia, PA
Arthur Sykes born Sep 20, 1888 in PA [7]

...................6. *Arthur Sykes Jr. born Sep 4, 1912 in Philadelphia died Jun 29, 1993 at 80* [7]

...................6. *Lorenda Sykes born Dec 6, 1924 in Philadelphia, PA*
Lorenda Sykes married Sidney F. Sneade on Jan 13, 1947 [7]
Sidney F. Sneade born Aug 11, 1923 in PA [7]

...................6. *Joan Sykes born May 5, 1928 in PA*
Joan Sykes married Harry Walzer on Nov 6, 1948 in Philadelphia, PA
Harry Walzer born May 16, 1921 [7]

...................7. *Living Walzer*
...................7. *Kathleen Walzer born Apr 14, 1953 - died on same day* [7]

...............4. Robert McKay born born Mar 17, 1856 in Boston, MA died Jun 5, 1945 at 89
Robert McKay married Harriet C. Selsor
In 1900, Robert is an Episcopal Minister in Chester, NJ [17]
In 1920, he is a minister in Daytona, FL [19]

...................5. Nellie Selsor McKay born Sep 2, 1883 - died Nov 21, 1883 *at 11 weeks in Philadelphia of <u>inflammation of the stomach</u> and is buried in the Ivy Hill Cemetery* [6]

...................5. Robert Barnes McKay born Feb 12,1886 - died Jan 12,1974 at 87

APPENDIX 4 - McKAY FAMILY GENEALOGY

Robert Barnes McKay married Mariella Perkins
Jun 4, 1912 in Detroit, MI
In 1910, he was a student at the Philadelphia
Divinity School on Woodlawn Ave. in
Philadelphia, PA [18]
In 1920, he is married with 3 children and is a
Clergyman in Little Falls, Passaic, NJ [19]
In 1930, he is a Rector in an Episcopal Church
in Little Falls, NJ [20]

..........................6. Robert McKay III born Feb 17, 1913 *in NJ* [19]
Robert McKay III married Dorothy Darling Sturges
on Oct 17, 1941

..........................6. Henry Perkins McKay *born Aug 4, 1914 in NJ* [19]
Henry Perkins McKay married Elsie Boyce on
May 13, 1939 [19]

..........................6. John Perkins McKay *born Sep 14, 1917 in NJ* [19]
John Perkins McKay married Inez Crosset on
Jun 20, 1942 [24]

...........................7. Gordon Robert McKay born Aug 31, 1943 -
died Dec 4, 1947 at 4 years old

...........3. David McKay born in Shelburne Oct 14, 1819 - *died*
Feb 12, 1907 at 87 in East Boston of old age
and is buried in the Woodlawn Cemetery,
Everett, MA [6]
David was a ship carpenter and a shipwright in
*East Bosto*n [14,17]
David McKay married Mary Riley *in Gloucester, MA on*
Jan 7, 1849 [6]
Mary Riley born abt 1830 and died before the
1900 census [15] [17]
In 1900, David was living with his daughter, Mary
(McKay) Lang and her family at 147 Maverick
St. in East Boston. [17]

................4. *Honora McKay born Sep 2, 1849 in Gloucester, MA -*
died Sep 12, 1849 at 10 days old [6]

................4. Annie McKay born Aug 24, 1850
Annie McKay married John Mulloy
John Mulloy was born in Ireland
In 1880, John is a stone cutter living at 269
Wood St. in Dorchester, MA [15]

...................5. Mary Elizabeth Mulloy born Apr 2, 1876
...................5. Catherine Agnes Mulloy born Oct 21, 1877
...................5. John Joseph Mulloy born Aug 19, 1879
...................5. Frederick David Mulloy born Jul 4, 1881 - died
Dec 10, 1881 at 5 months old

..................5. Annie Mulloy born Mar 22, 1883
              Annie Mulloy married Duncan R. McEachern
......................6. Ronald David McEachern born Aug 7, 1891
......................6. Allan Joseph McEachern born May 8, 1894
................4. John McKay born Oct 14, 1853 - died Jul 22, 1892 at
             38 years old
             In 1870, he was a waiter at Moinken Oyster House
             in Boston, MA
...............4. William McKay born Feb 3, 1856 - died Mar 5, 1856 at
             1 month old.
             *When I checked the death records I found these
             dates to be in error. The correct dates should
             be : born May 30, 1854 - died Jun 30, 1854 in
             East Boston of convulsions at 1 month old . [6]
             The family was living on Trenton St. in East
             Boston, MA at the time.*
...............4. Matilda McKay born Jan 5, 1858 - died Jul 7, 1860 at
             2 years old
             *These dates are also in error. They should be
             (Aug, 1855 - Feb 15, 1857). Matilda's death
             certificate shows that she died Feb 15, 1857
             in Boston of scarlet fever and was living at
             Marion St. & Trenton St. in East Boston. She
             is buried in the East Boston Cemetery. It
             also says that she was 1 year 6 months old,
             which would put her birth in Aug, 1855, not
             Jan 1858.*
...............4. Nathaniel Joseph McKay born Feb 14,1860 - *died prior
             to the 1910 Census*
             *In 1900 Census, he is listed as a day laborer in
             East Boston* [17]
             Nathaniel Joseph McKay married Elizabeth Mary Shea
             on Feb 15, 1887 in Boston, [6]
             *Elizabeth Mary Shea was the daughter of John
             and Hannah Shea* [6]
             *Elizabeth Mary born Nov 1859 - died after 1920
             Census* [17]
             *Nathaniel is listed on the marriage certificate as
             a stevedore. They did not have any children* [17,18]
...............4. Mary McKay born Nov 9, 1865
             Mary McKay married John Frederick Lang *Aug 11, 1886
             in East Boston by the Rev. B.P. McCarthy* [6]
             *John Frederick was born Aug 22, 1864 in Boston.
             He was the son of Augustus and Mary Lang and
             is listed as a salesman* [6]

APPENDIX 4 - McKAY FAMILY GENEALOGY

> *In the 1900 Census, he is listed as a grocery clerk*
> *in East Boston* [17]

.................5. Mary Alice Lang born Mar 21, 1889

.................5. Annie Gertrude Lang born Dec 1, 1891

.................5. Frederick Augustus Lang born Oct 5, 1892

.................5. *Francis McKay Lang born Apr 1895* [17]

.................5. *Margaret E. Lang born Jan 15, 1900 - died*
> *Jun 22, 1901 in Boston, MA of* marasmus
> *(severe malnutrition) for 6 months. She*
> *was less than 1 ½ years old. They were*
> *living at 147 Maverick St. in East Boston at*
> *that time.* [6]

.................5. *Unknown child born after 1900 - died before*
> *1910* [17,18]

..........3. John McKay born in Shelburne Jan 20, 1822 - *died*
> *May 13, 1897 at 75* [12]

John McKay married Mary Brothers

...............4. Richard Brothers McKay born Nov 2, 1845 - *died*
> *Nov 23, 1895 at 50* [12]

Richard Brothers McKay married Mary Bill *on*
> *Nov 8, 1875 in Shelburne, NS* [7]
> *In the 1881 Canadian Census, Richard is an*
> *engineer in Lockport, Shelburne, NS*

.................5. Jessie McKay born Aug 31, 1876 - died Mar 12, 1877
> at 6 months

.................5. Elizabeth McKay born May 21, 1878

.................5. Gordon Bill McKay born Apr 11, 1879

.................5. John Lauchlan McKay born Jan 21, 1882

...............4. Hugh McKay born Mar 8, 1847 - died Oct 7, 1869 at
> 22 years old

...............4. Nathaniel Lang McKay born Dec 13, 1848

Nathaniel Lang McKay married Ida Gray
> *Ida Gray was born Aug 26, 1862 in Nova Scotia* [16]

.................5. Mary Jane McKay born Aug 1, 1889

.................5. Nina Gordon McKay born Aug 15, 1891

.................5. *Jessie McKay born Nov 18, 1895 Hunts Point,*
> *Shelburne, NS* [16]

.................5. *Annie McKay* [12]

...............4. Mary Ellen McKay born Jun 12, 1852

Mary Ellen McKay married Donald McKay

.................5. Mary Janet McKay born Oct 20, 1883 - died
> Jan 17, 1885 at 1 year

.................5. William Lawrence McKay born Jan 6, 1885

.................5. Warren Clement McKay born Aug 15, 1889

APPENDIX 4 - McKAY FAMILY GENEALOGY

...............4. John Lauchlan McKay born Jan 30, 1854 - *died prior to 1920*
John Lauchlan McKay married Emily B. Margeson *on Nov 21, 1883 in Boston, MA by Rev. William W. Colburn* [12]
In the 1900 & 1910 Census, John is a building superintendent living at 46 Frances St. in Melrose, MA.
In the 1920 Census, Emily is a widow and Richard 19 and Marjorie 17 are living at home.
...............5. Marion Anetta McKay born Aug 9, 1885
...............5. Ermine Mariah McKay born Apr 1, 1888
...............5. *Richard McKay born Mar 17, 1900* -died Feb 1984 [17]
Richard McKay married Isabelle McCleary [25]
Isabelle was born in 1902 and they had three children (names unknown) [25]
...............5. *Marjorie E. McKay born abt 1903* [18]
...............4. *Barbara McKay born Jan 19, 1857 in Jordan River, NS* [1]
...............4. *Elizabeth Jane McKay born Sep 22, 1858 in Jordan River, NS* [1]
...............4. Annie Cornelian McKay born Apr 14, 1860
Annie Cornelian McKay married Michael Fitzgerald
...............5. Austen Fitzgerald born Dec 5, 1880

...........3. Simon McKay born in Shelburne on Feb 6, 1823 - died Nov 25, 1882 at 59 *in Boston, MA after suffering for 2 years with* <u>*consumption*</u>. [6] *They were living at 38 White St. in East Boston at the time of his death.* [6]
Simon McKay married Sarah Jane Osgood *on Feb 21, 1848* [7]
Sarah Jane was born on Apr 1, 1828 in Salisbury, MA and died Apr 20, 1850 at 22 [7] *She is the daughter of Timothy and Eunice (Varnum) Osgood* [6]
...............4. Roland Campbell McKay born Mar 20, 1850 - died Sep 28, 1885 at 35
Roland Campbell McKay married Celia C. Smith
In 1880, Roland was a clerk for a naval contractor in Philadelphia, PA [15]
...............5. Clement Blethen McKay born Jun 9, 1878 in PA
...............5. Harold C. McKay born May 6, 1881 *in PA* [18]
Harold C. McKay married Patricia E. ___ abt 1910 [18]
Patricia E. was born abt 1885 in Vermont [18]

In 1910, Harold is working in an electrical supply company and living with his wife Patricia, his mother Celia and his uncle, Donald K. Smith at 108 Phillips St. in Quincy, MA [18]

3. 2nd marriage - Simon McKay married Mary Jane Worthen *on Jul 27, 1853 in Portland, ME* [7]

Mary Jane Worthen was born Jun 19, 1831 in Amesbury, MA - died Feb 9, 1895 at 62 in Cambridge, MA of pneumonia. [6]

Mary Jane is the daughter of Joseph and Dorothy Worthen. Mary Jane had three brothers and three sisters.

In 1880, Simon and Mary Jane are living in the same house as Simon's sister, Matilda, at 168 Lexington St. in East Boston and he is listed as a ship carpenter. [15]

......3. Mary Ann McKay born in Shelburne born Sep 11, 1824 - died Apr 14, 1888 at 63 *of Apoplexy for 1 week (stroke) in East Boston, MA* [6]

Mary Ann McKay married Patrick McKenzie *on Jan 4, 1841* Patrick McKenzie was born abt 1812 in Nova Scotia to John and Mary McKenzie. [6] *He died on Aug 17, 1850 at 38 of Dysentery in East Boston, MA.* [6]

Patrick was a ship carpenter [6]

......4. Alexander McKenzie born Aug 1841 - died Jul 28, 1850 at 8 years 11 months *in Boston of Measles. He is buried in the East Boston Cemetery* [6]

......4. Hugh McKenzie born born May 1845 - *died Aug 2, 1850 at 5 in Boston of Diarrhea. He is buried in the East Boston Cemetery* [6]

......4. *Unnamed child baptized Sep 15, 1848 - St. John's Kirk, Shelburne, NS* [1]

3. 2nd marriage - Mary Ann (McKay) McKenzie married John Kean *on Dec 14, 1853 in East Boston by E. T. Taylor* [6]

John Kean, born abt 1828, son of William Kean, [6] *was a ship carpenter in East Boston.* [14]

In 1880, they are living at 114 Saratoga St. in East Boston [15]

......4. William Lawrence Kean born Sep 23, 1854 - *died Jun 15, 1923 at 68 and is buried in the Mt. Auburn Cemetery, Cambridge, MA* [8]

APPENDIX 4 - McKAY FAMILY GENEALOGY

William Lawrence Kean married Eliza Jane Hacker in
Boston, MA on Feb 11, 1895

*Eliza Jane was born Oct 12, 1846 in Bridgewater,
MA - died May 25, 1924 at 78, is buried in Mt
Auburn Cemetery, Cambridge,MA* [8]
*She was the daughter of Captain William and
Mary Hacker* [8]
*In 1880, at 25, before he was married, William was
a bookkeeper in a bank in East Boston.* [15]
*In 1900, William and Eliza are living at 620 Warren
Street in Roxbury section of Boston and
William is retired at 46. They continue living
there for the 1910 and 1920 census.* [17, 18, 19]

...............4. Matilda Kean born Aug 11,1856 - died Sep 10, 1861
at 5 years old
...............4. Alonzo Kean born Sep 13, 1859
Alonzo Kean married Martha A. Jackson *abt 1892*
*In 1880, at 20, before he was married, he is
living at home and working as a clerk in a
grocery store in East Boston.* [15]
*In the 1900 Census, Alonzo is an electrician living
with his wife Martha and her widowed mother,
Lydia McKie, on Princeton St. in East Boston.*
*In 1920, Martha is still living there with her 86
year old mother and Alonzo is divorced and
living in Los Angeles, CA working as railroad
electrician* [19]

...........3. Charlotte Sprot McKay born in Shelburne Jun 14, 1826 -
died Nov 19, 1899 at 73 [12]
*Charlotte was named after Charlotte Sprot, the wife
of the Rev. John Sprot, a Presbyterian Minister* [1]
Charlotte Sprot McKay married James Albert German *on
Jun 12, 1845* [1]
*In 1880, Charlotte, James and their daughter
Annie are living at 38 White St. in East Boston,
down the street from where her brother Donald
lived, and in the same house as their sons
James and John.*
James is a ship joiner. [15]
...............4. Walter McKay German born Apr 14,1846 - died
May 14,1878 at 32
*In 1870, Walter was single and a coachman in
Cleveland, OH* [14]
...............4. John Crocheron German born Sep 16,1848
John Crocheron German married Eliza Golden

APPENDIX 4 - McKAY FAMILY GENEALOGY

>*In Jun of 1880, John is a machinist living with his wife Eliza and his daughters Florence and Evelyn in East Boston in the same house as his father and brother James Jr.* [15]

....................5. Florence Gertrude German born May 27, 1872

....................5. Georgie Evelyn German born Apr 5, 1878 - died Dec 11,1890 at 12

................4. Mary Annie German *born Sep 14, 1852 - died Sep 18, 1854 at 2* [1]

................4. Annie McPherson German born Dec 23, 1854 - died May 23, 1883 at 28

Annie McPherson German married William C. Pinney

................4. James Albert German born Oct 21, 1856 - died Apr 22, 1883 at 26

>*In June of 1880, James is a flagstone Dealer living with his wife Katherine at 38 White St. in East Boston, MA.* [15]

James Albert German married Katherine F. Creelman

....................5. Annie McPherson German born Oct 12, 1880 - died May 8, 1886 at 5

............3. Anna Lang McKay born in Shelburne born Dec 11, 1829 - died Nov 30,1894 at almost 64 *in Chelsea, MA of dilation of the heart. She was living at 114 Chestnut St. at the time.* [6]

>*According to Nathaniel McKay's book, she was born Dec 13, 1829* [9]

Anna Lang McKay married James D. Alley on July 7, 1853 *in Boston, MA* [6]

>*James D. Alley was born abt 1826 in Maine - in 1870, James was a painter living in Chelsea, MA* [14]

................4. Alden Gifford Alley born May 9, 1854

Alden Gifford Alley married Hannie O. Dixie *abt 1878 in Chelsea, MA* [17]

>*Hannie (Hannah) O. Dixie was born Jul 1853 in MA* [17] *She died prior to the 1910 Census*
>*In 1870, Alden was a vest maker.*
>*In 1900, he was a salesman* [17]
>*In 1910, he was a widower and a silk manufacturer still in Chelsea* [18]

....................5. Alden Gifford Alley born Feb 7, 1879

....................5. Anna Lang Alley born Jan 3, 1881

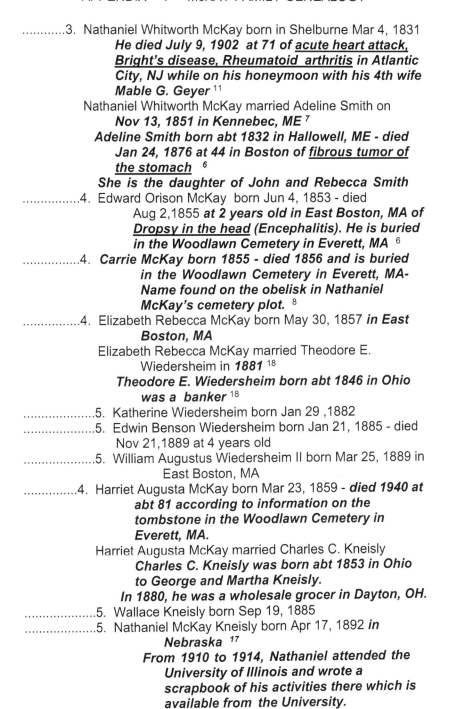

...........3. Nathaniel Whitworth McKay born in Shelburne Mar 4, 1831
*He died July 9, 1902 at 71 of <u>acute heart attack,
Bright's disease, Rheumatoid arthritis</u> in Atlantic
City, NJ while on his honeymoon with his 4th wife
Mable G. Geyer* [11]
Nathaniel Whitworth McKay married Adeline Smith on
Nov 13, 1851 in Kennebec, ME [7]
*Adeline Smith born abt 1832 in Hallowell, ME - died
Jan 24, 1876 at 44 in Boston of <u>fibrous tumor of
the stomach</u>* [6]
She is the daughter of John and Rebecca Smith
...............4. Edward Orison McKay born Jun 4, 1853 - died
Aug 2,1855 *at 2 years old in East Boston, MA of
<u>Dropsy in the head</u> (Encephalitis). He is buried
in the Woodlawn Cemetery in Everett, MA* [6]
...............4. *Carrie McKay born 1855 - died 1856 and is buried
in the Woodlawn Cemetery in Everett, MA-
Name found on the obelisk in Nathaniel
McKay's cemetery plot.* [8]
...............4. Elizabeth Rebecca McKay born May 30, 1857 *in East
Boston, MA*
Elizabeth Rebecca McKay married Theodore E.
Wiedersheim in *1881* [18]
*Theodore E. Wiedersheim born abt 1846 in Ohio
was a banker* [18]
..................5. Katherine Wiedersheim born Jan 29 ,1882
..................5. Edwin Benson Wiedersheim born Jan 21, 1885 - died
Nov 21,1889 at 4 years old
..................5. William Augustus Wiedersheim II born Mar 25, 1889 in
East Boston, MA
...............4. Harriet Augusta McKay born Mar 23, 1859 - *died 1940 at
abt 81 according to information on the
tombstone in the Woodlawn Cemetery in
Everett, MA.*
Harriet Augusta McKay married Charles C. Kneisly
*Charles C. Kneisly was born abt 1853 in Ohio
to George and Martha Kneisly.
In 1880, he was a wholesale grocer in Dayton, OH.*
..................5. Wallace Kneisly born Sep 19, 1885
..................5. Nathaniel McKay Kneisly born Apr 17, 1892 *in
Nebraska* [17]
*From 1910 to 1914, Nathaniel attended the
University of Illinois and wrote a
scrapbook of his activities there which is
available from the University.*

APPENDIX 4 - McKAY FAMILY GENEALOGY

*In the 1920 census, he is at 3129 Forest Ave.
in Kansas City, MO and is an auto
accessories salesman* [19]

3. 2nd marriage - Nathaniel Whitworth McKay married Ella J.
Kneisly
Ella J. Kneisly was born abt 1845 in Ohio. [15]
.............4. William Kneisly born *abt 1868 in Ohio - Ella's son
by prior marriage* [15]
William Kneisly married Ida B. __ abt 1892 in Ohio [19]
Ida B. was born in Aug 1874 in Ohio [19]
.................5. *John H. Kneisly was born in Jul 1894 in Ohio* [19]
4. *2nd marriage - William Kneisly married Florence S.__
in Ohio* [19]
*In 1920, William was a traveling salesman for
display fixtures living with his mother 75 in
Dayton, OH - Florence was a bookkeeper for a
butter Co.* [19]
.............4. Nathaniel McKay born Oct 29,1880 - died Oct 25,1883
just before his 3rd birthday

3. 3rd marriage - Nathaniel Whitworth McKay married Jenny
Wilson Pope *on Jan 9, 1889 in Brooklyn, NY* [11]
*Jenny Wilson Pope was born in May 1853 in
Georgia. Her father was Gideon Pope and in
1880, they were living at 323 McDonough St. in
Brooklyn, NY* [15]
Nathaniel and Jenny did not have any children.

3. *4th marriage - Nathaniel Whitworth McKay married
Mable Grace Geyer on Jun 26, 1902 in Crisfield,
MD (Nathaniel died 2 weeks later)* [11]
Mabel Grace Geyer was born Sep 1878 in Virginia [17]
*Mable lived across the street from the Dewey
Hotel, which Nathaniel owned. She was 23
when they were married and Nathaniel was 71.*

.........3. Matilda Nancy McKay born in Shelburne Oct 14, 1832 -
died May 15 1878 [12]
Matilda Nancy McKay married Donald Dewar *in Boston
on Sep 19, 1850* [6] *by the Rev. J. D. Bridge* [6]
*Donald Dewar, born on Prince Edward Island, was a
ship joiner. He died Feb 18, 1852 in East Boston
of* <u>*consumption*</u> *(Tuberculosis)* [6]
.............4. Elizabeth Smith Dewar born Jul 17,1851

APPENDIX 4 - McKAY FAMILY GENEALOGY

3. 2nd marriage - Matilda Nancy (McKay) Dewar married
John A. C. Geddes

*John A. C. Geddes was born abt 1829 in Nova
Scotia and was a ship joiner in East Boston,
MA* [14]

...............4. Simon McKay Geddes born Jan 8,1855 - died
Oct 7,1884 at 29

Simon McKay Geddes married Emma Jordan *sometime
after the 1880 census*

*In 1880, at 25, he is living at home at 169
Lexington St. in East Boston and he is a
manufacturer of clothing.* [15]

...............4. Mary Jane Geddes born Aug 3,1869 - *died
Nov 25, 1910 at 41 in Boston of Progressive
Pernicious Anemia for 2 years (body does
not create enough red blood cells - vitamin
B12 deficiency)* [6]

Mary Jane Geddes married Alvin George Jr. *abt 1892* [18]

*Alvin George, Jr. born Jun 1860 was a druggist
in Boston* [17]

In the 1910, Census they are in Northfield MA. [18]

*In the 1920, Census, after Mary Jane died,
Alvin is married to Bessie still living in
Northfield* [18]

...................5. Marion Matilda George born Jan 9,1893

ABBREVIATIONS

AZ	-	Arizona	MI -	Michigan
CA	-	California	MO -	Missouri
CT	-	Connecticut	NJ -	New Jersey
DE	-	Delaware	NS -	Nova Scotia, Canada
FL	-	Florida	NY -	New York
IA	-	Iowa	OH -	Ohio
IL	-	Illinois	PA -	Pennsylvania
KS	-	Kansas	RI -	Rhode Island
LA	-	Louisiana	TX -	Texas
MA	-	Massachusetts	VA -	Virginia
MD	-	Maryland	WA -	Washington
ME	-	Maine	WI -	Wisconsin

APPENDIX   4 - McKAY FAMILY GENEALOGY

FOOTNOTES

1....... "The Family of Donald McKay - The McKays and
McPhersons" by Marion Robertson
2.......Ancestry.Com Marriage records
3.......Ancestry.Com Birth records
4.......Death Certificate - see Appendix 1
5.......Boole Family Genealogy - Robin Ogilvie - Appendix 2
6.......City or Town Vital Records
7.......Family Search.Org
8.......Cemetery Records
9......."Nathaniel McKay" book by Nathaniel McKay
10.......Kate (Michel) Silvernale's family history
11.......Brooklyn Eagle Newspaper
12.......Notes in Dr. Donald McKay's copy of Kean's book
13.......1850 Census
13a.....1860 Census
14.......1870 Census
15.......1880 Census
16.......1901 Canadian Census
17.......1900 US Census
18.......1910 US Census
19.......1920 US Census
20.......1930 US Census
21......."History of Weymouth"   Weymouth Historical Society 1923
22......."History of the Town of Hingham" published by the Town
in 1893
23.......Art Cunnington family history
24...... Genealogy.com
25.......Rootsweb.com
26.......Obituary
27.......Donald Gunn Ross Family History
28.......Harrow School Records (Harrow, England)
29.......Reay McKay's Family Genealogy
30.......New England Historic Genealogical Society - Boston, MA
31.......Donald James Reay McKay History
32.......Thurston Genealogies by Brown Thurston - pg 192
33.......Sarah Woodbury Haug's Genealogy
34.......Family Search.org - Donna Whitehouse
35.......1820 Census
36.......English Census
37.......Gordon Wells Moore Genealogy

APPENDIX 5
McPHERSON FAMILY GENEALOGY
Edited by Paul Donald Hamilton

The following genealogy of the McPherson family is largely taken from "The Family of Donald McKay - The McKays and McPhersons" by Marion Robertson, reprinted in 1996. This 39 page document was obtained for me at a bookstore in Shelburne by the Shelburne County Genealogical Society. This book is very well written and very well documented, but since the book is written in regular text format, I have extracted the genealogical information and put it into a genealogical format.

All of the following information is from this book except the information that is in *Italics*. *This is information, from various sources, that has come out of my research.*

.....1. Lauchlan McPherson born in Glasgow, Scotland in 1766 - died Jan 8, 1832

Lauchlan McPherson married Elizabeth Urquhart

Elizabeth Urquhart was born in Edinburgh in 1763 - died Jun 25, 1816. She was the daughter of a British army officer stationed in India. They were on their way to Pugwash in 1787 when a big storm came up and they were forced to seek shelter in Shelburne, Nova Scotia.

They decided to stay in Shelburne and settled on some land by the Jordan river, where most of their children would be born and grow up.

..........2. David McPherson born in Scotland Apr 23, 1786 - lost at sea in 1807

..........2. Donald McPherson born in Scotland Sep 12, 1787 - presumed to have died before 1793

..........2. **Ann McPherson** born in Shelburne, NS Nov 4, 1789 - died in Boston, Ma. Nov 14, 1856

Ann McPherson married Hugh McKay on Oct 15, 1808 in Shelburne, NS

...............3. Elizabeth Anne McKay born in Shelburne Oct 14, 1809 - died Feb 18, 1869 at 59

Elizabeth Ann McKay married John Crocheron *on Aug 23, 1827*

John was the son of Abraham and Penniah Crocheron [2]

APPENDIX 5 - McPHERSON FAMILY GENEALOGY

        3. 2nd marriage - Elizabeth Ann McKay married Robert
             Major
.............3. Donald McKay born in Shelburne Sep 4, 1810 - died
             Sep 20, 1880 at 70
         Donald McKay married Albenia Martha Boole In New York
             in 1833.
            Albenia Martha Boole was born Sep 4, 1815 - died
               Dec 10, 1848 at 33
            ***Donald was one of the most famous clipper ship
            builders in the world.***
        3. 2nd marriage - Donald McKay marries Mary Cressy
             Litchfield in Boston Massachusetts on Oct 7, 1849
            Mary Cressy Litchfield was born Sep 30, 1831 - died
              Feb 6, 1923 at 91
.............3. Lauchlan McKay born in Shelburne Dec 16, 1811 - ***died
            Apr 3, 1895 at 83 in Roxbury,MA.***
        Lauchlan McKay married Judith Coombs
.............3. Sarah McKay born in Shelburne Feb 26, 1813 - died
             Sep 22, 1868 at 55
        Sarah McKay married George ***Washington*** Thurston -
            son of William and Nance (Foster) Thurston [2]
.............3. Margaret McKay born in Shelburne May 2, 1814 - died
             Aug 29, 1867 at 53
        Margaret McKay married Solomon Thurston ***on
            Jan 14 1833 - Solomon drowned in Boston
            harbor in 1847.*** [2]
        3. 2nd marriage - Margaret McKay married Ambrose
             Salisbury
.............3. Jennett McKay born in Shelburne May 4, 1815 - died
             May 20, 1817 at 2
.............3. Ann McKay born in Shelburne Jan 27, 1817 - died
             Feb 10, 1824 at 7
.............3. Hugh Robert McKay born in Shelburne Mar 21, 1818 -
             died Apr 23, 1886 at 68
        Hugh Robert McKay married Margaret McKay - ***Margaret
            was the oldest daughter of Robert and Janet
            (Murray) McKay***
.............3. David McKay born in Shelburne Oct 14, 1819
        David McKay married Mary Riley
.............3. John McKay born in Shelburne Jan 20, 1822
        John McKay married Mary Brothers
.............3. Simon McKay born in Shelburne Feb 6, 1823 - died
             Nov 25, 1882 at 59
        Simon McKay married Sarah Jane Osgood
        3. 2nd marriage - Simon McKay married Mary Jane Worthen

APPENDIX 5 - McPHERSON FAMILY GENEALOGY

...............3. Mary Ann McKay born in Shelburne Sep 11, 1824 - died
Apr 14, 1888 at 63
Mary Ann McKay married Patrick McKensie *on*
Jan 4, 1841.
  3. 2nd marriage - Mary Ann McKay married John Kean
...............3. Charlotte Sprot McKay born in Shelburne Jun 14, 1826
Charlotte Sprot McKay married James Albert German on
Jun 12, 1845
...............3. Anna Lang McKay born in Shelburne Dec 11, 1829 - died
Nov 30, 1894 at 64
Anna Lang McKay married James D. Alley **on May 9, 1854**
...............3. Nathaniel Whitworth McKay born in Shelburne
Mar 4, 1831
Nathaniel Whitworth McKay married Adeline Smith
  3. 2nd marriage - Nathaniel Whitworth McKay married E.
Kneisly
  3. 3rd marriage - Nathaniel Whitworth McKay married
Jenney W. Pope
  3. 4th marriage - Nathaniel Whitworth McKay married Mabel
Grace Geyer
...............3. Matilda Nancy McKay born in Shelburne Oct 14, 1832
Matilda Nancy McKay married Donald Dewar
  3. 2nd marriage - Matilda Nancy McKay married John A. C.
Geddes

**(See Appendix 4, "McKay Family Genealogy", for a more
detailed genealogy of Hugh McKay and Ann McPherson's family)**

..........2. James McPherson born in Shelburne Mar 24, 1791
James McPherson married and made home in Liverpool - he
was a poet

..........2. Evan McPherson born in Shelburne May 16, 1792 - died
1845 at about 53
Evan McPherson married Elizabeth Demings
Elizabeth Demings was Baptized Dec 17, 1794. She
was the daughter of Anthony and Almira (Morris)
Demings of Roseway, Shelburne, NS
They lived in Shelburne for a while and then moved to
Pugwash, NS
...............3. Rachel Almira McPherson born in Shelburne, NS
Jun 20, 1814
...............3. Daniel Urquhart McPherson born in Shelburne, NS
May 21, 1816

APPENDIX 5 - McPHERSON FAMILY GENEALOGY

..............3. Elizabeth Urquhart McPherson born in Shelburne, NS
          Apr 1818
          Elizabeth Urquhart McPherson married Amos Eaton *on*
              May 26, 1836
              Amos Eaton born Oct 6, 1815 in Oxford, NS [1]
..............3. *Alexander McPherson was a sea captain* [1]
          Alexander McPherson married Mary Anderson of
              Pugwash, NS
..............3. *Catherine McPherson*
          Catherine McPherson married George Demings [1]
..............3. *Margaret McPherson*
          Margaret McPherson married William Demings [1]
..............3. *Isabel McPherson*
          Isabel McPherson married Anthony Demings [1]
..............3. *John Wesley McPherson born Jan 22, 1829*
          John Wesley McPherson married Phoebe Ackerly on
              May 3, 1850
              Phoebe was born Sep 10, 1830 in Wallace, NS -
              she was the daughter of Isaac Ackerly and
              Esther Doherty White - from Long Island, NY
...................4. *Amelia McPherson born Mar 11, 1851* [1]
          Amelia McPherson married Amos B. Ripley on
              Sep 4, 1873
          4. 2nd marriage - Amelia McPherson married John A.
              Oldham of Central Falls, RI on Jun 2, 1884
...................4. *Mary Adelia McPherson born Aug 12, 1852* [1]
          Mary Adelia McPherson married Joseph Howe
              on Feb 11, 1871 `
              In 1920, Mary is Mary A. Eaton living at 48
                  Elmwood St. in North Attleboro, MA with her
                  sister Flora and Flora's son Harold [8]
...................4. *Alexander McPherson born Jan 16, 1855* [1]
...................4. *John Wesley McPherson Jr. Born Aug 15, 1859* [1]
              (1900 Census shows Aug 1861) and shows
              John as a bench hand [6]
          John Wesley McPherson Jr. married Nina Ackerley
              of Pugwash abt 1882 - Nina was born
              Aug 1862 in Nova Scotia [6]
.....................5. *Ethel M. McPherson born Jul 1883 in MA* [6]
.....................5. *Leroy C. McPherson born Dec 1884 in MA* [6]
.....................5. *Rosa J. McPherson born Apr 1888 in MA* [6]
...................4. *Fletcher McPherson born Nov 22, 1861 - never*
              married [1]
...................4. *Flora McPherson born Mar 3, 1863 in Canada* [1]
              (The 1900 Census shows Mar 1866 [6]*)*

> *Flora came to this country in 1886 and became a*
> *citizen in 1887* [8]
> *Flora McPherson married Charles P. Day of*
> *Attleboro, MA (present day North Attleboro)*
> *abt 1866*
> *Charles P. Day born Nov 1854 in MA* [6] *- died*
> *prior to 1910* [7]
> *In 1900, Charles was a trimmer* [6]

.........................5. *Harold R. Day born Jul 1886 in MA* [6]
> *In 1910, he was a typewriter salesman living*
> *at 41 School St. North Attleboro, MA with*
> *his mother*[7]
> *In 1920, he is still single living with his mother*
> *at 48 Elmwood St. in North Attleboro, MA*
> *and is a caretaker at a livery.* [8]

.........................5. *Gertrude J. Day born Mar 1890 in MA* [6]
.....................4. *Rosa McPherson born Jul 9, 1867 - died in infancy* [1]
.....................4. *Ada McPherson born Mar 6, 1869* [1]
> *Ada McPherson married George Simpson of Galt*
> *Ontario*

.....................4. *Emma McPherson born Feb 4, 1875* [1] *- died prior to*
> *1920* [8]
> *Emma McPherson married Edgar C. Oldham of*
> *Central Falls, RI*
> *Edgar C Oldham born Jul 1874 in RI* [6]
> *In 1900 and 1920 Edgar is a mail clerk for a*
> *railroad in Central Falls, RI* [6,8]

...............3. *Mary McPherson*
> *Mary McPherson married Angus MacDonald* [1]

...............3. *Fletcher McPherson - was not married - lost at sea* [1]

.........2. Donald McPherson born in Shelburne Aug 23, 1793
> Donald McPherson married Letitia Parker - they lived in
> Brookfield, Queen County, NS

...............3. Irene McPherson
> Irene McPherson married her cousin John McPherson on
> Dec 12, 1841

...............3. Harriet Sophia McPherson
> Harriet Sophia McPherson married her cousin Lauchlan
> McPherson son of John and Elizabeth (Martin)
> McPherson

.........2. Lauchlan McPherson born Jun 18, 1795 - died May 7, 1860 at
> 64 years old
> Lauchlan McPherson married Margaret (Martin) McNutt on

236

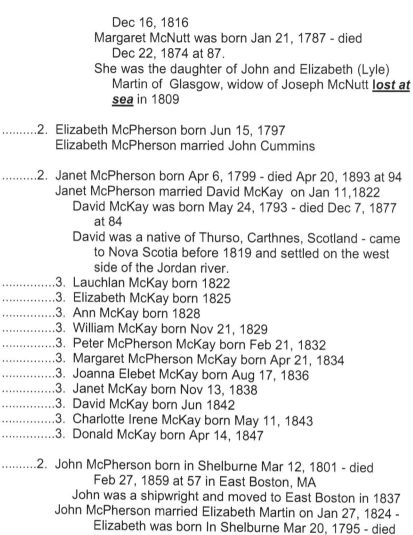

Dec 16, 1816
Margaret McNutt was born Jan 21, 1787 - died
Dec 22, 1874 at 87.
She was the daughter of John and Elizabeth (Lyle)
Martin of Glasgow, widow of Joseph McNutt **_lost at
sea_** in 1809

..........2. Elizabeth McPherson born Jun 15, 1797
Elizabeth McPherson married John Cummins

..........2. Janet McPherson born Apr 6, 1799 - died Apr 20, 1893 at 94
Janet McPherson married David McKay on Jan 11,1822
David McKay was born May 24, 1793 - died Dec 7, 1877
at 84
David was a native of Thurso, Carthnes, Scotland - came
to Nova Scotia before 1819 and settled on the west
side of the Jordan river.
..............3. Lauchlan McKay born 1822
..............3. Elizabeth McKay born 1825
..............3. Ann McKay born 1828
..............3. William McKay born Nov 21, 1829
..............3. Peter McPherson McKay born Feb 21, 1832
..............3. Margaret McPherson McKay born Apr 21, 1834
..............3. Joanna Elebet McKay born Aug 17, 1836
..............3. Janet McKay born Nov 13, 1838
..............3. David McKay born Jun 1842
..............3. Charlotte Irene McKay born May 11, 1843
..............3. Donald McKay born Apr 14, 1847

..........2. John McPherson born in Shelburne Mar 12, 1801 - died
Feb 27, 1859 at 57 in East Boston, MA
John was a shipwright and moved to East Boston in 1837
John McPherson married Elizabeth Martin on Jan 27, 1824 -
Elizabeth was born In Shelburne Mar 20, 1795 - died
in East Boston on Sep 3, 1878 at 83.
She was the sister of Lauchlan's wife Margaret (Martin)
McNutt.
..............3. Elizabeth Lyle McPherson born in East Jordan Dec 17,
1824
*In the 1900 census, she is single, living with her
brother Ebenezer* [6]
..............3. Lauchlan McPherson born in East Jordan Apr 2, 1826 -
*died May 5, 1866 at 40 of Congestion of the lung
He was living at 23 White St. in East Boston when
he died.* [11]

APPENDIX 5 - McPHERSON FAMILY GENEALOGY

> *Lauchlan McPherson married Harriette ___*
> *Harriette was born abt 1830 in Nova Scotia* [3]
> *In 1860, Lauchlan is a ship carpenter living with his family in East Boston along with his sister Elizabeth, his mother Elizabeth and brother Ebenezer, an accountant.* [3]
> *In 1870, Harriet is living in East Boston without Lauchlan. She is living with her family, her mother-in-law Elizabeth and her sister-in-laws Elizabeth and Agnes. Her son, John, is working as a clerk in an office.* [4]

...............4. *John McPherson born abt 1851 in MA* [3]

...............4. *David McPherson born abt 1855 in MA* [3]

...............4. *Harriet R. McPherson born abt 1861 in Boston, MA* [4]

...........3. Agnes Russell McPherson born in East Jordan Mar 31, 1828

...........3. John Martin McPherson born in East Jordan May 25, 1830

...........3. David McPherson was born in East Jordan Aug 1, 1832 - He was a shipwright who worked in the Donald McKay shipyard in Boston.
He moved to Halifax and was a prominent shipbuilder, an Alderman for 15 years, the Mayor of Halifax for 4, and the Provincial Legislature for 15.

...........3. James Evan McPherson was born in East Jordan Aug 25, 1834

> *James Evan McPherson married Henriette ___*
> *Henriette was born abt 1837 in Maine* [3]
> *In 1860, James is a ship carpenter living with his family in East Boston* [3]

...............4. *Charles McPherson born abt 1856 in MA* [3]

...............4. *Eliza McPherson born Jan 1860 in Boston, MA* [3]

...........3. Ebenezer Martin McPherson was born in East Jordan Oct 24, 1836 -

> *Ebenezer Martin McPherson married Elizabeth R. ___ abt 1890 and they did not have any children.*
> *Elizabeth was born Sep 1841 in RI* [6]

Ebenezer was the President of the Security Safe Deposit Co. of Boston, a member of the Massachusetts State Legislature for 2 years, member of Governor Ames's Council for 2 years, State commissioner of Foreign Mortgage Corporation for three years, and trustee of the East Boston Savings Bank.

APPENDIX 5 - McPHERSON FAMILY GENEALOGY

In the 1900 census, they were living at 171 Trenton St. in East Boston, **MA** [6]

.........2. Peter McPherson was born in Shelburne, NS Dec 19, 1804
Peter McPherson married Martha Irving
2. 2nd marriage - Peter McPherson married Sarah Collins

.........2. Margaret McPherson was born in Shelburne May 6, 1807 -
died Apr 22, 1848 at 40

FOOTNOTES

1. Family Tree Maker - Local and Family Histories: New England 1600 - 1900's
The Eaton Family of Nova Scotia, Chapter IX
2. "The Genealogy of Hugh McKay and his lineal descendant" by William Lawrence Kean
3. 1860 US Census
4. 1870 US Census
5. 1880 US Census
6. 1900 US Census
7. 1910 US Census
8. 1920 US Census
9. 1930 US Census
10. City Directory
11. Death Certificate

ABBREVIATIONS

AZ - Arizona	MI - Michigan
CA - California	MO - Missouri
CT - Connecticut	NJ - New Jersey
DE - Delaware	NS - Nova Scotia, Canada
FL - Florida	NY - New York
IA - Iowa	OH - Ohio
IL - Illinois	PA - Pennsylvania
KS - Kansas	RI - Rhode Island
LA - Louisiana	TX - Texas
MA - Massachusetts	VA - Virginia
MD - Maryland	WA - Washington
ME - Maine	WI - Wisconsin

APPENDIX 6
BIBLIOGRAPHY

Alexander, E. P. - "Iron Horses - American Locomotives 1829 - 1900" - Bonanza Books - 1941 - (Picture of McKay & Aldus Iron Works Locomotive - Chapter 9)

Brooklyn Eagle newspaper - 1841 to 1902 available on-line

Bunting, W. H. - 'Portrait of a Port - Boston 1852 - 1914' - published by Harvard College - 1971

Cheney, Robert K. - "Maritime History of the Merrimac - Shipbuilding" - Newburyport Press, Inc. 1964

Cushing, James Stevenson - "Genealogy of the Cushing Family" - self published 1905

Huber, Leonard - "New Orleans, A Pictorial History" - Crown Publishers 1971

Kean, William L. - "Hugh McKay and his linear decedents" - Boston, Mass. Feb 11, 1895 - Updated by Robert McKay III - Detroit, MI Jul 4, 1976

Maryland Historical Society - Portrait Vertical File - 201 West Monument Street, Baltimore, MD

McKay, Nathaniel - "Nathaniel McKay" - published in 1901

McKay, Richard Cornelius - "Some Famous Ships and their Builder, Donald McKay" - First printed in 1928 - 2nd revised edition 1969 - 7 C's Press, Inc.

McKay, Richard Cornelius - "South Street - a Maritime History of New York" - Published 1934 - G. P. Putnam's Sons: New York

Michel, Elsie Jeanette - "Jules-Jerome Michel - 1884-1961" Family story of some of Frances McKay's descendents written by Jules Michel's daughter-in-law

Mjelde, Michael Jay - "Glory of the Seas" - Wesleyan University Press 1970

Mugnier, George François - "New Orleans and Bayou Country" edited and introduced by Lester Burbank Bridgham - Barre Publishers

Robertson, Marion - "The Family of Donald McKay - The McKays and McPhersons" - reprinted from Collections of the Nova Scotia Historical Society, Vol 37 - 1996

Rootweb.com - "Lockport & the Lockes of Shelburne Count"

Rowe, William Hutchinson - "Shipbuilding Days in Casco Bay 1727 - 1890" - The Bond Wheelwright Company Freeport, ME 1929

Rowe, William Hutchinson - "The Maritime History of Maine - Three Centuries of Shipbuilding and Seafaring" - by W.W. Norton and Company, Inc 1948

Town of Hingham - "History of the Town of Hingham" - published by the Town of Hingham - 1893 - Vol III

Wallace, Frederick William - "In the Wake of the Wind-Ships" - published by George Sully & Company 1927

INDEX

Paul Hamilton
at the McKay Family Plot in the Oak Hill Cemetery
Newburyport, Massachusetts - 2005

Made in the USA
Charleston, SC
11 April 2010